We Are the Ramblers

A Reflection on Windber High School Football

Carl D. Mayer

Front Cover
Photo in Center: 1941 game at Delaney Field
Photo on Left: Jim "Scoop" Camile-1925
Photo on Right: Josh Simon-2001

Back Cover
Center: Programs of 1933 and 1937 Championship games
Programs: Representing Eight Decades of Windber High School football

Copyright © 2008 Carl D. Mayer

All rights to this book are reserved. No part of this publication may be reproduced, stored in a retrieval system, or transmitted, in any form or any means, electronic, mechanical, photocopying, recording or otherwise, without the prior written permission of Carl D. Mayer

Published by Carl D. Mayer
1616 Fern Ave.
Windber, PA 15963
814-467-4653
www.fern1616@verizon.net

Dedication

This book is dedicated in loving memory of Curtis L. Mayer, my seven year old son, who died from childhood cancer and was not given the opportunity to become a Windber "Rambler".

Carol, my wife, you are everything to me!
I love you!

Charlie, my son, you continue to instill
a father's pride!

To my mother, Nova,
who sacrificed everything for her sons
love always!

To all former, current, and future Windber Football "Ramblers"
carry on the tradition!

Contents

Dedication --- iii
Content --- iv
About the Author --- v
Foreword --- vi
Acknowledgements --- vii
Song of the Ramblers --- viii

Chapters

1	How it All Got Started	9
2	The First Official Team	15
3	Formative Years	19
4	The 1920's	22
5	The Glory Years	27
6	We Become the "Ramblers"	45
7	Following the Glory Years	49
8	The Glory Years Return	57
9	Gridiron Venues	63
10	Camp Hamilton	75
11	Football Camp	83
12	Nicknames	93
13	On to College	97
14	Reflections on Windber High School Football	99
15	Most Notable Rambler Football Player	107
16	Myths, Incidents and Circumstances	113
17	Student Managers	121
18	Songs, Cheers, and Yells	125
19	Impact Individuals	133
20	Tidbits of Information	141
21	Heckler's Reflection in Drawing and Caricature	153

Appendixes

I	Team Photographs and Records: 1914-1950	183
II	Team Photographs and Records: 1951-1989	223
III	Team Photographs and Records: 1990-2007	263
IV	Opponents, Coaching Records, Four Year Letter Winners and Miscellaneous	281

Bibliography

Bibliography, Interviews, Newspapers, Internet Sources, and Photo Credits --- 302

About the Author

Carl D. Mayer

Carl D. Mayer was born in Windber, Pennsylvania, January 18, 1944, twin son of Charles L. Mayer and Nova (Lochrie) Mayer. He married Carol M. Cotz of Windber on October 5, 1968. They are the parents of two sons; Charles J. Mayer and wife Karrie, parents of two children, Jakson and Mackenzie and Curtis L. Mayer (deceased).

Mr. Mayer earned a bachelor's degree in education in 1966 from Indiana University of Pennsylvania. He then taught Earth and Space Science for 11 years at Richland Junior High School. In 1977 he left the teaching profession and worked as an underground coal miner for five years, where he earned certification as a fire boss. He then worked as a shift foreman at Snyders of Berlin for two and a half years before entering the Pittsburgh Institute of Mortuary Science where he graduated summa cum laude. Mr. Mayer has worked, as a funeral director, in Windber for 18 years, and is currently employed as a funeral director for the William Kisiel Funeral Home. He also works part time as a substitute teacher for the Windber Area School District.

Currently, he is president of the Windber Rambler Lettermen's Club, and member of the Windber Coal Heritage Foundation. He is a former president of Windber Fire Company # 1.

Mr. Mayer played varsity football for Windber High School from 1959 through 1961 and graduated in 1962. He then played football for Indiana University of Pennsylvania from 1962 through 1965. During his sophomore year he was presented with an award for being the most promising player in the future. He then coached junior high school football for four years at Richland Junior High School before becoming an assistant varsity football coach at Richland High School for seven years. In 1984, he was an assistant varsity football coach for the "Ramblers" of Windber.

The Mayers now reside in Paint Township.

Foreword

For nearly 100 years the fall spectacle of football has been played in Windber, Pennsylvania. This town located in northern Somerset County in the southwestern part of the state has been noted primarily for coal mining and winning football teams.

The Berwind-White Coal Mining Company named the town by reversing the two syllables in Berwind, and carefully planned this community to suit its need for the production of bituminous coal. With the need for many laborers and supervisory personnel, people moved to this community in great numbers. Most of these people were immigrants from Europe, representing many ethnic groups.

This "melting pot" of people, in small town, U.S.A., is the reason for Windber's reputation for producing winning football teams. The story of Windber High School football, lies in the individual players, coaches, managers, and fans who make up this community.

There have been years when the wins were less than the losses but the reputation of hard nosed football did not lose any ground, unlike underground coal mining, which no longer takes place in Windber today The reputation for winning football teams continues.

Approximately 20 years ago, while waiting for a haircut at Bill Gorgon's barbershop on Graham Avenue, Bill asked me if I had ever seen the list of offensive starting lineups for Windber High School football teams that had been compiled. This list included the teams from 1914 to 1959. Bill challenged me to update this list. After further research I found this list had been compiled by William "Bill" Zepka, a member of a twelve man committee in 1959, who took on a project sponsored by the Windber American Legion Post #137 to identify the most outstanding players and coach for a Windber High School Football Hall of Fame. This 1959 Hall of Fame list can be found in Chapter 20, Tidbits of Information, on page 146.

The challenge was accepted, and over the past 20 years I have enjoyed adding to this list. As of this writing, the teams from 1914 to 2007 have been compiled. Following the 2002 season, someone suggested that I make this list available. I was very hesitant because of the accuracy of such a list, and began to research some of the player's names from the early years.

This research led me to believe that a more accurate record was needed, and this record of Windber High School Football should include; team photographs, factual and mythical stories, and interesting tidbits, and might be an interesting topic to write about.

It is my hope that this Reflection on Windber High School Football will be enjoyed, promote pride, and be continued for years to come. This story is so huge it could never be considered completely done. My goal was to record as accurately as possible this history within limitations of this publication. Any corrections or additions would be appreciated.

Carl D. Mayer

Acknowledgements

Facts for this publication were gathered from files of newspapers, programs, high school yearbooks, maps, photographs and interviews.

I am grateful to many individuals who volunteered to share materials, information, or just reminisce, especially the following: Bill Gorgon, Pat Freeman, Jack Lochrie, John and Judi Pruchnic, Geno Stevens, Phil DeMarco, Ralph DeMarco, Jack Gallagher, Jason Oyler Charles W. Beckley, Dennis Zahurak, James "Peachy" Miller, Ray Wozny, Leonard Mayer (twin brother), Joe Dressick, Mike Webb, Jerry Simon, Jim Boburchuk, Matt Grohal, Tom Congersky, A.J. Cannoni, Joe "Gunda" Kush, Larry Betcher, Kristen Lochrie, Pam Gyurik, Gary DiGuilio, Roger Ripple, Glenn Gaye, Jr., Joe Yasko, Charlie Puckey, John Csordas, Shaz Yuhas, Stacey Zeglin, Barb Korhut, Leonard LaPlaca.

Special thanks go to Noah Martin for his editing and proof-reading, Lillian Kochinski, Windber Area High School librarian, who made available the many yearbooks used, and Edward Surkosky who made available the micro-film of the *Windber Era* from the Windber Area Museum.

A very special thanks goes to Bob Daniels for his guidance with the publishing and help with photographs.

A very special thanks, with deep gratitude, goes to Terry Heckler for sharing his drawings and caricatures.

Song of the Ramblers

Song of the Ramblers

Tune--"Notre Dame Fight Song"

Cheer, Cheer for Old Windber High,
We are the Ramblers, we're riding high,
We can pass and we can kick,
To make a touchdown, we'll pull a trick,
Whether they're big or whether they're small,
Old Windber High will win overall,
While our team goes marching forward,
Onward to victory.

Written by Mary Elizabeth Solomon (Class of 1941)

1

How it all Got Started

Windber High School football officially began in the fall of 1914, the first year all members of the squad were students and the first year record keeping started. However, leading up to this first official year of scholastic football, I felt it necessary to try and find the origin of how this fall spectacle began in Windber.

Windber, Berwind-White's model coal mining town, was born in 1897, but it has not always been known for football. During the early days of Windber, a number of organized sports were played, which included; boxing, basketball, track teams, rugby, soccer, and baseball. Baseball, by far, was the most popular and teams from surrounding communities would compete.

Most of these baseball teams were made up of older boys and young men, who were out of school or had never attended high school because of the need to work. Baseball was played during the summer months and into the fall at Dewey Field or Recreation Park.

The fall season sports were rugby and soccer; they were probably introduced by the English and Scotch immigrants who came to the new coal fields. The rugby games were probably played with some American football flavor. After reading *The Way We Played the Game* by John Armstrong, I discovered that high school football actually started in Boston, Massachusetts, in 1862.

The first information regarding football in Windber was located in the September 1, 1904 issue of the *Windber Journal*. An announcement by Joe Mills and Will Jones read: "A football team is being organized and anyone interested can leave their name at Mill's Pool Room."

This brand of football was rugby, with each team having 11 players on the field. This first football team which was composed of town's people of various ages must be considered an independent team as opposed to a scholastic team. The first report of a game (location unknown), probably Dewey Field, was found in the October 13, 1904 issue of the *Windber Journal:*, "Windber beats Scalp in football."

A second game was played November 7, 1904 at Dewey Field. The opponents were Windber and Llanfair (a small village near Dunlo); the Llanfair team won the game 3 goals to 1. According to the account in the *Windber Era*, Windber claimed Llanfair had twelve men on the field, and even some of the members of the Llanfair team said that Llanfair had twelve men on the field in the last half. The referee, S.H. Mills, did not notice the "stuffing" (a term used for too many men on the field today) until the game had ended. Was this the first infraction by a team against Windber and the first oversight by an official during a Windber football game?

In the third game of 1904, Windber defeated Ehrenfeld by a score of 3 to 2, and in a fourth game, Windber beat a team from Bakerton 1 to 0.

According to an article in the October 12, 1905 issue of the *Windber Era*, representatives from Windber, Ehrenfeld, Dunlo and Llanfair met in the office of Burgess S.H. Mills (the official in charge of the Windber vs. Llanfair game, November 1904) on Tuesday, October 10, 1905 to form an Association Football League. This form of football was rugby, I am sure, with some American football influence. There is very little information available to put together an actual visual picture of how the game was played.

This league, however, was short lived, according to an article in the November 23, 1905 issue of the *Windber Era*, It was decided at a meeting of the local Association Football League "to abandon the present schedule because most of the boys work in the mines and cannot get off work, thus weakening the team to such an extent that it is impossible to win."

This brand of football continued to be played in the area during the fall season as teams from surrounding communities would get together and play. These independent teams played sort of a free for all game as standard rules had not yet been adopted. The teams always were out to get each other, and very rough play was the result.

An article in the October 10, 1907 issue of the *Windber Era* attests to this rough play. "It was reported that Thomas Bertram (30 years old) of Altoona was fatally injured in a football game at Portage. This is the first death caused by the game of football in the area."

The First UnOfficial Team

According to an article in the December 21, 1937 issue of the *Hi-Times* (Windber High School-newspaper), the founding father of football in Windber was the late Dr. B.J. Smith of Windber, a graduate of Maryland University, who made an attempt to coach a team in Windber. The team, however, did not only consist of Windber High School students but older boys as well.

As of this time I have not been able to find any information on Dr. Smith or the year this attempt was made. Also, in this article it is mentioned that in 1908 an attempt was made by a younger group of boys to organize a team, however, they were not all high school students. This may have been the team coached by Dr. B.J. Smith, but no information can be found to verify this. They called themselves the Windber High School Team.

With continued research I did come across an article in *The Johnstown Daily Tribune* dated September 18, 1908, it reads as follows: "Windber Y.M.C.A. football team has been organized for the season with William Peightal as manager and Sherman Rodgers as captain. The eleven will average about 125 to 135 pounds. The first game is being played tomorrow afternoon at Dewey Field with the Coopersdale team from Johnstown." (Both William Peightal and Sherman Rodgers names appear in the starting line-up for this 1908 team.)

The outcome of this game was reported in the September 19, 1908 publication of the *The Johnstown Daily Tribune* an article began with the following head line: **First Rugby in Windber, Northern Johnstown A.C. wins first football contest of season.** The article under the headline reads: "The first rugby football game ever played in this place was pulled off on the gridiron on Dewey Field yesterday afternoon with the local Y.M.C.A. eleven and the Northern Johnstown A.C. as the contesting teams. The Johnstowners won 11 to 0, scoring two touchdowns and a goal in the second half by better team work. The Y.M.C.A. players were slightly outweighed and lacked the coaching of the visitors."

In the October 3, 1908 publication of *The Johnstown Daily Tribune* an article mentioned that the Johnstown Scrubs (Johnstown High School's second team) will play Windber High School at 3:15 at the Point, following the high school game. "The scrubs think they are strong enough to give Windber High School a tussle that they will not forget in a hurry." The most interesting thing in this article is that this is the first mention of the team being called Windber High School. The result of this game appeared in the October 5, 1908 issue of the *The Johnstown Daily Tribune* with the Johnstown Scrubs defeating Windber 5 to 0.

A very interesting article appeared in the Monday, October 12, 1908 issue of the *The Johnstown Daily Tribune*. The headline read: **Rowe College Triumphs--Windber High School could not stop rushes of Johnstown Eleven in Saturday's Game.** The most interesting thing was who is Rowe College? After some conjecture the only conclusion I could come up with is that this was a team from the current day Cambria Rowe Business College located on Central Avenue in Johnstown. The accompanying article reads: "The football team representing Rowe College played its first game of the season at Windber Saturday afternoon and came home with a victory, 21 to 0, over the Windber High School eleven. The Rowe College eleven under the leadership of Coach and Manager About and Captain Joe Nokes, played rings around the Windber team. The feature of the game was the rooting by a delegation from Johnstown, mostly girls from the school."

Following this game with Rowe College the Windber High Team probably played the South Fork All-Stars. An article in the Monday, November 23, 1908 issue of the *The Johnstown Daily Tribune* reads, "The South Fork All-Stars who were defeated at Windber some time ago, challenge the Windber High School eleven for a return game". No report of a score of this game or the date it was played could be found. The next reported game was found in the Monday, October 26, 1908 issue of *The Johnstown Daily Tribune* and read, "Eighth Ward-5, Windber H.S.-0."

The Windber High School eleven played a game at the end of October with the Dale Borough football team. In the Monday, November 2, 1908 issue of *The Johnstown Daily Tribune*, it was reported "Tie game at Windber. The Dale Borough football team played a no-score game with the Windber High School eleven in the coal town on Saturday afternoon".

The next game of this 1908 unofficial Windber High School football team was played on Saturday November 21, 1908. An article in the Monday, November 23, 1908 issue of *The Johnstown Daily Tribune* reads, "Windber High wins. The Windber High School football team on Saturday afternoon defeated the Eighth Ward eleven by the score of 9 to 0. The Johnstowners won a couple of weeks before by the score of 5 to 0." Another line in this same article read, "St. Francis College of Loretto will send a team to Windber next Thursday for a game." This appears to have been the last game played by the 1908 team, however, there was no information found as to the score.

The outcome of this 1908 Unofficial Windber High School football year:

Northern Johnstown A.C. (Coopersdale) 11 Windber High 0

Johnstown Scrubs 5 Windber High 0

Rowe College 21 Windber High 0

South Fork All-Stars ? Windber High ? (game won by Windber)

Eighth Ward 5 Windber High 0

Dale Borough 0 Windber High 0

Eighth Ward 0 Windber High 9

St Francis of Loretto ? Windber High ?

Another interesting item, besides the mention of a team representing Windber High School was a published starting line-up of the Rowe College team and Windber. This starting line up and the one in the 1937 *Hi-Times* article are very similar except for a few names. (See following page for line-ups and photograph of the 1908 team.)

After checking class lists for the years 1904 through 1909 I did discover that three boys on the 1908 team where high school students and graduated in 1909. They include; Bill Pieghtal, Harry Wrye, and Bill Farber. I also found the graduation year for two of the older boys on the team, Lou Middleman-1904 and Ben Phenocie-1907. None of the other names in the starting line-ups or substitute list could be found in any class list.

The 1937 *Hi-Times* article goes on to say: "This team was greatly handicapped because nothing in the line of materials or equipment was furnished for them. They considered themselves very lucky if they met the expenses of the team scheduled to play. Therefore most games were scheduled to be played in their own vicinity."

Starting Line-up
Windber vs Rowe College

Position	Last Name
Left End	Redpath
Left Tackle	Wrye
Left Guard	Reed
Center	Hoffman
Right Guard	Seese
Right Tackle	Olson
Right End	Breth
Quarterback	Farber
Lft. Halfback	Peightal
Rt. Halfback	Rodgers
Fullback	Crubbs

Starting Line-up for the 1908
Windber High School Team
Information obtained from the December 21, 1937 issue of the *Hi-Times*

Position	Name
Left End	John Breth
Left Tackle	Bert Murphy
Left Guard	Ben Phenocie
Center	Lou Middleman
Right Guard	Irvin Faust
Right Tackle	Jaye Reed
Right End	Harry Wrye
Quarterback	Bill Pieghtal
Rt. Halfback	Sherman Rodgers
Lft. Halfback	Melvin Seese
Fullback	Bill Farber

Windber High School Team of 1908

Top photo shows Windber Football Team in 1908, They are; Sherm Rodgers, Harry Wyre, Bill Farber, Bert Murphy, Mel Seese, Gaud Buckwalter, Ben Phenocie, Bill Livant, Jaye Reed, Irvin Faust, Bill Pieghtal, McKendreck, and Middleman. Lower photo shows the team in uniform. (Photo taken from December 21, 1937 *Hi-Times*)

A report in the Monday, October 11, 1909 issue of *The Johnstown Daily Tribune,* under football results shows the Eighth Ward team defeating Windber High by a score of 10 to 0. This is the only mention of a Windber High School team that could be found following the 1908 Unofficial Team. In the Monday, October 18 issue of *The Johnstown Daily Tribune* a write up reads, "Berwind A.C. defeated by a husky Altoona team 38 to 0. A couple of Johnstown boys were in the Windber lineup. The Windber eleven was the same aggregation defeated recently by the Eighth Ward team." The only conclusion I could draw was that the Windber High team mentioned in the article from October 11, 1909 was the independent Berwind A.C. mentioned in the October 18, 1909 article.

From this point in 1909, up to 1913, the only information about football in Windber dealt with the independent team known as the Berwind team. This team gained notoriety because it was organized and had supervision. In the October 2, 1913 issue of the *Windber Era,* prior to Berwind playing South Fork at Dewey Field, this list of players, managers and substitutes were given.

Manager	Peter Sharp
Asst. Manager	Ernest Faust
Quarterback & Capt.	William Lochrie
Left End	Phenicie
Left Tackle	Keirn
Left Guard	Taylor
Center	Simpson
Right Guard	Morris
Right Tackle	Smith
Right End	Buckwalter
Left Halfback	Foust
Right Halfback	Lloyd
Fullback	Skinner
Substitute	Watyko
Substitute	Kreger

The rugby teams, independent football teams, and the 1908 team played a very special part in preparing Windber High School football for the next 100 years. The game has changed in many ways over this time frame but the foundation had been provided and the stage set for the first official team.

2

The First Official Team

The 1914 Windber High School football team has the distinction of being the first official high school football team. When, exactly, plans were made to field this team cannot be found. An article on the sports page of the September 25, 1914 issue of the *Johnstown Daily Tribune* reads:

Windber High Has Material for a Nifty Eleven
Varsity about Chosen and There Are Still Over 30 Players

Special to the Tribune

Windber, Sept. 25---Windber's High School football team, the first put in the field by the local school for some years, promises to make an excellent record. The training of the Pitt eleven near this place has stirred up interest in the game among the local boys and every afternoon about 40 lusty youths turn out for practice and testing.

A "Varsity" has been practically selected as follows: Left end, James Hyde; tackle, George Hasson; guard, Leroy Williams; captain and center, Frank James; right guard, David Bantley; tackle, Homer Hoenstine; end, Sheridan Hughes; left half, William Severn; right half, Edward Hughes; quarterback, Will McKendrick; fullback, David Parfitt.

With over 30 boys from whom to pick first and second scrub teams, there will be ample material against which to send the regular team for practice. Elmer Daley, the pitcher, has been selected as head coach and is also coach of the Berwind Club's eleven, so that he will have lots of work in the next six weeks.

The high school "Varsity" asks the Tribune to announce that they would like to play the Colonials, of Johnstown, a week from tomorrow. The Colonials can answer direct or through the Tribune.

There are a number of things unique to this article:

First, the article leads you to believe there had been previous teams put on the field by the high school prior to this year. The only evidence of this was the 1908 team, which consisted of high school age students with possibly some older boys and the independent teams made up of older boys and young men.

Second, you almost feel as this is preseason practice when a game had already been played on September 19, 1914, as was reported in the September 22, 1914 issue of the *Johnstown Daily Tribune* in which the Berwind Junior Team defeated the Windber High School eleven 6 to 0.

Third, the head coach selected was Elmer Daley, "the pitcher". Upon further investigation, Mr. Daley was found to be a highly talented pitcher for the independent baseball team known as the Windber Collegians. This selection of Daley as head coach contradicts the record, which indicates W.W. Lantz, Principal of Schools, as head coach.

An article in the September 19, 1914 issue of the *Johnstown Daily Tribune* announces that the Windber High eleven will open the season this afternoon on famous Dewey Field and the opponent will be the Berwind Club Juniors. William Severn, manager of the team has asked one of Pitt's football players to referee and would like to schedule a game with the Colonial team of Johnstown; the manager of the Colonials may talk to manager Severn by calling Bell phone 470, Windber.

Unique to this article is that William Severn is listed as manager of the team and is also listed as the starting right halfback for the game. What happened to Coach Daley or Coach Lantz?

As the reader can tell the record keeping and newspaper accounts during this time period has led to some confusion as to whom the coach might have been and the number of games Windber High School played in 1914.

In all fairness, keeping with the present records, the coach of Windber High School's first football team will be listed as W. W. Lantz.

The very first football game played by Windber High School was on September 19, 1914. This game was played on Dewey Field and the first opponent was the Berwind Club Juniors of the independent football team known as the Berwind Club.

The sports page of the *Johnstown Daily Tribune*, September 22, 1914 reads as follows:

Berwind Juniors Win Opening Game

Special to the Tribune

Windber, Sept. 22-The junior team of the Berwind Club celebrated the opening of their football season Saturday afternoon by clubbing a 6 to 0 victory, out of the Windber High School eleven. The students excelled in the open formations getting off a number of pretty forward passes, but they couldn't stand up under the grueling pounding of their line.

The line-up:

Berwind-6   High School-0

Berwind-6		High School-0
O'Rourke	L E	Hyde
Murray	L.T	Honestein
L. Mills	L.G.	Hasson
Haggan	C	James
Noble	R.G	Reed
J. Buck	R.T	Williams
R. Mills	R.E	S. Hughes
McKenrick	Q.B	L. Buck
Smith	L.H	E. Hughes
Breth	R.H	Severn
Morris	F.B	Parfitt

Touchdown-J. Buck; Referee-Rodgers
Linesmen-Smith and Buck

This account is the first of many articles to be written about Windber High School football. Little did this first group of boys know they had started Windber High School football teams toward the reputation it has today.

Other members of this first football squad include: Bill Mckendrick, the starting quarterback in all of the other games played, Wilfred Nevling, John Hritz, Angelo Marinelli, Mike Metz, Al Berkey, Dave Bantly, (?) Phenicie and (?)Thomas.

The second game of the 1914 season was played at Dewey Field on October 3, 1914 against the Colonials from Johnstown. This was not the Johnstown High School football team; it was an independent team. According to the write-up in the October 5, 1914 issue of the *Johnstown Daily Tribune*,

"Windber High School defeated the Colonials, a strong Johnstown team, in an interesting and hard fought game here Saturday afternoon, 7 to 0. Bill Severn starred for Windber, scoring a touchdown for the locals after a hard 35 yard run, with Dave Parfitt scoring the "goal from touchdown."

This "goal from touchdown" as reported in the write-up, led to some confusion on my part. Upon further investigation, I found this was the way the extra point following the touchdown was reported. The method of scoring this extra point was probably by kicking; however, the kicking method was not as we know it today with a holder involved. The method used was that of a "drop kick" in which the ball was centered or snapped directly to the kicker who would drop the ball to the ground in front of him, and then kick the ball from the ground toward the goal posts.

The third game of this inaugural season was a return match with the Colonials at Point Stadium, Johnstown, on October 17, 1914. The following article from the October 19, 1914 issue of the *Johnstown Dailey Tribune* describes this game:

"Keeping their opponents on the jump from the opening kickoff, the Colonials downed the Windber High School football team at the Point, Saturday afternoon 19 to 6. At no time did the visitors appear dangerous. Windber's only score came in the last quarter when Ed Hughes grabbed a fumble and ran the entire length of the field for a touchdown.

The Colonials carried the ball well, their short end runs being especially productive of good gains. Dannenbaum (quarterback for the Colonials) was pushed over in the first quarter for a touchdown. Both failed to score in the second and in the third, Vogel (fullback for the Colonials) went across on a short end run for a touchdown. In the final round, Vogel intercepted a forward pass and sprinted almost the length of the field for the last touchdown of the game. Fleming (left tackle for the Colonials) kicked goal."

The fourth game was scheduled with Hooversville on October 31, 1914 at Dewey Field, however, there are no records indicating the outcome of this game. Because of the records indicating a tie, I am going to assume this must have been the game ending in the tie.

The fifth and last game of this first Windber High School football season was played on November 14, 1914. The opponent was Cresson, Windber was defeated by a score of 6 to 0. There is no indication of where this game was played.

The present day record shows the 1914 team with zero wins, one loss and one tie. With the information now available the correct record should reflect; one win, three losses and one tie. However, the P.I.A.A. at this time only recognizes the current record.

This inaugural team of 1914 laid the ground work for the next 93 years. Watching this team today, play their brand of Windber football, would be somewhat hilarious, a little difficult to understand, but very interesting. Although our modern day version of Windber football is very different, the dedication of players, coaches, fans and community has remained ardent. Windber High School Football history had begun and continues into the 21st century.

3

Formative Years

Beginning with this 1914 team, up to and including the 1919 team, a six year period, when Windber High School football was in its infancy I have duped as the formative years. That time frame when; very few games were played, small number of participants were involved, and record keeping was at a minimum.

During this period, the losses (12) outnumbered the wins (9), with one win being a thrashing of South Fork, 58-0 during the 1915 season when only three games were played. The last game of the 1915 season was the inaugural game with Johnstown High School, a game Windber lost 0-13, but one that would start a very intense rivalry for years to come. The 1916 season saw the Windber "Coaltowners," as they were called then, win three games, South Fork was defeated twice and the only loss was to Johnstown. The third win was against Scottsdale, at least that is what is reported; no score is available to verify the win.

All home games were played at Dewey Field in 1914. The 1915, 1916, and 1917 teams played their home games at Recreation Park, due to the renovation of Dewey Field.

The 1917 team played five games; two against Somerset, which they split, and two against Altoona, which they also split, and the fifth against Johnstown, losing by a lopsided score of 40 to 0. An article in the *Hi-Times*, Windber High School's newspaper, dated February 1962, relates a little known fact concerning this 1917 squad. The origin of this information is a mystery. The information appears to be factual due to the picture which accompanies it and needs to be shared. (Picture and Article appear on next page.)

1st row, (left to right)—Edgar Kyle, Bernard Duncan, Arnold Long, Nick Nazad, Elbridge Kyle, Tony Buscaglia, Allen Mathewson, Edward Mills. 2nd row, (left to right)—Donald Mathewson, Carl Hoenstine, George Moore, Ben Adams, David Latz, Colored Man, Wilfred Nevling; Victor Zack, Elmer Dailey, coach.

"1919---the highlight of that season was the game with Johnstown. A week before the game was to be played the Windber squad of 14 players became riddled with injuries. Only ten men were available for the game. Roxy Roach, a big league baseball player, pulled into town two days before the game with a colored chauffeur. Elmer Daily, coach of the squad, lassoed the color chauffeur and put him on the team. Eleven men played the entire game and held the strong Johnstown team to 40 points."

Why was this included with the 1917 team information? The article gives the year 1919, but after checking team records, a real sports oddity occurred. Windber did not play Johnstown in 1919 and the coach of the 1919 team was Jim Hyde. How factual the story is of Coach Daily and the chauffeur can't be verified. The picture, with names, appears to be authentic because in the background of the team photo is the old Windber Brewery next to Delaney Field.

The 1918 team played only two games, the others were cancelled due to a flu epidemic throughout the region. That lone win was against Altoona and there is no record of the score with Somerset the second opponent. The record shows an undefeated season, but is not considered for that accolade because of the cancellations due to the flu epidemic.

The 1919 team has the distinction of being the first winless team, compiling a record of zero wins, four losses, and one tie. An interesting note concerning one of the four defeats was that it occurred at the hands of Indiana Normal School, a college team from Indiana, Pennsylvania, now known as Indiana University of Pennsylvania.

This formative period, when Windber football was in its infancy of scholastic competition, presented many challenges to the fledgling players and coaches at Windber High School. These challenges were overcome, and little did these first participants know they had established a firm foundation for Windber High School football to build upon.

4

The 1920's

This era saw the number of teams increase on the schedule and produced Windber's first undefeated season, along with two of the worst defeats in school history. Teams such as Huntingdon, Bellefonte Academy, Turtle Creek, Lock Haven, Latrobe, Clearfield, Greensburg, St. Francis College, Indiana Normal School, and Westinghouse Tech were opponents. Both Altoona and Johnstown were scheduled each year during this era, setting up two of Windber's biggest rivalries.

Coach Jim Hyde, the first player/coach, was at the helm for the first three years of this decade. The wins, 14, outnumbered the losses, nine, with five ties, although two of the worst defeats occurred during these three years.

The worst official defeat of any Windber High School football team came at the hands of Huntingdon in 1920, Windber 0, and Huntingdon 64. However, the worst defeat of any Windber High School football team occurred on November 11, 1921 at the hands of Greensburg. The score, Windber 0 and Greensburg 94. The outcome of this game is not included in the records of 1921, as it was not a regular season game.

The October 17, 1927 issue of the *Windber Era* reports, that Coach Jim Hyde was contacted by Greensburg High School officials in September of 1921. They offered to pay a sum of 350.00 dollars if Windber would come and play in Greensburg. There was an attachment to this offer; the jerseys of the players must include a number, which were not used at that time by Windber. Coach Hyde cut numbers from oilcloth and sewed these numbers on the jerseys to comply with the offer. At that time all players were on their own to get to the game and back to Windber.

Jim Hyde left Windber following the 1922 season. His 1937 Erie East team would end Windber's 41 game winning streak by the score of 6 to 0.

In 1923, H. L. Koehler took over the reins and produced the first official undefeated team in the history of Windber High School Football.

**The First Official Undefeated Windber High School Football Team
1923**

No identification of players could be found

Besides being the **First** official undefeated team with a record of nine wins, zero losses and one tie, this team also holds a number of other **Firsts**. The **Second First** is that of holding their opponents to no touchdowns and only one field goal for the entire season. The three points scored is the lowest number of points scored against Windber in any of the 94 seasons of scholastic football. The **Third First** is that of beating Johnstown since the rivalry began in 1915; and the **Last First** is that of defeating both Johnstown and Altoona in the same season. Windber had defeated Altoona in the 1918 season.

Shown below is the offensive starting line-up, record, and opponents played:

			W.H.S.		Opponent
LE	Pete White		20	South Fork	0
LT	Philip DePolo		25	Clearfield	0
LG	Wenard Kough		32	Johnstown	0
C	Fred Sell		32	Meyersdale	0
RG	Raymond Wilson		13	Lock Haven	0
RT	Rodney Wirick		34	Beaverdale	0
RE	Louis Fruhlinger		24	Altoona	0
QB	Jim Hagan		13	Huntingdon	3
LH	Eugene Murphy		13	Hollidaysburg	0
RH	James Delehunt		0	Conemaugh	0
FB	Desiderius Polansky				

WINDBER HIGH SCHOOL
1923

Banquet

TUESDAY EVENING, DECEMBER 18, 1923
LEISTER HOUSE, WINDBER, PA.

The booklet shown at the left is a photo of the cover of an actual banquet booklet honoring the undefeated 1923 team.

The booklet contains the program with the toastmaster, speakers and various guests listed. Included: are the menu, list of letterman, list of substitutes, and managers.

The Leister House is the present day Windber Hotel on 15th Street and this banquet booklet is on display.

As Windber's reputation as a staunch opponent continued to grow, larger schools were scheduled, although some of these larger schools dominated the smaller Windber teams, as was the case in 1924, when they lost by large margins to Greensburg, 60 to 0, and to Indiana Normal School (now Indiana University of Pennsylvania), 41 to 0. However, some larger schools were defeated; in fact, with wins over both Altoona and Johnstown in 1923, 1924, and 1925, the only three year consecutive defeats in the 51 year rivalry of both Johnstown and Altoona occurred.

The 1926 team defeated Altoona 70 to 0, the largest margin of defeat by an Altoona team in this heated rivalry. This 1926 team also held Indiana Normal School to a scoreless 0-0 tie.

It was probably during this decade that the blue and white colors were selected for game jerseys. These jerseys had no numbers and the only markings were white circles around the sleeves extending from the shoulders to the wrist. The pants, made of canvas, continued to be the dirty yellow or khaki color. Exactly what year this blue and white color combination for jerseys began is not known. The only theory that I was presented with, was by my mother, Nova (Lochrie) Mayer (class of 1935). She seems to think that one of the senior classes, during the mid to late 20's, could have selected those colors to represent the senior class, a very common practice back then. As a result the blue and white color combination could well have been adopted by the athletic teams.

Joe Congersky, who played left guard on the 1925 team and right tackle on the 1926 team, whose picture is shown at Delaney Field, typifies the uniform used during the 1920's. This picture was contributed by his son, Tom Congersky, who was the starting right tackle on the 1958 team

Jim "Scoop" Camille was a member of the undefeated 1923 team and started at quarterback for the 1924, 1925, and 1926 teams. Jim latter became the caretaker at Windber Stadium. His picture, in uniform, appears on the front cover.

Harold "Duke" Weigle, whose teams never suffered a loss under his tenure as head coach at Windber, was a starter on both the 1926 and 1927 teams.

Niles Dalberg, the second four year letter winner, got his start as a tackle on the 1927 team; the third four year letter winner Oscar Ripple started as a halfback on the 1929 team.

The teams of the 1920's produced a 59 percent winning percentage, and Windber High School was starting to get a reputation of playing hardnosed football, even though they were outweighed by most teams. Their reputation was growing in Western Pennsylvania and provided the groundwork on which the teams of the 1930's would expand upon. Windber High School football would soon gain statewide recognition.

5

The Glory Years

Windber High School football has been in existence now for 94 years. Among these 94 years there have been periods, which people continue to debate today, that are referred to as "The Glory Years." Some individuals feel it should encompass the years 1921 through 1945, while others feel this period covers the time frame from 1930 through 1961, others feel that the decade between 1930 and 1939 best suits this title. Also, the years 1998 through 2003 have to be included, as this time frame includes 49 consecutive regular season wins, the most by any Windber High School football team.

After much consternation, I decided the time frame between 1930 and 1943 should be referred to as the "Glory Years." This 14 year period produced two state championship teams, four undefeated teams, a 41 game winning streak, a 77% winning percentage, with only one season when losses outnumbered wins, and the nickname "Ramblers" was attached. Also, a great deal of information concerning players, coaches, and game exploits are available as Windber gained state and nationwide recognition, because of playing many teams outside the local area. Between 1930 and 1943, the W.H.S. football teams compiled a record of 120 wins, 24 losses, and 12 ties.

An article in "*The Evening Star*," a Washington D.C. paper, quoted on Tuesday, October 1, 1939: "Last week's squib about the high school team with the largest winning streak brought a flock of replies. Right now, Ankeny, Iowa, is on top with 45, Massillon, Ohio, next with 44 and Windber, Pennsylvania, third with 41."

Also, in 1939, Windber High School Football was given the rating of "All American" by Jimmy Powers, sports writer for the "*New York Daily News*." and was rated one of the best in the country by Coach John "Jock" Sutherland, former nationally famous University of Pittsburgh coach. Coach Sutherland's name can be found listed among the group of Pitt football players to use Camp Hamilton for pre-season practice in 1914.

The 1930 team compiled a record of 8 wins, 2 losses and 1 tie. The first win of the season was a sound beating of the team from Carrolltown, 82 to 0. The tie was against Johnstown during the regular season and led to the scheduling of a post-season charity game for the unemployed, contested at Point Stadium in Johnstown. Windber defeated Johnstown, champions of the Central Pennsylvania Interscholastic Football Conference, by a score of 7-0. An interesting fact related to this game was that two starters for Johnstown, John Kawchak, left tackle, and Steve Terebus, left halfback, would become head football coaches at Windber.

Another interesting fact was found in the September 29, 1930 issue of the *Hi-Times*. The story began with the headlines:

Daily Classes in Football Held

"Windber High gridders have their daily lessons in football as other pupils have in English and Math. A few days ago Coach Allen inaugurated a daily football class during the second period in Room 105.

The purpose of this class is to teach the boys the rules of the game so that they may be able to understand the game better.

Football rule books and mimeographed contract sheets have been given out. The rule book is to be studied, and the contract sheet gives an actual play on the field. The player is to untangle the situation and be able to tell whether the play was legal. He must also know what he would have done in that certain situation. This tends toward better understanding of the game and increased efficiency, says the coach."

Increased efficiency. Was this Coach Allen's method of introducing a game plan for an upcoming game, thus providing less time needed at practice to learn plays? What an advantage this provided. Can you imagine the uproar heard from students, parents, and administrators today if these classes were a part of the present day curriculum?

The 1930 team had a special treat on Friday October 24, as reported in the October 28 issue of the *Hi-Times*, when they attended the college night game between Thiel College and St. Vincent College at Johnstown's Point Stadium. "The whole squad was able to go because of the efforts of Coach Allen who secured complimentary tickets through the courtesy of St. Vincent's Athletic Department. Coach Allen secured permission from Thiel authorities to let Captain's Marron and Gates watch the attitude taken by a college team before the game. Marron and Gates were much impressed by the absolute seriousness shown by all the players."

Another interesting article from the October 28, 1930 issue of the *Hi-Times* was a piece of correspondence received from a group of either players or fans from La Salle Institute, located in Cumberland, Md. The article read:

FROM THE LASALLE INSTITUTE

Attention Ye Loyal Followers of the
Windber Hi School Football Team:

Forward March and Read
La Salle 44, Rowlesburg 0.
La Salle 6, Mt. St. Mary's College Frosh 0.
La Salle 20, Martinsburg Hi 0.
La Salle 32, Gonzago Hi (Washington, D.C.) 0.

That makes it more interesting. Windber is undefeated. Get pepped to look at a snappy football team. It's going to be a battle and we are coming plenty strong.
(Signed)
Mike, Ike, Spike, Wilbur, Jerry, Anthony,
Horne, James, and the gang.

I can just imagine the effect this article had on the 1930 squad. Was this a ploy by Coach Allen to fire up the team? We shall never know, but to hold a team to seven points with that record was impressive. Even though, as reported in the November 10, 1930 issue of the *Hi-Times*, the Windber gridders outplayed and outfought the larger opponents at Delaney Field on Saturday, November 8. The final score was LaSalle 7, Windber 6.

Two members of this team were four year starters (1927-1930); Niles Dalberg, at tackle, who did not pursue a college career and died in 2004 at the age of 95 and Joe Gates, at quarterback, who went on to play college football at Duquesne University and St. Francis College, Loretto, PA, He returned to Windber to coach for four years (1939-1942).

The 1931 and 1932 teams with a combined record of 13 wins and 6 losses, provided much needed experience for the younger players who would provide Windber High School with its first state championship. John Murphy, the captain of the 1931 team, went on to become a prisoner of war during World War II, and Oscar Ripple went on to play football at Concord College, West Virginia, and returned to the area to teach and coach at Shade High School. Charles Mayer, my father, was the starting right tackle for the 1932 team, and after high school, worked for Berwind-White, and continued work until his untimely death at the age of 38 in 1953.

The 1933 "Coaltowners", as they were known then, became the first W.H.S. football team to win a state championship by defeating John Harris High School of Harrisburg at Point Stadium in Johnstown under the tutelage of Coach T. T. "Tubby" Allen. An article in the December 21, 1933 *Hi-Times* reports that an estimated crowd of 20,000 fans witnessed this game on Saturday, December 9, 1933, with Windber leading 7-6 as a result of a touchdown by Jim Cavacini, followed by an extra point kick from Bill "Cooney" Farkas. Late in the fourth quarter Windber was forced to punt, presenting the "Jonnys," as they were called, with an opportunity to win the game. This punt, by Jim Cavacini, who went on to play Big Ten Football at Indiana University, according to statistics, traveled 76 yards and put John Harris in a big hole. The "Jonnys" methodically moved the ball closer to the Windber goal line. The game ended with Windber making an amazing goal line stand in the last minutes and John Harris at the Windber eight yard line.

Another other first this 1933 team provided, occurred on Thursday, September 28, 1933. The first night game played by a Windber High School football team, under the lights. The game was played at Point Stadium in Johnstown, against Ferndale, whom they dispatched 18-0.

It was also during 1933, after defeating Hollidaysburg, that a 41 game winning streak started. This regular season streak continued through the 1937 season when it was ended by Erie East, score, 6-0. There were six ties during this period. This 41 game regular season winning streak is the second longest in the history of W.H.S. football.

Photograph of Jim Cavacini taken from the 1934 *The Little Stylus* (W.H.S. Yearbook)
The caption underneath read:
   Triple Threat Jim Cavacini

1933 State Champions

Row 1 T.T. Allen-Head Coach, R. Morgan-Mgr., H. Weigle-Asst. Coach, M. Mock, J. DeArmey, J. Cavacini, J. Wagner, M. Stringer-Mascot, T. Marron, G. Gordon, L. Fancourt, B. Murray-Manger, M. Beam-Faculty.

Row 2 W. Lamb, C. Bartholomew, T. Harding, J. Carliss, A. Garlathy, W. Farkas, J. Bell.

Row 3 B. Allison, A. Sendek, W. Wilson, V. Couperthwaite, M. Heckler, J. Daily, F. Sakon, W. Beckley, F. Purcelli, W. DePolo, W. Gahagen.

Row 4 E. Larson, E. Yocca, C. Gilroy, A. LaMonaca, R. Parnell, A. Dzierski, W. Kinney, G. Katchmerick, W. Manotti, J. Sherlock, J. Freeman, T. Senella.

Row 5 E. George, M. Durbin, W. Cook, J. Bednar, R. Sherlock, E. Fagnani, J. DiGuilio, C. Wilson-Mgr., C. Pierre, J. Mastrolembo-Mgr., P. Ciotti, F. Hoffer-Mgr., A. Abbatte, A. DePolo, J. Mansour, T. Moraca.

In 1934, "Tubby" Allen moved to Pottsville High and was replaced by J. Harold "Duke" Weigle, captain of Windber's 1927 team and assistant coach to T.T. Allen. During the 1934 season, Allen faced his former assistant on the Pottsville gridiron with the game ending scoreless. In 1935, Windber defeated Pottsville, 27-6, at the Point Stadium. This 1934 team concluded the season with a record of seven wins, five ties, and no defeats.

1934 Starting Offensive Line-up

Offensive Line: Left to Right
RE-Tom Harding, RT-John Daily, RG-Charles Bartholomew, C-Bernard Allison, LG-Wilson Lamb, LT-Arthur Garlathy, LE-Andy Sendeck.
Backfield: Left to Right
RH-Jack Bell, FB-John Carliss, QB-Bill Manotti, LH-Bill Farkas.

The 1935 team continued Windber's undefeated streak with 11 wins and one tie. The experience gained during these two years set the stage for 1936. Bill Farkas, starting left halfback, went on to play college football at the University of Pittsburgh.

The 1936 team, guided by "Duke" Weigle, concluded the season with the best record in Windber High School football history, undefeated in 13 games. Due to an eligibility infraction, discovered after the Altoona game by the P.I.A.A., all games played up to that point in the schedule were forfeited. (Information on this controversy will be found in a latter part of this chapter.)

It was during this time a sportswriter for the *Windber Era* coined the nickname "Ramblers" prior to the Bethlehem game, however, the nickname did not stick. (An in-depth discussion of this nickname follows in a later chapter.)

This record setting team ran all over their opponents. A total of 535 points were amassed by the "Blue and White", while holding their opponents to 64 points. Windber averaged 41 points per game, while holding their opponents to five points per contest.

Charles William Beckley, better known as Bill Beckley or his nickname "Beck", was the captain of this 1936 team. I had the pleasure of interviewing him on November 24, 2002. Beck, as I know him, related a number of interesting stories. The first tale he spun was a dandy.

Beck lived on Locust Street, and his buddy, George Bokinsky, lived on Bridge Street, both in Scalp Level. Beck convinced George, who was going to join his dad in the mines, to try football because he was a big bruiser. They went to see coach Weigle. Coach asked Bokinsky, "What position do you want to play?" George responded, "Fullback." Coach Weigle just laughed. Little did he know that George Bokinsky would become one of the famous "Touchdown Twins" as they were called in 1937, along with his teammate, Bud Bossick.

The second story Beck related, concerned "the football click." He and a number of his teammates, along with their dates, stayed out past training rule hours any number of times, because they were the "football click." Coach Weigle got wind of this "football click" procedure. The very next practice he ran those boys until their tongues were hanging out and they couldn't run any more. Beck laughed about this at the time of the interview, 66 years later, but I could tell it made a lasting impression on him, even to this day.

The last story Beck related, dealt with Assistant Coach, Charles "Ding" Schaeffer. Coach Schaeffer was the line coach and would tie a rope between the goal posts in order to teach the lineman to stay low as they moved from their stance. Beck related that any number of times he almost hung himself when he didn't stay low enough. Coach Schaeffer, along with Coach Weigle, made up the combination duo known in Windber High School football lore as "Ding and Duke".

"Ding and Duke"

J. Harold "Duke" Weigle

Charles "Ding" Schaeffer

Following the Altoona game, which Windber won 20-12, the ninth game of this 1936 season, and prior to the scheduled game with Johnstown, a controversy arose concerning the eligibility of some Windber players. Someone from either Altoona or Johnstown notified the P.I.A.A. officials that possibly some of the Windber players may be ineligible because of their age. The P.I.A.A. officials came to the high school to investigate the allegations and uncovered the infractions.

In the November 5, 1936 issue of the *Windber Era* the headline reads:

"P.I.A.A. bars Windber Grid Players: All games ordered forfeit."
The article continues and explains the P.I.A.A. interpretation:
"Pertains to when a student passes only two subjects out of four in his freshman year and comes back the following year and passes four subjects, he would be classed as a sophomore in that year and the following year he becomes a junior".

The result of this interpretation was that two boys were playing more semesters than permitted and that the age of these boys was not a factor as originally thought. The Johnstown-Windber game on Thanksgiving Day probably would have been played without these two star players had it not been for the reaction of Windber fans and players.

In an October 1936 issue of the *Windber Era* it was reported that eleven members of the Windber football team invaded Johnstown High School and went to Coach William "Foxy" Miller's room, calling him out of the classroom and threatened to "pay him back" because of the ineligibility charges against Windber. Also, reported in this article, the Johnstown School Board pointed out a boycott against Johnstown merchants by the Windber fans because of this incident.

The article continued to explain that mutual cancellation of the game by both Windber and Johnstown was recommended by Edmund C. Wicht, secretary of the P.I.A.A. The Johnstown board stated that the cancellation of the game was made because it felt that the tension would not be lessened by Thanksgiving Day and the move would give both schools time to secure a Thanksgiving Day attraction.

The following is the Johnstown School Board statement:

"The board of school directors has decided to cancel the Thanksgiving Day game with Windber. The action is not in the nature of a reprisal or a 'run out' on Windber.

"The board could not overlook the high spirit of tension that has developed in Windber. The visit of 11 members of the Windber football squad to Johnstown High School, where they called Coach W. H. Miller from his room, with a bodily assault averted only by the courage and levelheadedness of Coach Miller, is an illustration of the violent spirit abroad."

"The boycott of Johnstown business houses by Windber people shows also an unreasonable attitude. It is a type of coercion that the board resents, and we believe the public resents."

"Secretary Wicht of the P.I.A.A. has conferred with Principal J. Ernest Wagner of Johnstown High School and Principal J. L. Hackenberg of Windber High School and has advised mutual cancellation in view of the existing tension."

The result of these games being forfeited prevented Windber from representing the western conference in the state championship game. The team from Curwensville, who Windber had defeated 39-0, was declared the western conference winner and played in the state championship game against Kingston, the eastern representative. The result of that game was Kingston-6 and Curwensville-0

A number of questions regarding this incident have been debated many times among Windber fans. Following are three such questions:

Who informed the P.I.A.A. that a possible eligibility problem existed?

Why would someone want to stir up such a situation?

Could Windber have competed for another state championship?

The answers to these questions will never be known, but it is interesting to try and answer some of these questions with questions that I am sure many Windber fans and players of that era have wondered about. Some of these questions are:

Was a disgruntled Altoona fan jealous of Windber's win?

Were the Johnstown fans worried about Windber defeating them?

Should Windber have been permitted to participate in another state championship?

Memories have faded and debate ended, but the fact remains; those thirteen games were all played and Windber was undefeated in 1936. This team also received an invitation to play in Miami, Florida on Christmas Day in 1936. The invitation was declined because of travel expenses.

J. Harold "Duke" Weigle completed his tenure at Windber following this 1936 season and took a coaching position at Tamaqua High School. His winning percentage still remains the best in Windber history with a record of 31 wins, no defeats and six ties, from 1934 through 1936.

With "Duke" Weigle leaving, the school board selected Charles "Ding" Schaeffer as the new head coach. "Ding" had been Coach Weigle's assistant for the past five years. The assistants to Coach Schaeffer were Ralph Weigle, brother of "Duke," who came from Ferndale High School were he was serving as an assistant coach, and Jimmy Daub, who came from Emporium High School, where he was serving as athletic director.

Coach Schaeffer chose not to serve as head coach. Instead he followed "Duke" Weigle to Tamaqua High School and served as an assistant. Coach Weigle spent one season at Tamaqua compiling a record of five wins and six losses. Following the 1937 season, he accepted the head coaching position at Phillipsburg, New Jersey. Coach Schaeffer remained at Tamaqua and became head coach.

The Second State Championship-1937

The 1937 team laden with talent from the previous undefeated season earned the second state championship for Windber. This team was coached by Ralph Weigle, brother of "Duke" Weigle, who had been selected as head coach when "Ding" Schaeffer decided to follow "Duke" Weigle to Tamaqua. The 41 game winning streak ended during the second game of this season, with Windber losing to Erie East 0-6. The game was coached by former Windber High School head coach, Jim Hyde.

Hobart Sherlock, a halfback on this '37 team, related his experience in an interview for an article in the December 10, 1989 issue of the *Tribune-Democrat*, by Mike Mastovich, about the big road game with Erie. "The game was close and some guy with no teeth chased me around the whole time," Sherlock said. "I'll never forget my dad when we were leaving for that three-day trip," Sherlock added. "You know how much he gave me? Fifty cents. That's it for three days."

This defeat did not hinder Windber as they vanquished all foes including a sound drubbing of Bethlehem High School with a 75-12 score.

In an article from the *Bethlehem Republic Newspaper*, October 17, 1937, the headline reads:

Touchdown Twins Rout Bethlehem

The article compares Bud Bossick the quarterback for the 1937 eleven to "Slinging" Sammy Baugh, Texas Christian's great passer. "Maybe, the least said about the Bethlehem High-Windber game the better it will be....but anyone who saw the fray couldn't pass over it without saying a few words for Bossick and Bokinsky, Windber's touchdown twins.... Bossick was a scholastic edition of "Slinging" Sammy Baugh....and Bokinsky caught most everything he threw. . .their performance was remarkable."

Picture of Bud Bossick (on left) and George Bokinsky (on right) "The Touchdown Twins", taken from the 1938 *Stylus*.

I wonder what Coach "Duke" Weigle would have thought about Bokinsky's effort, after laughing at his request to play fullback when they first met, as related to me in the interview with Bill Beckley.

This 1937 squad compiled a total of 391 points while holding their 13 opponents to a mere 39 points, including seven shutouts. The highlight of this 1937 season was the state championship game contested at Point Stadium, Johnstown, with the eastern representative, Steelton. A banner headline in the Dec. 9, 1937 edition of the *Windber Era* proclaimed:

"Blue and White Again State Champions" a sub-head read: **"Windber's Juggernauts display speed and air attack in 21-0 victory."**

In an article, published in the December 10, 1989 issue of the *Tribune-Democrat*, **"Ramblers' indomitable style ruled the '30s,"** by Mike Mastovich, sportswriter for the *Tribune-Democrat*, describes the game as follows:

"Like the '33 game, this championship also was played at a packed Point Stadium. Two stars of the team, the late Bud Bossick and George Bokinsky, were labeled the "touchdown twins."

"There was a marching band extravaganza before the game, with the bands from Windber, Johnstown, Southmont, Westmont, Conemaugh and Steelton putting on a show.

"Bossick then staged his own performance, returning the opening kick-off 95 yards for a score to set the tempo of the day and later scored on a 10-yard run after a lateral. Bokinsky completed the scoring with a four-yard run over center."

Mr. Mastovich continued the story of this game from interviews with former members of this state championship team. "We didn't realize it at the time, but that was pretty darn good," said Hobart Sherlock, a halfback on the '37 team. "The one thing I learned off the Weigles was that it doesn't matter how big they are. We still could play. We still could win."

"The togetherness of the team is something I'll always remember," added Paul Toth, a tackle on the '37 squad. "It was the coaching staff, the teachers, the students, just everybody together. Back then, you played not to lose. You played to gain and you weren't satisfied by just going out and playing a good game because you always wanted to win."

This attitude, expressed by Paul Toth, has emanated through every decade of Windber football. I feel sure it existed prior to this 1937 season and continues today.

1937 State Champions

Row 1 Pete Gorgone, Pete Pierzchala, Frank Durbin, George Wirick, George Bokinsky, Edward Bossick, Joe Rodgers, Paul Toth, William Hayes.
Row 2 Alvin Hagan, Victor Surina, Joe Tverdak, Hobart Sherlock, Frank Kinney, Joe Pierre, John Badaczewski, Steve Hienrick.
Row 3 Arthur Daub (Asst. Coach), Earl Ripple, George Balog, Jack Morgan, John LaPlaca, Edward Sakon, Joe Bell, William Racine, John Tomaczewski, Nick Boblick, Ralph Weigle (Head Coach).
Row 4 Richard Mickle (Faculty Manager), Joe Flori, Edward Stanish, Andy Allen, Earl Berkey, David Latz, Robert Holsinger, James Verna, John Visnovsky, Charles Obbets, Steve Izing (Manager).
Row 5 Robert Sherlock, Elmer Barna, Robert Hamilton, Leo Turcato, Walter Dressick, Felix Guss, Mike Kundar.

Coach Ralph Weigle left Windber after the 1937 season and was replaced by Don Fletcher. The 1938 squad did not have a very impressive season compared to the previous two years with a record of seven wins, four loses and one tie, but the schedule was very formidable. With the likes of Erie East, Scott High (now North Braddock), Pottsville, Dubois, Sharon, Curwensville and Johnstown, this team faced one of the toughest schedules up to this time.

The left tackle on this 1938 team, Dave Latz, Jr., from all indications, is the first son of a former Windber High School football player to follow in his father's footstep. Dave Latz, Sr. played on the 1916 team and was captain of the 1917 and 1918 teams. There have been numerous sons that have followed in their father's footsteps. I would like to include in this document all father and son combinations as well as grandfather and grandsons, but the list is now just too long.

An article in the October, 7, 1938 issue of the *Hi-Times* gives some insight as to how serious Coach Fletcher was about coaching. The article states, "Leo Turcato, our varsity end, had to carry a football to all of his classes because the coach spied him carrying the ball improperly on the field."

One of Windber's very few four year lettermen started his high school career in 1938. This boy, Joe "Gump" Polansky, went on to play three more years and became an icon at Windber. He helped with football from 1942 until his retirement in 1976. "Gump" worked as a janitor all those years for the school district. It was a job, I'm sure that some people might look down upon, but he was doing that in order to be around high school football, a game he loved. His contribution to Windber High School football can not be equaled.

The 1938 season ended with a banquet at Recreation Hall. An article in the December 18, 1938 issue of the *Windber Era* provides some understanding of the spirit of Windber football. "A crowd of approximately 250 people, including the mothers and fathers of the pigskinners, jammed the hall for the affair sponsored by the Windber Businessmen's Association. It was said at the banquet that more than 200 additional requests for tickets could not be filled because of the limited seating capacity of the hall."

In a later portion of this article, Coach Fletcher said he was greatly impressed by the crowd. "This is the first time I ever saw a turnout like this for a high school football banquet," he said. "This is truly an example of the spirit that prevails in Windber. I have begun to understand why Windber has a good football team every year. Windber not only has a good football spirit, but a good spirit throughout the town."

Two members of this 1938 team; quarterback, Pete Gorgone, went on to play college football at Muhlenberg College, Allentown and professional football with the New York Giants, while his teammate, right end, Joe Pierre played college football at the University of Pittsburgh and professional football with the Pittsburgh Steelers in 1945.

Coach Fletcher moved on to New Kensington at the end of the 1938 school year. Joe Gates, an assistant of Fletcher's, was named head coach. As head coach for the 1939 team, Gates started with an impressive record of ten wins, one loss and one tie. Playing a very impressive schedule, they vanquished such foes as Erie East 40-14, Scott High 20-7 and Rankin 21-6. The only loss came at the hands of Pottsville, coached by T.T. Allen, Gates' mentor at Windber, by a 12-0 score.

The most impressive win in 1939 was the defeat of Paterson High School, New Jersey, at Delaney Field. Windber 20, Paterson 6. Paterson had won their city championship 8 out of 14 times and was the reigning state champions in their division.

The most notable player on this 1939 team was John Badaczewski, who went on to play college football at Western Reserve and participated at the professional level with the Boston Yanks of the NFL. Earl Ripple, quarterback, for this 1939 team was the first Windber High School football player to earn All State honors. He was named to the 1939 Associated Press (Over All Format) Second Team as a back and earned an athletic scholarship to the University of Pittsburgh.

The 1940 team was the only team during these glory years that did not have a winning record. This team posted four wins, six losses and two ties. Steve Kaplan was the quarterback of that team and would return to Windber High School after college to coach both football and basketball.

The 1941 team, with third year coach Joe Gates at the helm and Nunzio Marino at quarterback, along with four year starter Joe "Gump" Polansky, at right halfback, and Walter Cominsky at left halfback, provided stiff competition for the opponents. The only two losses were to powerful Johnstown and Farrell. These boys on the 1941 team gained valuable experience and set the stage for the only back to back undefeated seasons in Windber High School football history. The 1942 and 1943 teams have the distinction of being the only two teams in school history with back to back undefeated seasons.

The 1942 team opened with an impressive victory over Shade by a score of 64 to 0, the largest point total against Shade in the 43 years that Windber and Shade have clashed on the gridiron. The victory over Johnstown was the first since 1933 and the victory over Altoona the first since 1928. The 1942 team concluded the season with eight wins and no defeats. Ray Torquato, who played center on this team, was the second W.H.S. football player to be selected as an All State player. He was chosen for the Second Team Associated Press All State for Pennsylvania.

Coach Joe Gates moved on to Greensburg following this 1942 undefeated season. He was replaced by Ray Jones, an assistant coach with Gates at the time. Jones led the 1943 team to an undefeated ten win season. The win over Johnstown would be the last until 1948. Coach Jones moved on following this undefeated season.

The 1943 team had a plethora of talent led by Nunzio Marino at fullback. Five players on this team were honored in the inaugural *Tribune-Democrat* All Scholastic Team in 1943. The selection of five players for this starting line up is unprecedented in the 25 year history of this first All-Star format. No other school, in the subscription area of the *Tribune-Democrat*, has had this many players selected for the first team. The five first team selections from Windber High School were: Joe Campitell-tackle, Joe DelSignore-guard, Arthur Toth-center, Walter Cominsky-quarterback, Nunzio Marino-fullback.

Inaugural Tribune-Democrat All Scholastic Team
1943

Top Left: Nunzio Marino. **Bottom Left to top right:** Steve Slobozien, John Bowman, Jim Pinelli, Arthur Toth, Joe DelSignore, Joe Campitell, Craig Kunkle. **Center:** James Davis, Harry Hunt. **Bottom right:** Walter Cominsky.

Photograph from the December 2, 1943 issue of the *Tribune Democrat*.

The most talented individual on this 1943 team was Nunzio "Touchdown" Marino. Beside the selection of first team for the Tribune-Democrat All Scholastic Team, he also was selected on the first team of the 1943 Associated Press All State Team for Pennsylvania, the first Windber High School football player to achieve that honor. Marino, also was presented the George S. Fockler Memorial Trophy, emblematic of the outstanding amateur sports achievement at the Point Stadium, Johnstown, in 1943, (now known as the Point Stadium Award), the first non-Johnstown resident to do so. With his talent and these awards for scholastic gridiron greatness he earned a scholarship at Notre Dame University.

Marino played for the "fighting Irish" for two years and transferred to St. Bonaventure, in New York state were he completed his college career. He then coached football and basketball at St. Bernard High School in Bradford, Pennsylvania from 1950 through 1955. Nunzio Marino at the age of 29 was stricken with an illness and died. An article in the *Bradford Journal,* dated November 23, 1955 reads: "The Great Referee" has called the games end for Nunzio Marino and Nunzio has left the field of play."

Nunzio "Touchdown" Marino

Marino at Notre Dame-1946
Photo courtesy of Geno stevens

Photograph taken in 1942 or 1943 at Point Stadium during the Johnstown - Windber game. Photographer unknown, possibly taken by the *Tribune Democrat*. This scene at Point Stadium during the "Glory Years" provides evidence of Windber's football prowess. Photo courtesy of Shaz Yuhas.

The "Glory Years", those years where Windber football teams became known throughout the state and the nation. I must agree with Robert B. Baylor of the *Harrisburg Patriot* when he wrote on August 31, 1975, "Windber High School Early Football Giant in Allegheny Mountains." The exploits of these teams and individuals will continue to make up a large part of the history of Windber High School football, but least we forget, everyone of those teams from the '30's and early 40's, just as every team from decades to come were trying their best. Coaching, scheduled teams, community spirit, and individual efforts have all played a factor in this period of the history of Windber Football.

The choice I made in selecting the '30's and early 40's as the "Glory Years" was entirely personal. Some readers may disagree and I apologize if this choice offended anyone. The decades that follow are just as important to Windber football as the "Glory Years".

During the back to back undefeated seasons, in 1942 and 1943, the newspaper accounts of games began to use the name "Ramblers" as a nickname to identify the team. Gone were the "Coaltowners", "Miners", and "Blue and White Gridders." Windber High School football had a new identity. How was this nickname derived?

6

We Become the "Ramblers"

Throughout the first 30 years of W.H.S. athletics, a number of different nicknames were used to identify athletic teams. The most common used were; "Coaltowners" and "Miners." These obviously were selected because of the community's involvement with underground coal mining.

In some newspaper accounts of football games, the team is identified by using the nickname "Blue and White Gridders", because of the color combination of the game uniforms.

The nickname "Ramblers" did not become attached until 1942 or 1943. The exact year is difficult to pin point. The nickname was used sporadically at the end of the 30's and beginning of the 40's, however, most of the newspaper accounts continued to use "Coaltowners" or "Miners" for identification purposes.

How did the nickname "Ramblers" for W. H. S. athletics get its origin?

When was this nickname coined?

These questions have been asked by many Windber fans, opponents, and the media for many years. Different theories have been proposed. I would like to present a few of these theories on the origin of this nickname "Ramblers", that were shared by various individuals as I researched this topic.

Coal Mining Term Theory: This theory was presented to me by an individual who thought the term was used in the past as a way of describing a job performed by an underground coal miner. For example: buggy runner, brattice man, lamp man, bolter, cutter, and shot firer; Some miners could have been called "ramblers" for the job they performed. During my five years as an underground miner I never heard the term "rambler" used for any job performed.

The Sandwich Theory: This particular theory was suggested by an individual who remembered eating submarine sandwiches prepared by the cafeteria staff at the high school. They told me the high school athletic teams were named after the sandwich which was called a "Rambler."

The Piglet Mascot Theory: Of the different theories suggested, this one holds the least amount of possibility. Someone told me that they heard the name "Rambler" was the piglet mascot that someone began to use as a caricature to represent Windber athletic teams. How did this caricature come into existence? I have not been able to find a clue; it is no longer used today.

The Rambling Theory: This theory appears to have a basis of fact. Different people suggested to me that the nickname "Ramblers" originated as a result of the football teams having to travel far and wide in order to find competition willing to play because of their reputation. They had to ramble or they went rambling to find opponents.

It was during the 1936 season that the nickname "Ramblers" was first used to identify the football team. In the October 15, 1936 issue of the *Windber Era*, a sportswriter, referred to this team as the "blue and white ramblers", as they were preparing to play a game with Bethlehem.

In trying to discover why this sportswriter used the name "Ramblers", I found some information at a Notre Dame web site (*www.nd.edu/sieghall/history.html*), which included nicknames used by the University of Notre Dame before the "Fighting Irish". Nicknames such as the "Notre Dame Ramblers", "Rockne's Ramblers", "Rambling Irish", and the "Nomads" were listed. It was explained that Knute Rockne's football teams could not find opponents within easy traveling distance to compete because of their football prowess and had to travel (ramble) in order to find competition.

W.H.S. football teams during the mid 1930's were experiencing this same dilemma. This sportswriter for the *Windber Era* in 1936 must have recalled these former Notre Dame football nicknames, and as a compliment to the 1936 team prior to playing the away game with Bethlehem, used the adjective "Ramblers." In the October 22, 1936 issue of the *Windber Era*, this same sportswriter gives an explanation of why he choose the name "Ramblers":

> "Close followers of the Windber High Football team are becoming curious to know where the title "Ramblers" came from. Well, to make a long story short, the writer recalls the great teams the late Knute Rockne turned out on the football fields of Notre Dame. They were named the "Ramblers". I rather consider it a compliment to the gridders and Coach "Duke" Weigle to likewise bear this name. So whether I am on the frying pan or in the fire, I still claim the 1936 Windber High Team is the "Ramblers."

I could not find the name of the individual sportswriter responsible for writing any of the articles, but I have a feeling it was Mike Serrian who at that time was doing some writing for the *Windber Era.*

Although we know the year the nickname "Ramblers" was coined, it is difficult to determine when this nickname began to be used extensively as a means of identifying Windber High School athletic teams. During the late 1930's, the nickname was not used very often and teams were referred to by their old nicknames. The write-ups of football games during the 1942 and 1943 undefeated football seasons, used this nickname very often. What year, exactly, this nickname became permanently attached, I don't think will ever be known. We are the "Ramblers" now and the athletic teams of Windber Area High School can probably thank the sportswriter for the Windber Era in 1936 for giving us this nickname.

A very peculiar thing occurred as I searched across the United States for high school teams using the nickname "Ramblers". The nickname "Ramblers" is not unique to Windber High School alone. I came across three other high schools which also use this same nickname.

The first is a high school located in our state of Pennsylvania. The Cathedral Preparatory School in Erie, also uses the nickname "Ramblers." Cathedral Prep. is an all boys catholic high school founded in 1921 and competes at the Quad-A level. After contacting Cathedral Prep., I was referred to an individual who had written a history of Cathedral Prep football. The follow up phone call to Daniel J. Brabender author of *Ramblers, The History of Cathedral Prep Football,* proved to be very interesting After thirty minutes of conversation I had found a person with the same passion about high school football. Mr. Brabender sent me a copy of his book and after a brief search I found information that a sportswriter for an Erie newspaper coined the name "Ramblers" in 1929. The nickname "Ramblers" was a direct reference to Notre Dame. What a coincidence that two high schools in the same state would be given nicknames the same way.

The second high school using the nickname "Ramblers" is located in Winthrop, Maine. I came across this name as a result of reading an article in a medical magazine while waiting for a doctor's appointment. This article dealt with teen suicide, a problem at this school, because of the pressure playing football. I then accessed the web site for Winthrop High School and found that in the past the high school had no playing fields and had to travel in order to compete. The nickname "Ramblers" evolved because of this need to travel. The teams used an old school bus as a means of traveling and as a result use a picture of a bus for its mascot.

The third high school using this nickname is located in Moosehart, Illinois. It was very serpenditious that I came across this team. I was looking at the latest edition of *Moose* a quartley publication by the Moose Organization and saw a story with the headline: **Ramblers Get Huge Media Coverage**. Of course, with the name Ramblers in the headline I quickly turned to the article and was informed that the high school team was nicknamed the "Ramblers". After further investigation, by use of the internet, I discovered this high school was established in 1913 and started football in 1914. The football team developed into a power house and as a result found it difficult to schedule area teams. Sounds very familiar, doesn't it. The result, you guessed it, they had to travel throughout the country to find worthy opponents.

The article by the *Chicago Tribune*, high lighted the "Red Ramblers" of Mooseheart during their 2007 season. Upon further investigation, on the newspapers web site, I discovered the adjective "Red" is used proceeding the name "Ramblers" because of the school's colors.

Go Ramblers!!

7

Following the Glory Years

Windber continued to field competitive teams following the glory years but the domination of opponents and number of wins began to decline. The 1944 through 1947 teams had a combined record of 20 wins, 15 defeats and 4 ties. What contributed to this decline? I feel there are a number of factors involved.

First, the talent pool was affected by some of the older boys enlisting in the service during World War II and others who could not devote their time to football because fathers or older brothers had been drafted into the service and they needed to work in order to supplement the family income.

Another impact of this talent pool occurred at the end of the 40's when Berwind Coal Company began to shut coal mines down because the demand for coal became less as oil replaced coal as a choice of fuel for industry. Miners and their families were forced to relocate to other industrial towns and cities to find employment. This exodus of families had a tremendous impact on the talent pool.

Windber football was affected by this decline in the talent pool but continued to field competitive teams. Names such as Paul Kutch, quarterback on the 1945 and 46 teams, who earned Second Team Offense-All State recognition both years and Frank Kush, starting lineman, during the 1945, 1946, and 1947 seasons, who went on to become the most notable football player from Windber, will attest to the ability of smaller players being capable of competing against larger schools, with a larger talent pool. The win-loss record of the late 1940's didn't compare to that of the "Glory Years" but player attitude and community support did not diminish. In fact, football fever continued under new coach John Kawchak and the opening of Windber Stadium in 1949.

The Kawchak Era 1948-1960

This era of Windber football began in the fall of 1948, the last year Delaney Field would be used as a home field venue and the first year John Kawchak would direct the Ramblers. The record of seven wins and four losses doesn't sound very impressive for this 1948 season, but three of those losses were against very large schools, and Johnstown was defeated. The construction of Windber Stadium had begun and football fever in the community was high.

One of the highlights during this 1948 season was the game with Allentown. Windber lost the game, played on Thanksgiving Day, but the fanfare associated with Allentown's dedication of its new stadium was college like and players along with fans still talk about this game. As a sidelight, it should be noted that all four losses in 1948 were to teams beginning with the letter A; Aliquippa, Adams, Ambridge, and Allentown.

The only damper of this 1948 season was the injury to Eddie Chupek, a junior tackle on the Shade Township team. During the game with Windber at Delaney Field on September 11, Eddie, in the act of tackling a Windber ball carrier, was critically injured. This injury left Eddie Chupek paralyzed and he remained so until his death on March 15, 1990. On Monday, October 25, 1948, "Eddie" Chupek Night was held at Point Stadium in Johnstown, participating in exhibition football games were teams from: Berlin, Boswell, Conemaugh, Conemaugh Twp., Johnstown, Meyersdale, Richland Twp., Shade Twp., Somerset and Windber. The proceeds from Chupek Night were used to establish a trust fund in order to defray expenses incurred as a result of this unfortunate accident.

The 1949 season brought a close to the 40's but opened up a new venue for Windber football, Windber Stadium. Windber's first game at the new stadium was played September 9, 1949, with Windber defeating Shade Township 40-to-0 before almost six thousand fans. With this new stadium and the 1949 team losing only one game, a renewed spirit which had waned for a couple of years was rekindled. The teams of the early and mid 1950's compiled a record of 46 wins, 19 losses and two ties. John Kawchak never had an undefeated season during his 13 year tenure but did have four one loss seasons. These four losses were all to local schools except for Punxsutawney in 1950. Most of these wins were over schools similar to Windber in size, but the schedule was going to change. In 1951 Beaver Falls was added and each consecutive year even bigger schools were added. Schools such as Pittsburgh North Catholic, Har-Brack, McKeesport, Chambersburg, Indiana, along with the old rivals, Johnstown and Altoona.

The last four years of the Kawchak Era saw the toughest schedules any Windber team had faced, in each of those four years the Ramblers competed against some of the biggest schools in central and western Pennsylvania. The games were very competitive, but because of the larger talent pool, size, and speed of the boys from these larger schools, the Ramblers found it difficult to win. This is not to say the boys were any less aggressive or the coaching was not as good, on the contrary, these boys and coaches worked as hard or harder because of the competition.

A good example of one of these teams during the last four years of John Kawchak's tenure was the 1959 Rambler team. They faced some formidable opponents and their only two losses were to Johnstown and Altoona, while tying Pittsburgh North Catholic. Nine of the starters on this team went on to play college football. The photograph below shows the starting line up at the conclusion of pre-season camp at Camp Hamilton in 1959. Photo courtesy of Terry Heckler, starting quarterback for the 1959 Ramblers.

Kneeling-Left to right, John Boruch, Don Martell, Pat Sherlock, John Dailey, Paul Wozniak, Tom Bossi, Robert Oyler, Ed Hadix
Standing-Left to right, Jack Creek, Joe Gavalak, Joe Stopko, Tom Sherwin, Terry Heckler, Dave Dunmire

Photo taken by *Tribune Democrat, 1959*

Individual accomplishments by players continued and Windber's football tradition held its own. Indiana High School, a school three times the size of Windber, was first scheduled during the 1957 season and defeated Windber by eight points, this might sound somewhat trivial to a Windber fan, but to an Indiana fan, that win, followed by ten consecutive losses left a big impression, it was not until the 1967 season that Indiana defeated Windber for the second time. Indiana had a wealth of talent; some players went on to play at major colleges and the professional level. The most notable of these was, Jim Nance, who went on to play for Syracuse University and the Cleveland Browns of the NFL.

Windber teams continued to dominate schools of equal size and remained competitive with the larger schools. However, Windber's football prowess had begun to wane, as a result of this very competitive schedule. Community spirit was also declining; the stadium was no longer filled with excited fans expecting to see Windber win. The Kawchak Era came to a close at the end of the 1960 season.

A Rambler Low Tide-1960 thru 1963

Throughout the early 60's, a very formidable schedule was played each year, almost identical to the last years of the Kawchak Era. John Lochrie coached the 1961 and 1962 teams which had a combined record of five wins, 12 losses and two ties. Ronald "Link" Younker took over the head coaching position in 1963 and finished the season with two wins and eight losses. Windber football had reached a very low point with both fans and the community. The schedule was changed for the 1964 season as teams the size of Windber were added, although Johnstown and Altoona continued to feast on the smaller Windber players. The 1964 team had a respectful seven win, three loss season, but the close followers of Windber football were clamoring through the Sports Readers Forum published by the *Tribune-Democrat* about the Ramblers being over-matched by the likes of Johnstown and Altoona and they should be dropped from the schedule. An article in the Sports Reader's Forum of the *Tribune-Democrat* from a Rambler Fan follows:

Windber Football, Windber, Nov. 13,1965.-Just how much pride do the people who arrange the Windber football schedule think Windber fans have?

It was, at one time, enough to be able to say we gave Johnstown or Altoona a tough time even though we lost. We can't say that anymore. All Windber is to these two schools is, as one Altoona radio station put it after the Windber-Altoona game, an "easy touch"

Right now most people are saying to themselves, "These are big money games." Did anyone look around at the Windber-Johnstown game of 1965 and then remember the same game in 1956?

Nine years ago, Windber Stadium was filled to standing-room-only. This year the main reason a handful of people stood was to keep warm, certainly not from the lack of seating. My question is, why doesn't Windber swallow some of its past pride and drop these two schools from its schedule?

I don't think I'm alone in saying that Altoona and Johnstown are way out of our class, and we have no business playing them. If it's a matter of money, wouldn't it be safe to assume that, were Windber to play an 8-game schedule of schools its own size and make a good showing, many of the no longer avid fans would return to the games?

Maybe these two games keep Windber's team in uniforms, I don't know. If such is the case, I say drop them and start having "sub sales" to put uniforms on the Ramblers.

I wasn't around when the first Windber-Johnstown game was played, but it probably wasn't a sellout. Why not look around and try to find a school our own size and see if we can make it a "bread winner," since money seems to be the object of the game.
Rambler Fan

An article in the November 24, 1965 edition of the *Tribune-Democrat* under the feature **Touring with Torr** by James H. Torr reflects on this clamoring.

Football at Windber High School

"There was a time when Windber took on all comers, with no quarter asked or given. In those days, the Ramblers were derided for playing and whomping teams in their own class. The fans wanted the king-sized teams and delighted in using that "the bigger they are, the harder they fall" chant after their warriors hung up another scalp to dry

Windber once was a torrid football town. On Saturday afternoon, the air was filled with tension and business practically stopped between 2:30 and 4:30 o'clock. The high school band marching down Graham Avenue to old Delaney Field brought out the "goosepimples"

It was a proud town, a proud football team and a proud band. Windber could have been playing Hogback Tech, with an 0-7 record, and Delaney Field nevertheless still would be packed. It is not for us to say that Windber should or should not drop Johnstown and Altoona. Despite its reverses, Windber is still a proud town and the Ramblers are a proud football team. Naturally, it is disturbing to be beaten by one's formidable rivals year after year, but deep down Windber must be dreaming that the time will come when it once more can take the field with more than just a glimmer of hope.

It may never come in numerical strength, but the return of the old Windber spirit could be the equalizer. Yes, that old Windber spirit. We remember it well."

Windber continued to play Altoona, who was dropped after the 1966 season and Johnstown, who was dropped following the 1968 season.

Following three consecutive losing seasons, 1966, 1967 and 1968, the schedule started to change, schools the size of Windber were added, and some of the large AAA and AAAA schools were dropped. With a more competitive schedule, in relationship to the size of the student body, Windber's football fortunes began to show signs of resurgence.

The Old Windber Spirit Returns-1968-1971

Harold Price took over reigns as head coach in 1968, following a disappointing two win, seven loss season, the Ramblers followed up with back to back nine wins, one loss seasons in 1969 and 1970. The only losses in each of those two years were to Richland coached by Windber alumnus, Emil DeMarco.(1950) Richard Zepka starting center on the 1970 team was selected to play in the 1971 Big 33 game. Price concluded his coaching tenure at Windber in 1971 with six wins, three losses and one tie before moving on to Hollidaysburg.

The Flori Era-1972-1980

Under coach Joe Flori, who was on the 1937 State Championship team and the 7th alumnus to take over as head coach, along with a staff of former Windber players as assistant coaches, continued this renewed spirit of winning claimed during the 1969 and 1970 seasons. They dispatched teams with regularity in 1972, 1973, and 1974 going 28 and 3.

The 1972 team lost one game and in 1973 after 30 years, the Ramblers captured their 7th undefeated season with a record of 10-0. This team permitted only 53 points to be scored against them and held five teams scoreless while scoring 268 points.

1973 Undefeated Team

See Appendix II, Page 245 for team roster and records.

Flori coached teams continued their winning ways in 1974, 1976, and 1977 with a combined record of 22 wins, seven losses, and one tie. The 1975, 1978, and 1979 seasons all produced five wins and five losses. Two very talented players; Bill Elko, right guard on the 1977 team went on to play at Arizona State University and Louisiana State before being drafted by the San Diego Chargers of the National Football League and Rodger Shepko, halfback on the 1978 team became only the 4th player from Windber to be selected to play in the Pennsylvania 'Big 33" game in July of 1979. He then continued his football career at Lafayette.

Bill Elko

The "Old Windber Spirit" began to wane as the 1970's were drawing to a close, the wins became less in number and the losses were mounting up. What precipitated this? Pardon me if I get on the soap box. Football was changing, there were more things for boys to do, the high tech world of computers, mini-bikes, etc, began to provide outlets not provided in the past. Parental influence also became more prevalent. Conflict between players, coaches, and parents made it difficult to maintain the team philosophy required to field competitive teams.

Rodger Shepko

Players, coaches, and parents must work together for the team concept to materialize. Players must make a one hundred percent commitment, coaches must adjust to change, and parents must rely on the ability of the coaching staff to use players to benefit the team concept. Without this unity, the team will exist but not at the level required to produce winning teams.

You must also remember that the skill players required to execute an offensive and defensive in football have to be present. The cyclic nature of average players out numbering skill players and waiting for younger players to mature are a high school coach's nightmares. Without players filling the skilled positions, the average high school team will be just that. Jumping off the soap box at least for the time being, I will continue with the chronological history of "Rambler" football.

Rambler Football Hits Rock Bottom

During the 1980 season, Windber football reached rock bottom, a record of zero wins and ten losses were recorded, this had not occurred in 61 years, when the 1919 squad went winless in five games. Needless to say, school spirit and community pride, also at rock bottom, provided the impetus for an immediate change. As in most cases, when a team has been losing, the blame is attached to the coach. That is exactly what took place and a coaching change occurred. Unfortunately, the next four years provided only nine wins combined with 32 losses.

I must again jump on the soap box and attempt to give the reader some insight why this period of Windber football might possibly be the low tide in its history. As I pondered why this five year period between 1980 and 1984 proved to be rock bottom for Windber High School football, a number of factors came to mind. The experience of losing had been accepted, there had only been eight wins in five years, player's attitudes reflected this. Other schools had enhanced their program with weight training and the preverbal nightmare of average players outnumbering skill players all played a role.

Windber Football is Resurrected

At the conclusion of the 1984 season all coaching positions were opened and a search for a new head coach began. After a thorough review of all candidates the school board selected Phil DeMarco, a 1967 graduate of Windber High School who played left guard on the 1966 team and was selected first team *Tribune-Democrat* as an offensive guard. He was faced with a daunting task, how to return Windber football to respectability, the 1985 team had a few skill players and coach DeMarco who had assembled a staff of very knowledgeable assistants used these boys along with the average players to resurrect the program. The team finished with four wins and seven losses but, players, coaches, parents and the community started to believe Windber football could return to respectability.

The 1986 team led by Paul Romanchock at quarterback along with Brian Costa, a skilled receiver, Don Koshute and Virg Palumbo, halfbacks and a well coached offensive and defensive line righted the sinking Rambler football ship by winning nine games while losing only one and tying another. The only loss was to Bedford in the District V Championship game by two points. Paul Romanchock was selected to play in the Pennsylvania "Big 33" game in July of 1987, the 5th player from Windber to do so. Paul continued his football career at the University of Maryland.

Paul Romanchock

Coach DeMarco and his staff continued to build the program, there were years when loses outnumbered wins but the "Old Windber Spirit" had been reborn and players began to see how they could become part of the winning tradition Windber football was noted for in the past.

8

The "Glory Years" Return

Not to take away from the Glory years of 1930 to 1943, this contemporary "Glory Years" which began in 1997 and continues today parallels Windber football's domination of teams much like the original "Glory Years".

During the 1997 season, which concluded with six wins and four loses, an 11 year consecutive winning season streak was started. The 2007 team finished with a record of seven wins and three losses. During this time frame the "Ramblers" compiled a record of 100 wins while losing only 23. A 49 game regular season winning streak would also begin with a win over Berlin during the ninth game of the 1997 season This winning streak would continue into the 2003 season and ended with a loss in the third game of that season to Meyersdale.

What is unprecedented is that over a span of five seasons, 1998 to 2002, the Windber Ramblers were undefeated in regular season play. No Windber team had ever achieved that feat. Windber High School football dominated the class A teams of the area and gained statewide recognition, just as they had done during the original "Glory Years". During this period of the contemporary "Glory Years" there were 55 wins and five loses.

There were numerous outstanding players during this contemporary "Glory Years" much like the original "Glory Years" and it would be remiss of me not to mention a few.

Nick Rizzo, quarterback of the 1999 squad, lead the Ramblers to a ten and one season. As result of his outstanding play, Nick earned the *Tribune Democrat* Offensive Player of the Year award and went on to play for the University of Pittsburgh.

Junior, Frank Tallyen, was recognized as a second team All State linebacker by the Associated Press-Small School Format and by Pennsylvania Football News. Frank also made Pennsylvania Football News second team defense as a linebacker in 2000.

Nick Rizzo

Frank Tallyen

Jeff Slatcoff took over the role as quaterback on the 2000 squad and earned the *Tribune Democrat* Offensive Player of the Year award, a Windber player had now won this award two years in a row.

Steve Slatcoff, Jeff's brother, made the Pennsylvania Football News second team defense as a defensive back in 2001 and 2002. He earned First Team Defense on the *Tribune Democrat* All Area Team in 2002.

Jeff Slatcoff

Steve Slatcoff

In 2001, John Curlej, made the Associated Press Small School Format second team defense as a punter and the Pennsylvania Football News second team defense as a punter. He was selected by Pennsylvania Football News on the third team defense as a punter in 2002.

In 2001 and 2002, Philip DeMarco, son of head coach Phil DeMarco, earned All State-first team defense by the Associated Press-Small School Format, as a defensive lineman. and Pennsylvania Football News, also, as a first team defensive lineman.

John Curlej

Philip DeMarco

Following a successful 7 win, 3 loss season in 2003, Coach DeMarco decided that a change in offensive was needed in order to use his players to the best of their ability. He changed the offensive to a single wing, much like what was used during 1930's and 1940's. This very radical change, from the contemporary offense used by most schools today, required a commitment on both the players and coaches' part in order to operate this offense the way it is designed. The 2004 season was a learning year with mixed reactions, particularly with close followers of Windber football.

Although the team concluded with a six win, four loss record, the frame work was in place to execute this offense. Signs that this offense would present problems to teams showed up with the season finale against Portage.

That was one of the best Windber football games I ever witnessed. Portage was a two or three touchdown favorite and Windber with the single wing attack confused the Portage defense enough to equalize the line of scrimmage. The defense played with tremendous heart and this team effort produced a surprising 12 - 7 win.

The 2005 season began with three a day practices at Camp Hamilton in August. I was fortunate enough to attend a number of these practices and more closely observe the drills necessary to mold this group of Ramblers into a winning team. The single wing offense was being honed and the defensive unit worked on learning different formations. The hard work, dedication, and loyalty required of a winning football team were evident.

The winning started with the first game at Blacklick Valley and continued through the eighth game with a victory over Ferndale. This set the stage for a showdown with Portage, who was also undefeated, in the last game of the regular season. The game was at Portage with a rabid crowd expecting to see the mighty Mustangs roll over Windber as they had done with their eight previous opponents. The ardent Windber fans showed up in great numbers on a very cold evening and filled the visitor's sideline. Windber held the upper hand for the first two quarters and went into the locker room at half time leading. The second half went back and forth with Portage scoring a touchdown as the clock ended the game with the score, Windber 14, Portage 14.

Overtime was required to determine a winner; I am in favor of overtime but in this particular case both teams should have been declared a winner as it was one of the best high school football games I have ever seen. Both teams played their hearts out.

Portage won the coin toss and optioned to play defense. On Windber's second play from scrimmage they scored and kicked the extra point setting the score at 21- 14. Portage went on offense and scored on their first play from scrimmage. Portage then decided to go for two points too win the game and, following an offside penalty by Windber, ran the ball around left end into the end zone for the winning score. Windber 21, Portage 22.

Although the Portage fans celebrated with great enthusiasm while the Windber fans stood stunned in the stands, this spectacle of high school football exhibited by both teams will be remembered for years to come.

This was not the last game Windber would play in 2005 as they had qualified for the District 5 Class "A" playoffs with their 8-1 record; in fact, they were the first ranked team in District 5 and earned a by-week for the up coming playoffs. The first team they played was Meyersdale who they had dispatched during the regular season. This first playoff game proved to be a real nail biter with Windber defeating Meyersdale, 13 to 6.

The second game, which was the third round of the district playoffs, would decide the overall champion of District 5 Class "A". Windber's opponent was Tussey Mountain who had upset second ranked Rockwood the previous week. I unfortunately did not see this game as I was attending the birth of my second grandchild in Atlanta, Georgia. It was a girl!! Windber didn't need my support as they easily defeated Tussey Mountain.

On to interdistrict play, the playoff format pits the District 5 Class "A" team against the District 7 Class "A" team. District 7 is from the Pittsburgh area and always has a very formidable representative. The Duquesne "Dukes" were the 2005 representative, with a record of 12-0. The Ramblers faced a well coached and athletic team, with most people feeling the "Dukes" would roll over Windber by four or five touchdowns.

The game was held at Churchman Stadium, East Allegheny High School, North Versailles, Pennsylvania on a frigid cold night with the temperature around 20 degrees Fahrenheit. Windber's single wing offensive attack presented trouble for the "Dukes" early and the defense did a fine job containing the Duquesne running backs. Going in at half time the Ramblers trailed just 6-0. The second half was all Duquesne, as mistakes were made, and the score at the end of the game was Windber 0-Duquesne 18.

The effort put forth by the Ramblers was solid and as Coach DeMarco stated "Our kids played with them. They turned the corner on us a few times, but, overall, our kids ran with them." Duquesne coach Patrick Monroe praised the Ramblers saying, "That offense, as sophisticated as it was, for us to hold them without a score is a real accomplishment for our defense. (*Tribune-Democrat*, November 26, 2005, Aaron Weaver, writer)

A stalwart on this 2005 team was junior linebacker Josh Kotula, who earned All State recognition on the second team defense as an all purpose back by the Associated Press-Small School Format, and was named the Defensive Player of the Year by the *Tribune Democrat* on the All Area Team. He also went on to earn All State first team defense as a linebacker by the Associated Press Small School Format in 2006 and first team defense as a linebacker on the *Tribune Democrat* All Area Team.

Josh Kotula

The 2006 season saw the "Ramblers" breeze through the regular season with their only regular season loss at the hands of Meyersdale. After handing North Star a defeat in the District 5 playoffs, they met Meyersdale again in the PIAA District 5 final. The game was a hard fought contest with both teams leaving nothing on the field. Unfortunately, Meyersdale prevailed in overtime by a score of 20 to 14.

The final fall spectacle of Windber High School Football covered in this document is the 2007 season. Coach Phil DeMarco working with a small nucleus of lettermen and many underclassmen started the year with five straight wins. Back to back losses in games six and seven slowed the development of the team, but they bounced back to win their final two regular season games. The 2007 team qualified for the district 5 playoffs and had a week off before meeting North Star in a District 5 Semi-final game. The "Cougars" handled the "Ramblers" with ease, winning by a score of 29 to 0.

The 2007 season of Windber High School football brought to a close 94 years of inter-scholastic football in this small former coal mining town. It is a proud history, developed from an ethnic melting pot of European immigrants who came to work in the coal fields and established a tradition of hard work that has carried over to the high school football team. With pride, dedication, and hard work the future football "Ramblers" of Windber High School will continue to write this proud history.

I have enjoyed presenting this chronological look at Windber High School Football. The research presented an interesting challenge and provided a stimulus for uncovering more and more information. This portion of the book condenses 94 years of high school football in Windber. Most of the story has yet to be revealed.

The real story is made up of such things as, gridiron venues, Camp Hamilton, nicknames earned, humourous stories, and cheers performed. All of the "things" which make Windber High School football unique to this community. It is my wish, by adding these "things", the story of W.H.S. Football will be better understood and enjoyed. Read On!!

9

Gridiron Venues

For the past 57 years the Windber Ramblers have played their home games at Windber Stadium. Because of the length of time involved, most people would find it difficult to imagine the Ramblers playing at any other venue. Prior to the use of Windber Stadium, home games for 31 years, were played at Delaney Field. During the years, 1915 through 1917, home games were played at Recreation Park. It is therefore necessary to look at all three of these venues a little closer to see the role they played in the history of Windber High School football.

Recreation Park

The first home games were played at Recreation Park, located at the top of 9th Street, along state route 160 North. This 25-acre park, previously owned by the Berwind-White Coal Company, was developed in 1910 and is situated in Windber Borough (Somerset County) and Richland Twp. (Cambria County). Except for the first official year of high school football (1914), the three-year period of 1915 through 1917 saw all high school games played at the park's combination baseball/football field. No pictures are available to give any indication as to exactly where this combination field was located. The following diagram of the present day Recreation Park, with buildings, swimming pool, playground, volleyball courts and roads, with the approximate location of the former football field superimposed, should provide some insight as to where these first games were played.

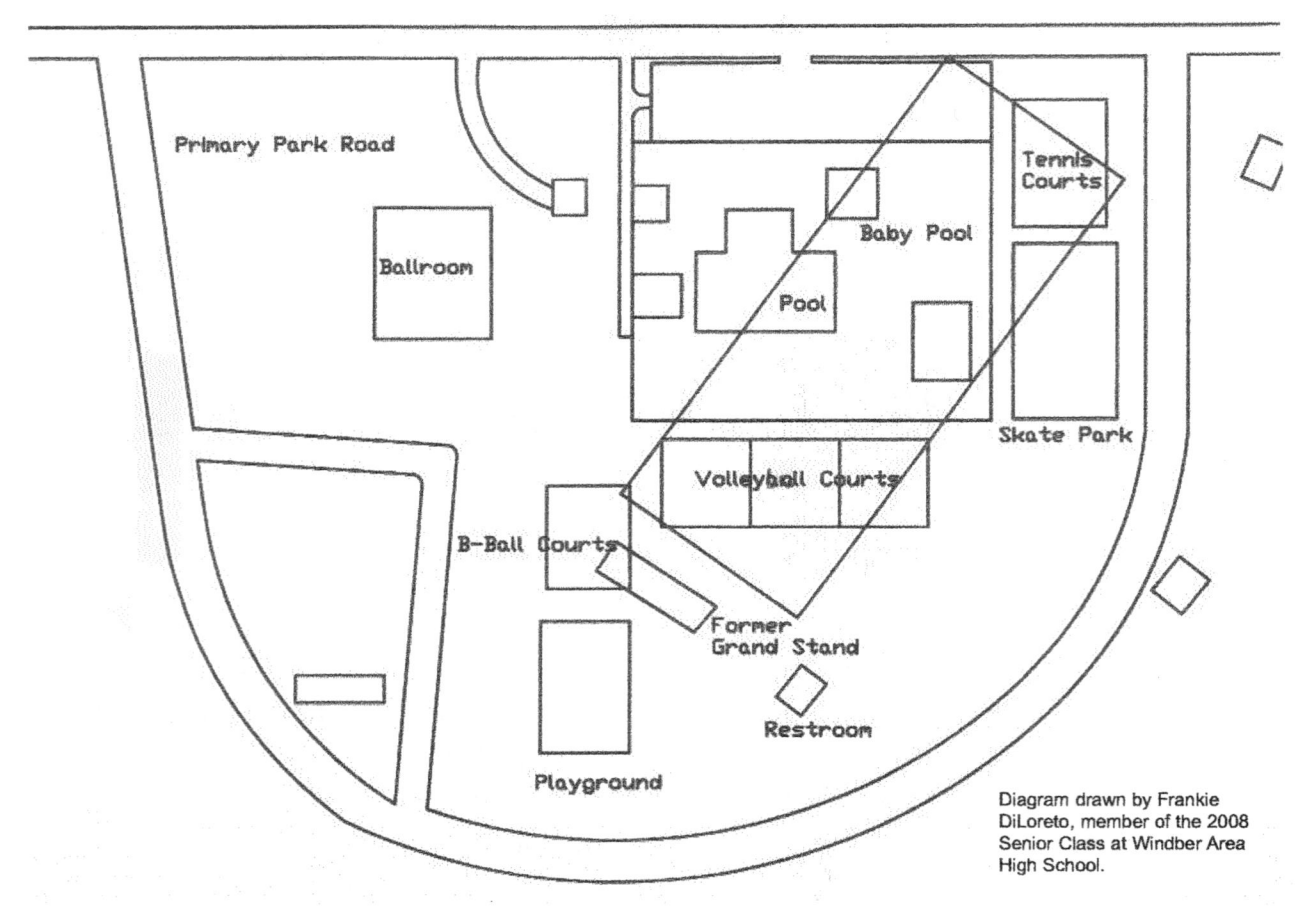

Diagram drawn by Frankie DiLoreto, member of the 2008 Senior Class at Windber Area High School.

The only remaining structure from that era is the ballroom or dance hall, which is still used for functions today. A grandstand was located directly behind home plate and is shown in its approximate location in the diagram above. A photograph of this grandstand is shown below, thanks to the Coal Heritage Museum were it was found.

Recreation Park, now owned by Windber Borough, has provided many memories for Windberites. They include, the many Fourth of July Celebrations provided by Windber Fire Company #1, the all steel swimming pool, former amusement rides, picnic facilities, and the dance hall where Sunday night record hops were held during the 1950's and 60's.

Today's athletic fields, located between route 160 North and the access road to the swimming pool, are primarily used for baseball, but during the fall, elementary aged students use a few of the fields for flag football. These future Ramblers are getting their start close to where some of the first high school games were played.

Delaney Field

The second venue of Windber High School football was Delaney Field; this facility was used for a period of 31 years (1918-1948). Some information refers to this field as a stadium, however, it was far removed from any stadium-like facility. The original name was Dewey Field, laid out mid-town in 1900 and surrounded by an eight foot high fence in 1904. Why the name Dewey was selected cannot be determined. Dewey Field was situated on land bordered by Stockholm Avenue, 17th Street, and Veil Avenue. Today this site is occupied by Calvary United Methodist Church, Quemahoning Towers, and Windber Area Water Authority buildings.

An article in the December 21, 1937 issue of the *Hi-Times* reports:

"When our field was but a plot of ground used for playing baseball, Chief Engineer Eugene Delaney saw visions of a beautiful athletic field for Windber. In 1917 he drafted a plan persuading the Berwind-White Coal Mining Company to lease the land for his project. The field and a grandstand, with a seating capacity of 800, were completed in 1918 and its old name, Dewey Field was still retained at the dedication.

"Mr. Delaney expired in 1920 after finding his dream was a reality. One of his last requests was that Berwind-White Company would keep the field in good condition. His favorite proverb was "Every man is a dreamer, but he must have strength and hope to make his dreams become realities." With this thought in mind, the town council changed the name Dewey Field to Delaney Field."

Eugene Delaney

(Picture of Eugene Delaney, found in the Illustrated Industrial Edition, supplement to the *Windber Era*, February 1, 1901)

In the fall of 1918 the high school team began using Delaney Field for practice and home games. For almost 20 years no improvements were made to this facility, except for some portable bleachers, which could be moved if other events were taking place. An interesting article in the November 14, 1940 issue of the *Windber Era* reports: "Delaney Field of yesterday (1921-1925), lights set on poles trying to pierce the falling darkness, the forward pass was just some new fangled method that coaches wouldn't touch with a ten-foot pole. Light was good for running plays."

This apparent improvement provided sufficient light for practice but was by no means intended for games. The fence constructed in 1904 undoubtedly had to be fixed periodically as a result of weathering and the relentless pursuit of youngsters trying to gain entrance to the field in order to watch their gridiron heroes.

I was talking to Charlie Puckey, starting left end in 1944 for Windber High School and former basketball coach for Richland High School, and mentioned to him about my interest concerning Delaney Field. He remembered an incident when he was a youngster about sneaking into Delaney Field. He said, "We would go down to the field during the week to scout out the best spot to try and jump over the fence. One Saturday, I took a running jump, hit the fence about halfway up and was over. Much to my surprise when I landed, there was a policeman standing right next to me. It didn't take me long to jump back over and try and find another place to sneak in."

Another story was related to me during an interview on April 20, 2001 with Niles Dalberg, a four year starter at tackle for Windber High School (1927-1930). This story dealt with Delaney Field and the eight foot high fence surrounding it. Niles said, "When I was a young boy and couldn't climb the fence, the only way I could see a game was by climbing one of the trees near the field." Bill Beckley, Captain of the 1936 team, told me of the times youngsters would carry the practice shoes and shoulder pads of their heroes from the high school to practice at Delaney Field.

Except for the grandstand located behind home plate or near the end zone at the east end of the football field, there was very little seating available. The *Windber Era* reported in the October 14, 1934 issue: "Additional seats for Delaney Field, 16 sets of bleachers with a seating capacity of 1000." A few bleachers show up in some team photos, but for the most part, fans stood on the sidelines or end zones to observe these games. Numerous photographs of games played at this field show the sidelines and end zones filled to capacity.

Games were played Saturday afternoons rain or shine. Playing conditions on this combination baseball/football field were dependent on the weather and must have been mixtures of dirt and grass or mud and grass. I suspect, mostly dirt or mud from all the photographs, and reports of game conditions from players.

Only two games were affected by weather in the 31 year history of Delaney Field. The first occurred in 1930 when Windber was scheduled to play Shade Twp. It was cancelled because of heavy snows. The second game was cancelled in 1940. Windber was scheduled to play Conemaugh Twp. on Thanksgiving Day but ice on Delaney Field prevented this.

Night games were not played because of the lack of adequate lighting. In the fall of 1939, however, as reported in the August 12, 1939 issue of the *Windber Era*, "Night football for the first time, a high powered lighting system will be used on a trial basis at Delaney Field to determine if it would be advisable or not to install permanently. Three night games are planned, Conemaugh on September 30th, Shade Twp. on November 4th, and a play-by play broadcast of the away game at Pottsville." No information can be found regarding how well the experiment of using this lightning system went. The Windber Era did report that the broadcast of the Pottsville game did not go well because the press box was not sound proof and there was considerable noise from the people seated there.

Arial Photograph taken in 1947 as the carnival sets up for the 50th Anniversary of Windber. Outline of baseball and football field can be seen. Photo obtained from the 50th Anniversary Photo book from 1947.

Photo courtesy of Bill Gorgon

Photo courtesy of Shaz Yuhas

Game action during the 1940's at Delaney Field.

Photo found in scrapbook originally owned by Steve Hritz

Game action at Delaney Field. This photo was taken during the 1941 season, opponent unknown. Photograph was donated by Tom Congersky. The color version of this photo appears on the front cover.

As the above photograph shows, the need for a new stadium was apparent. With no room for expansion, lack of seating, field conditions, and the need for permanent lighting led some individuals to begin formulating plans to construct a stadium that could be more suited for use by the community.

An article in the December 2, 1937 issue of the *Windber Era* reports, "New stadium proposed, a committee of ten individuals have been appointed to start action on constructing a stadium with a seating capacity of 10,000." I found this to be very interesting because it was not until 1947 that any indication of a plan for building a new stadium could be found.

Windber Stadium

Aerial view of Windber Stadium, taken by Jim Cover, Jr.

In November of 1947 the Windber Recreation Committee was organized and plans for a stadium that would seat over 9,000 people were formulated. In the book, *The Windber Story* by Frank Alcamo, a detailed history of the development of Windber Stadium is given, with facts, figures, and townspeople involved.

Wilmore Real Estate Company donated 22 acres of land, and plans were formulated for a stadium to seat over 9,000 people. Included in the plans were a football field, with state of the art lightning for night games, track, baseball diamond, swimming pool, and a large parking lot. The Windber Recreation Committee raised over $190,000 in pledges through special gifts and community support. Construction began in August of 1948. The new stadium was dedicated on September 7, 1949, following a parade through town. Windber High School played its first football game there on September 9, 1949 against Shade High School, with Windber defeating Shade, 40 to 0. (The football used in this game can be seen in a trophy case at the high school in the hallway near the present day gym.)

This stadium was the envy of many surrounding communities, with its impressive press box and elevated bleachers constructed on a concrete base. It had the appearance of a college stadium. On Saturday nights during the 1950's and 60's, the bleachers were packed with anxious fans waiting for the "Ramblers" to wage their gridiron conflicts. This stadium is located along a four lane highway known as State Route 56 East, and a traffic light at the intersection of 24th Street and the highway, provide access to the parking lot.

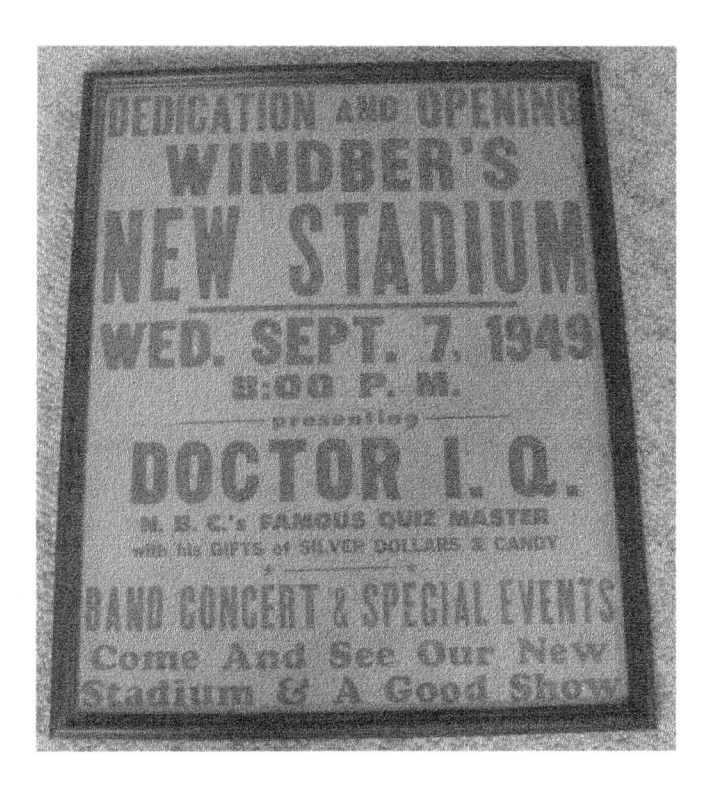

Photograph taken by the author of an original poster advertising the dedication of Windber Stadium in 1949. This framed poster was located in a storage room at the stadium.

Windber Stadium has also been used by various high schools in the area, especially when they needed a larger facility to accomodate crowds, for a rivalry game. Teams from Richland, Ferndale and Bishop McCort have used this facility for home games.

During the 1950's, the annual All Star Game of the West Central Pennsylvania Coahes Association was contested at Windber Stadium. All Star players, who had completed their high school eligibility, from schools in the area were divided up into a West squad and East squad. The game was held in early August and kicked off the new high school football season.

From 1971 through 1984 the Ken Lantzy All Star Football Game was held at Windber Stadium. This All Star game originated out of the need to help a young athlete, Ken Lantzy of the Cambria Heights High School football squad, defray medical bills and costs. Lantzy received an injury that would confine him to a wheelchair for the rest of his life. All Stars, selected by coaches, from area schools make up the North and South squads. This All Star Football game continues today and is contested in June at Point Stadium in Johnstown.

Windber Stadium has been used for various events besides football. The community has benefited from carnivals, high school band contests, and stock car races, to name a few. There was even a revival crusade during the summer of 1958 with a huge tent and an authentic evangelist. Johnny Weismiller, the famous Olympic swimmer who played Tarzan in the movies, was honored by the community at the stadium in 1950, because of the claim he was born in Windber.

Yes, the Windber community has greatly benefited from this stadium, but most of the memories revolve around the football games played there. Windber High School has never had its own home field, except for a field and synthetic track constructed in 1995 at a windblown site above 26th street. The high school continues to use Windber Stadium for home football games. The use of the stadium is compensated by an annual fee.

Beginning with that first game in 1949, and using five varsity home games per year over the 58 year period through 2007, the community has enjoyed approximately 300 Windber High School varsity football games. Many of the memories of these games by fans and players have faded. However, this icon of high school football stadiums in South Western Pennsylvania continues on. The restroom facilities need updated, and the light standard knocked down by a strong storm three years ago needs replaced, but the facility still holds a magnetic attraction for high school football games.

My first memory of this stadium, was not at a football game, but sitting in the bleachers at the ceremony honoring Johnny Weismiller in 1950. My father had taken my twin brother, Leonard, and myself to the stadium for this event. The thing that I remember most, was not the famous person being honored, but the size of the complex and the enormity of the field. At the age of six, a structure like this left a bigger impression than all the fanfare over a famous hometown hero.

I find it difficult to remember most of the games I attended as a youngster. The most vivid memories of Windber Stadium during that time of my life, involve playing tag and touch football on the steep hillside next to either side of the bleachers. This has not changed in the past 57 years. I still observe youngsters rolling down these inclines during games today. I, also, vaguely recall being in the end zone when the players entered the field, hoping to catch a glimpse or touch a football hero.

The most lasting memory of my youth, at Windber Stadium, occurred around the age of eleven or twelve. While in attendance at an afternoon football game, I was running down the bleachers when I suddenly tripped, the end result was an impact with a corner of a bleacher. This doesn't sound as if it should stand out as a memory of Windber Stadium except for the hole in my tongue after impact with the bleacher, and all the blood associated with a mouth wound.

During my 8th grade year in junior high school, while preparing for my first home football game in a "Rambler" uniform, I ran on the field for the first time. I will never forget the sensation of seeing those bleachers rise to the sky and the magical feel of running on the field where W.H.S. football heroes had trodden in years gone by. Even to this day, whenever I attend a game, I can still feel that rush of adrenalin as I ran on that field at age 14. I didn't get to play in any games during that eighth grade season. It wasn't until my freshman year that I actually played in a game on the field.

The games in junior high school were all played in the afternoon. Very few fans were in attendance except parents and a few die hard football enthusiasts. I was anxiously waiting for an opportunity to play under the lights. That opportunity didn't occur until my junior year while playing B-Team or as it is known today as the Junior Varsity. During my senior season (football of 1961) I actually played an entire game as a starting end on both offense and defense. Up to that point my playing experience at Windber Stadium consisted of kickoff and punt teams. Needless to say, my football prowess didn't measure up, and I was relegated to "riding the pines" or what is known as sitting on the bench. Prior to my senior year I only dressed for home games as a result of not having enough ability to make the traveling squad.

The first home game as a senior will never be forgotten, I no longer rode the pines, I had gained enough ability to earn a starting position. The crowd, lights, and most importantly the sensation of finally being looked upon as one of those gridiron heroes I had watched run out on the field as youngster was overwhelming.

I feel sure these same feelings were being experienced by many teammates and have been felt by most, if not all football "Ramblers" whatever field they played their first game on. Hopefully, some of these same feelings will be conjured up after reading some of this material and old memories of days gone by can be rekindled.

Windber Stadium, where wins and losses have occurred for 58 years, will continue to provide countless experiences and lasting memories for future gridiron heroes for years to come.

Game Action at Windber Stadium in 1961, during the Johnstown-Windber game, George Tobias, #40 and Ron Rubal,#61 run down a loose ball.

Game action at Windber Stadium, Joe Yasko fights for yardage in 1971.

The 2006 Ramblers on the sidelines

10

Camp Hamilton

This landmark, along the banks of Shade Creek, has played a vital part in the lore of Windber High School football. Camp Hamilton has a storied past concerning football, some not related to Windber High School football, while the majority of this storied past revolves around the almost 65 years this facility has been used as a pre-season training camp by Windber High School football teams. The physical plant has changed and new grass is planted periodically, but the fear of being an underclassman and the joy of finally attaining the status of senior remains the same as a new pre-season arrives. This late summer tradition with all of its hard work, blood, sweat, and tears along with the many stories both on and off the practice field, have added to the lore of playing football for Windber High School.

It is necessary to look at the historical development of this landmark in order to understand the significance it has played in the history of Windber Football.

Prior to being called Camp Hamilton, this scenic area was called Ott's Bridge Camp, the name being derived from the bridge constructed to carry the road across Shade Creek, near the entrance. Town's people, who enjoyed getting away from the hustle and bustle of the growing coal town, first used it as a summer retreat. The September 3, 1914 issue of the *Windber Era* reports: "Camping at Ott's Bridge, families would pitch tents and compartment cottages on the banks of Shade Creek at Ott's Bridge."

This land was owned by Alfred Reed Hamilton of Pittsburgh and was part of the Bonny Lee's Farm, known as an internationally famous sheep ranch, where Mr. Hamilton would spend his summers at his house called Mt. Orchard. This house and barn for the farm were located outside Mine 37, along what is now Eisenhower Blvd. and the Mine 37 road.

The first football players to plant their cleats on the turf at Camp Hamilton were not from Windber, but, from the University of Pittsburgh. It is believed that Mr. Hamilton was one of the first organizers of football at the university and provided this site to the University of Pittsburgh for training purposes. The first University of Pittsburgh team to use this facility as a training camp was the 1913 team. A report in the October 2, 1913 issue of the *Windber Era* reads: "University of Pittsburgh camp on Shade Creek was broken up last week and on Thursday, September 25, the boys took their departure for Pittsburgh, where most of the boys have already entered."

An interesting article in the September 4, 1914 issue of the *Johnstown Daily Tribune*, describes the opening of the University of Pittsburgh training camp in 1914.

Pittsburgh University Football Practice is Inaugurated at Camp

"Windber, Sept. 3---The first practice of the season for the football squad of the University of Pittsburgh was held at 9 o'clock this morning at Camp A. R. Hamilton at Ott's bridge, about four miles from here. At that time the candidates for positions on the rush line of the Pitt team were taken out to the big field and given their first instructions by Head Coach Joe Duff. An hour later the backfield candidates were given a session by Coach Duff. At 2 o'clock this afternoon general practice will probably be carried out during the training period in camp here.

"There will not be much work this week except what is necessary to round the players in shape. The first line plunging is scheduled for Saturday morning. There will be no work-out Saturday afternoon.

"The strictest rules of training are to prevail in the camp from now until the first string squad departs on September 22 for Ithaca to prepare for the opening game of the season with Cornell on September 26. Everybody must be in bed at 10 o'clock at night. The players must get out of bed at 6:30 o'clock in the morning and report for breakfast at 7 am.

"A. R. Hamilton the Pitt alumnus who provided the camp is remaining all the time with the football squad instead of living at his Mt. Orchard summer home near here."

Also, mentioned in this article from the *Johnstown Daily Tribune* dated September 4, 1914, was that there were 35 players in camp and a list of some of the candidates was given. Listed among those were John B. "Jock" Sutherland, who would return to the University of Pittsburgh and become head coach for 15 years. The last paragraph of the article reads as follows:

"The football camp is fixed up in the most up-to-date-manner and the players have the same convenience they would have in the city, plus the pure mountain air. There is hot and cold-water shower baths, a rubbing tent and a telephone booth. There are 22 sleeping tents, with cots, a large assembly tent for meetings, lectures and social purposes; two large mess tents, a large commissary tent and a kitchen tent with a stone oven. The water is piped here from a spring."

The picture below was found on the sports page of the September 22, 1914 issue of the *Johnstown Daily Tribune* and was titled "Scene from Yesterday's Scrimmage on University of Pittsburgh Football Field at Camp Hamilton, Near Windber." This must have been the last practice for the squad prior to their departure for Ithaca to prepare for the opening season game with Cornell.

"Chalky" Williamson carrying the ball in a long end run.

Photo from the *Johnstown Daily Tribune*, Sept. 22, 1914

The University of Pittsburgh used this gridiron facility, known as Camp Hamilton at Ott's Bridge for 22 years. The "Ott's Bridge" name was dropped and the name, Camp Hamilton continues to be used today.

Mr. Hamilton died in 1927 and the land was donated to the University of Pittsburgh that same year. The university continued to use this facility as a pre-season training camp for the football squads but, also, developed it as field camp for its civil engineering department and provided students with an opportunity to work in the field during the summer months. It was during the time frame between 1925 and 1930 that 15 cottages, with bunks, a mess hall, supply hut, cook's cabin, coach's cabin, classroom and shower room combination, restroom facilities, and numerous garages were constructed. In addition, recreational facilities were provided including: tennis courts, volleyball court, and a nine hole executive golf course.

As reported in the September 16, 1926 issue of the *Windber Era* "Unique golf course is furnishing much pleasure for men at Camp Hamilton, a 715 yard, par 30 course, with the following nine holes, #1--65 yd.--par 3; #2--60 yd.--par 3; #3--68 yd.--par 3; #4--120 yd.--par 4; #5--75 yd.--par 3; #6--89 yd.--par 3; #7--111 yd.--par 4; #8--70 yd.--par 3; #9--57 yd.--par 3." Included with the listing of all nine holes was also a description of where sand traps were located.

The location of this unique golf course, cottages, buildings, and recreational features can be seen in a topographic map prepared by civil engineering students in 1931. Don Weaver donated this topographic map in 2000 to the Windber Area School District. Don's uncle, J.P. Weaver, was a student with the university at Camp Hamilton during the summer of 1931.

The 1935 football season was the last year the University of Pittsburgh used Camp Hamilton as a pre-season training camp. The famous 1936 flood washed out all but nine cottages and other buildings, including extensive damage to the topography along Shade Creek. The July 25, 1936 issue of the *Windber Era* reported, "a face-lift was given to the huts and cottages and 87,000 tons of dirt was hauled into fill areas washed away by the 1936 flood."

The University of Pittsburgh continued to use Camp Hamilton following this face-lift as an engineering field camp. As reported in the September 24, 1937 issue of the *Windber Era,* "29 students in 1937, housed in cottages with a recreation and dining hall, tennis courts, and a mush ball field were involved in a ten week civil engineering course."

At this point in the historical look at Camp Hamilton and before I continue with where Windber H.S. football enters this historical involvement, I would like to include some interesting information obtained from an interview with Mrs. Irene (Geiser) Berkebile. Mrs. Berkebile, age 94, is the daughter of the former caretaker at Camp Hamilton, John Geiser. Mr. Geiser had been hired by the University of Pittsburgh to handle the caretaker responsibilities at Camp Hamilton. During the discussion with Mrs. Berkebile I was amazed by her memory. She was just a young teenage girl when her dad began working as the caretaker. As I mentioned some of the information I had found concerning Camp Hamilton, Mrs. Berkebile would add a story about various things she had experienced. The use of tents by the early Pitt players brought to her mind about the huge trucks that would deliver the tents and how her dad and brothers would erect these tents on wooden platforms providing a much needed floor. She then added that after football camp was over her brothers would supplement their income by finding coins which had fallen down between the boards of the wooden platforms.

Mr. John Geiser was a local farmer whose farm and farm house was located along Berkey Church Road, approximately one mile from Camp Hamilton. Mrs. Berkebile told me that the university constructed a storage building at the farm for various pieces of equipment used at the camp. She vividly recalled that everything from kitchen utensils to the wooden platforms for tents were stored in the building. She also said that all of the equipment had to be moved to the storage building by horse and wagon.

While in high school, Mrs. Berkebile remembered that the university provided a house near Camp Hamilton for the family. This house can been seen off to the left of the road before crossing the bridge over Shade Creek. This house for the Geiser family provided closer access to Camp Hamilton because of the need for caretaker Geiser to keep a closer eye on things. As Mrs. Berkebile continued with her story she made it very clear that on more than a number of occasions individuals would sneak into Camp Hamilton during the off season and remove everything, including lumber from the cottages. She said most of the individuals were from Mine 38, a Berwind-White mine located in the small village of Seanor, located down stream from Camp Hamilton along Shade Creek. The thieves would push hand carts up the railroad track from Seanor to Camp Hamilton. They knew the train schedule and would plan their pilfering accordingly. Mrs. Berkebile said her dad was able to control the pilfering for the most part because of living close by. Mrs. Berkebile then related a very amusing story told to her, by her father, concerning one of these pilfering escapades.

Mr. Geiser had caught on to the schedule followed by the thieves. One day, as the thieves made their way down the hill from the train tracks above Camp Hamilton, Mr. Geiser positioned himself out of sight near the dining hall. When the thieves were about to break the lock on the door to the dining hall he raised his shot gun, loaded with rock salt, and blasted a teenage boy in the butt. Needless to say, the band of marauding boys didn't return. Mrs. Berkebile laughed aloud as she continued the story, because, it didn't end with that shotgun blast. Some years later her brother, Hamen, was working in Mine 38 and was asked by a fellow worker if he was related to the Geiser who was the caretaker at Camp Hamilton. Hamen responded to the inquiry that the caretaker was his dad. The fellow worker then admitted he was the teenage boy who had received the blast of rock salt. Mrs. Berkebile said that her brother and his fellow worker laughed about the incident.

Mrs. Berkebile thanked me for sharing some of the information I had discovered about Camp Hamilton, a very cherished part of her childhood, as it had helped her recall many memories about her families involvement with Camp Hamilton. I thanked her for providing me with information that could add a personal touch to this landmark on the banks of Shade Creek.

During August of 1941, the first Windber High School football team used Camp Hamilton as a pre-season training camp, although it was still owned by the University of Pittsburgh. What arrangements the school district had with the university concerning the use of this camp and any rental fee involved could not be found. The football team continued to use this facility as a training camp from 1942 until 1949, when it was purchased by the school district. As reported in the September 30, 1949 issue of the *Hi-Times*, " On September 12, 1949, the Windber High School Athletic Association purchased Camp Hamilton from the University of Pittsburgh for $2000 dollars." An interesting article concerning the use of Camp Hamilton was found in the August 17, 1951 issue of the *Windber Era*, "July, 1951, school directors attempting to secure some college or pro-team to hold pre-season drills at Camp Hamilton." No information has been found to indicate any response from a college or pro-team to this inquiry.

Cabins one through four, date of photograph unknown, prior to 1977 flood.

Pre-season practice for W.H.S. football continued to be held there for 33 years. The only interruption that prevented 65 continuous years was the 1977 Flood, which inundated the entire area and destroyed the nine cabins, mess hall, shower room, and rest room facilities. Only the cook's cabin and coach's cabin, along with the football field, survived.

The 1977 through 1980 teams had to use the high school for their pre-season training camp. Cots were provided and placed in the hallways and gym for the players. Practices were held at Windber Stadium.

During the summer of 1980, this approximately 25-acre campsite was converted into an educational and environmental center. With the aid of a grant from the Federal Emergency Management Agency, a lodge consisting of a kitchen, dining facilities, and sleeping quarters for 60 people was constructed. Also included were nature trails, recreational areas, and playground facilities. This facility is used extensively by the school district during the school year for field trip activities, class outings, and various social events.

Aerial view of Camp Hamilton-2007, taken by Jim Cover, Jr.

Picture of the Lodge and Dorm-2007

Camp Hamilton continues to be used today as a pre-season football training camp and educational center. Isn't it interesting, after over 90 years, that a facility like this is still used for its original purpose? The most unique aspect of this community landmark is that is probably one of only a handful of camps in the United States owned and operated by a school district almost exclusively for football practice.

This historical look at the development of Camp Hamilton gives us an understanding of the physical make up of this facility. But the real understanding as to why this camp is significant in the lore of Windber High School Football revolves around the participants: players, coaches, and managers. These are the individuals who have contributed to this storied past and have provided the countless memories of Windber "Rambler" football camp.

11

Football Camp

Pre-season training camp is usually a two-week period near the middle of August each year. This two-week adventure, I use this term "adventure" with tongue in check, is interrupted by only a few brief hours on the Sunday between scheduled weeks. The participants have that time to attend church, wash clothes, and try to decide if they can make it through another week.

Memories have faded, but I can still recall my first trip as a participant. The year was 1958, I was a ninth grader, age 14. I, along with approximately 30 other ninth graders, were bused out to Camp Hamilton to begin football camp. Crossing "Ott's Bridge," you get a glimpse of this facility and wonder exactly what football camp is all about. You have heard stories and wonder how true they really are. Time has erased most all the memories of this first trip, except the feeling I had upon passing under the arch at the entrance to camp. That feeling was one of leaving a very comfortable world and entering the world of the unknown. A feeling most of us have experienced at some time in our lives. Here we were, at Camp Hamilton, about to experience an unforgettable journey into the life of a high school football player from Windber.

Unfortunately, almost 50 years have passed since that memorable day, and the erosional forces affecting the human mind have taken their toll, resulting in not being able to recall most of the details of that first year as a participant, except that initial glimpse of camp and the feeling of entering the world of the unknown.

A typical day at camp consisted of the following schedule. Even in this modern football era, the schedule remains about the same.

> Wake up call-6:30 am
> Breakfast-7:30
> Morning workout-9:00
> Lunch-12:00
> Afternoon workout-2:00 pm
> Supper-5:30
> Special teams on field with shorts or blackboard
>   drill-6:30 to 7:30
> Lights out-9:00

This schedule was modified on occasion by weather conditions, but for the most part was adhered to very strictly. With a disciplined schedule such as this, a team concept was being built, necessary for development of the individual player and team.

The morning and afternoon workouts were filled with conditioning, blocking and tackling drills, running plays and yes, live contact. Most players have long forgotten these tortuous workouts, although one individual, Pat Freeman, a retired teacher from Virginia, former Windber teacher/coach, and member of the 1947 through 1950 teams, shared with me an essay he had written for a creative writing course. The final project in this course was an essay on an event that had a lasting impact on the writer.

I have excluded the opening five paragraphs of this essay, as it deals with a little history of Windber and subject material already discussed.

"The Monster"

"For two weeks a year Camp Hamilton was a Dante's Inferno for sixty aspiring football players. Every minute of each day was regimented so we would not have time to wonder what the hell enticed us to come to this place. Two a day practices and evening skull sessions kept us busy and tired so that early curfews were a welcome respite.

"Practices were long and demanding. Running, contact, more running, and then more contact. But, for every torture devised by coaches, nothing was more devious than the "the monster." This implement of the devil was a canvas dummy filled with sawdust. A pulley system allowed the life sized, headless dummy to hang a foot off the ground. All that was needed was a horse to complete the saga of Ichabod Crane!

"As the dummy swayed above the pit, filled with sawdust of course, we were to tackle the beast. Everything was to be done in the proper order and using exact techniques. Drive through the dummy, lift it on our shoulders, and slam it into the pit.

"Since it was always hot and humid in August, the drill was an unwelcome part of our day. The beads of sweat poured off our bodies like a monsoon rain. Once we landed in the pit our bodies were covered with sawdust. Chips were under the helmet and hip pads, in our ears, in the socks and jock strap. It was everywhere and there wasn't any way to brush off the irritating particles.

"One hit was never enough to satisfy the sadistic coaches. They always found a mistake. "Your head was down; do it again." Or, "your feet were too close together; do it again - damn it!" Also, "God damn it, your feet were too far apart - do it again!" Possibly, "Piss poor tackle; my grandmother can do better." Since we were not allowed to swear at the coaches we took it out on the monster. As we drove through our common enemy it became a "son-of-a-bitch, a bastard or an ass hole." But the dummy always got the last laugh.

"Rain was a welcome sight for the team, except when we were on the monster. Not only was "he" twenty pounds heavier but then we had sawdust clinging like leaches to our eyes, lips, and neck. Our only prayer was for lightning to accompany the rain. God, we soon discovered, did not answer prayers from Camp Hamilton.

"We all survived the ordeal. Each year at the breaking of camp we vowed never to return. Each August we disgustedly returned as though in a trance. We came back because we remembered the old days at Delaney Field. We remembered waiting for the team to enter. We recalled the victories over bigger schools like Johnstown and Altoona. We came back because of the winning tradition. This year - we would be the heroes for a new generation of "Ramblers."

Pat Freeman - 1986

The photograph inserted in the essay was taken by the *Tribune-Democrat* during pre-season practice at Camp Hamilton in 1947. This is the "Monster" Pat Freeman described and the player tackling the "Monster" is Frank Kush.

This essay appears to indicate that football camp was nothing but pure torture. That assumption is not far off the mark because "camp" was designed to test your survival skills as well as prepare you for Windber football. This disciplined schedule separated those who wanted to play football from those who choose to "go over the hill," the phrase used to designate the boys who left camp because football was not for them. Most boys stuck it out, some because the ridicule of being called a quitter would have been worse. The major cohesive force, however, was the knowledge that if you survived "camp," you would be a member of the Windber Rambler Football Team.

Memories of those grueling practices have long disappeared but the periods of rest in-between and leisure time after the evening chalk talks still remain. Any free time following the morning practice was spent relaxing. This consisted of sleeping in your assigned cabin or a teammates, lying in a secluded shade covered grassy spot, if one could be found, playing cards, or watching the waters of Shade Creek tumble through the rocks. Some teammates would study playbooks, especially if they had problems remembering assignments during the morning practice. If morning practice was exceptionally difficult, this rest period following lunch was a much welcomed event, although it gave you considerable time to ponder how bad the afternoon practice would be.

Rest period, following morning practice, lasted approximately two hours, and as afternoon practice drew closer, some boys began preparing by attempting to dry out their equipment, even though it had lain in the sun for almost two hours.

Following afternoon practice, after hanging up you equipment in the open air drying room and a quick shower- not necessarily in that order-you looked forward to the dinner bell and the bug juice, lemonade, and milk you could drink to replenish all the fluids you had lost during practice. Even the nasty salt pills, required to prevent muscle cramps, tasted good. You knew the rest of the evening was not going to be strenuous. We all, in our own way, thanked God for permitting us to make it through one more day.

Dinner was the favorite meal of most players. You could eat as much as you wanted, unlike breakfast or lunch, because of the fear of losing it on the practice field. This meal, served family style, was enjoyed by the upperclassman in particular, because they had positioned themselves at the end of the table where the food was first served. Experience does have its advantage. After a short rest following dinner, or, perhaps, a visit to the trainer if you were experiencing some discomfort. (I use the word discomfort very loosely as you only saw the trainer if it was next to impossible to crawl there), chalk talk was held. This consisted of coaches outlining on a chalkboard the new series of plays and individual assignments for tomorrow's practice. We copied these in our play books as fast as we could, knowing that very shortly we would be "free." At last you could stop thinking football for awhile.

On rare occasions, you might go up the practice field and walk through plays and assignments in shorts, instead of the drudgery of chalk talk. This last regimented exercise of the day lasted approximately an hour.

The last two hours, before lights out at nine o'clock, were spent visiting with family and friends, but only on designated evenings; playing cards, listening to the radio, waving to girl friends standing on the bridge, especially if it was a non-visit night; stretching tight muscles or painting names of cabin members on the interior walls of your assigned cabin. The captain, usually a senior, assigned the underclassman the responsibility of leaving a lasting record of the inhabitants of this cabin for posterity. This annual ritual, usually done by someone with artistic talent, but not always, produced a smorgasbord of interesting "art" work.

The two photographs below show an excellent example of the interior of two cabins during the 1965 Camp Hamilton adventure. The names of previous players adorn the walls as members of the 1965 team pose for pictures.

Seated: Tom Portante, **Standing left to right:** Ron Chuta, Steve Pallo, Lou Elias, Tom Cover, Rick Meek.

Seated left to right: Bob Weaver, Lynn Durst, **Standing left to right:** Bee DeBias, Joe Elias, Augie Spadone, A. J. Cannoni.

Unfortunately the 1977 Flood washed away all nine of the cabins that were adorned with countless names and graffiti. Each year, when attending camp, you would check to see if your name was still on the cabin wall from the previous year. As you might suspect many names were painted over as a new crop of "Rambler" hopefuls inscribed their names for posterity.

Lights out took place at 9:00, when all shutters, which had been opened through out the course of the day to permit air flow through the cabins, were closed. The captain of the cabin would also check to be sure that all the assignments given to underclassman that day were completed. These assignments included sweeping the floor, picking up gum wrappers (sticks of gum were used in place of money for card games), opening and closing shutters, and making bunks. This captain was also responsible for maintaining control and getting seven other boys settled after lights out.

This job sounds easy in an environment where physical activity consumes most of the day. You must remember, these are high school aged boys and horseplay comes natural. The task of getting things under control after lights out was daunting.

I can recall an incident after lights out, during my junior year (1960), in Cabin Seven of which I was a member. A cabin mate's family had brought fried chicken as a treat for their son. Most of the time you shared treats with teammates. I repeat, most of the time. That evening, following lights out, this fried chicken hoarding individual decided to devour his treat. Thinking that no one would detect his hidden treasure, and not giving any thought to the delicious odor emanating throughout this small cabin crammed with hungry football players, a search began. Once the source was discovered, it didn't take long for pieces of fried chicken to be consumed, much to the dismay of the chicken hoarder who was being held down in his bunk. Captain Jim Stawarz tolerated this fiasco while the chicken was consumed, but when the chicken bones began being propelled like hand grenades, he ordered everyone back to their bunks. This short respite of flying chicken bones lasted ten minutes, until a chicken bone struck Captain Jim.

He jumped from his upper bunk, turned on the lights, and ordered everyone to stand at attention, like a drill instructor, next to their bunks. His next order, "pick up all those bones", did not fall on deaf ears. Everyone scrambled to pick up the mess. He then proceeded to inform us that the next chicken bone striking him or anyone else would result in disciplinary action by the senior members of the team. This threat, and the tone of voice used in giving orders, was well understood by all concerned and order was restored.

However, the approach used by Captain Jim resulted in him earning the nickname "Nicki," for Nikita Kruschev, premier of the U.S.S.R. at the time. This communistic tactic was effective, but from that night on until the end of camp, all Cabin Seven members would respond to orders from Jim, with the response, "awe Nicki."

As the reader might conclude, lights out meant just that, but activity didn't cease. Night life at camp was filled with the unexpected, ranging from pranks on one cabin from members of another, harassment by an upperclassman, to the anguish cry of a teammate suffering from a sudden cramp. From Cabin Three, during the 1960 season, the sound of guitar music could be heard for hours after lights out; hence the name "The All Night Satellites" was attached.

Morning arrived all too soon. Most players were sound asleep as the early rays of the sun pried their ways through the small cracks of the wooden sided cabins until Joe Polansky, adult manager, former four year letterman, and star player during the 1938 through the 1941 seasons, would lift a shutter and bang it down producing an alarm clock noise equal to that of a jet engine taking off. After your first experience of hearing that noise and the resultant banging of your head as you exited a lower bunk, the following mornings were not as traumatic but, nonetheless, unforgettable. It was approximately 6:30 and another day at "camp" was going to be endured. Breakfast was at 7:30, the cooks had obviously been up early in order to prepare a delightful culinary spread, but the majority of boys who had moved very slowly to the mess hall could only stare at this delight and wonder what it might look like on the practice field in about two hours.

Morning practice commenced promptly at 9:00. The time prior to this torture was spent on your bunk attempting to digest what little food you had consumed for breakfast. If you were a kicker or punter, along with the centers, practice started about 15 minutes earlier than the entire squad. As you watched these specialty players prepare for practice, the thought of having to go to the drying room and collect your practice equipment which had not dried out over night, was especially discouraging. The fresh socks and jock strap provided each day did inject a slight amount of relief, until you realized those personal pieces of clothing were soon going to be saturated with sweat and had to be worn for two practices. You also double checked your jock strap for "atom bomb," an analgesic ointment used to treat sore muscle when heat would be produced during exercise. Put there by a prankster teammate who had forgot to check his jock strap one time. You don't have to use your imagination to picture the outcome. Another morning practice began. Day after day we would follow the same schedule. Day after day we wondered why we were here.

The first Saturday of "camp" was looked on with much anticipation. A live scrimmage, scheduled with another school, took place at 10:00 am. We finally had the opportunity to hit someone other than our own teammates, get a break from the torturous grind, and look forward to the end of the first week of camp. This controlled scrimmage consisted of a team running ten offensive plays, called by the coaches, and interrupted after each play to go over any mistakes. The opposing defense likewise would be constructively criticized, and following this sequence of ten plays, would change from offense to defense. This cycle would repeat itself, even after a team scored a touchdown. Extra points were not attempted nor any kickoffs.

I can remember a very funny incident from the first scrimmage my senior year, I can't recall the school we scrimmaged. But I will never forget the play. We were on defense, and a ball carrier from the opposing team was stacked up at the line. After the whistle ended the play, a coach came running up to the ball carrier and asked him how many fingers were up.

This coach had four fingers pointing to the ground. The ball carrier responded, "four." The coach proceeded to kick him in the butt and said, "you dumb ass, they are down." This constructive criticism may have been great in math class, but I still haven't been able to figure out how it applied that day.

After lunch on Saturday and a brief recap by the coaches on the scrimmage, we were bused back to town and dropped off at the high school. The outcome of the scrimmage had already hit the streets. If we had dominated the opposition, you would walk the streets home and hold your head high. If the scrimmage carried a negative evaluation, you got home as fast as you could. The first week of "camp" was over. A good night sleep in your own bed, pampering from mom and dad, an enjoyable meal, maybe even a date with that favorite girl, and most importantly, knowing you would get up from that comfortable bed without having a cabin shutter go off in your ear. It was a sweet release from the torture of camp.

Sunday, a day that flew by like a 57 Chevy drag racing on the Elton Road, started with church where you began to contemplate your return to camp, buying more gum for card games, eating your favorite food, contemplating your return to camp, saying good by to that favorite girl, having your practice uniform washed by mom, contemplating your return to camp, buying batteries for the transistor radio, getting your clothes ready for next week, and did I forget, contemplating your return to camp.

The thought of two a day practices under that mid-august sun, coupled with all the inconveniences of "camp" life, occupied a great deal of your thinking on Sunday. However, you come to the realization that to become a "Rambler" and wear the blue and white uniform, a little sacrifice for the next week would be well worth the effort.

After arriving at camp, around 5:00 that evening, getting everything situated in your cabin, sharing a few lies with your teammates about that junior girl you took to the movies Saturday night, and trying to find out who might have gone "over the hill," the dinner bell rang- the first signal that the second week of camp had started. You made your way slowly to the mess hall where a meal for a condemned man was waiting, at least that was the feeling you had. Week two had started; the disciplined schedule was going to repeat itself. Practices again would seem an eternity, and putting on those sweat soaked uniforms, which never seemed to dry, continued each day.

Week two of torture went by fast. Soon it was apparent that camp would be ending, and the sacrifice endured in preparing yourself for another football season at Camp Hamilton would be over. On Saturday, the last day of camp, the second pre-season scrimmage was planned with an opposing team.. This scrimmage was organized in the same manner as the first, except a few extra points were tried following a touchdown. At the conclusion of this scrimmage, "camp" was officially over. The confusion of showering, a hurried lunch, packing clothing, and tearing your bunk down was done with precision. We were now a team, ready to be included in the history of Windber High School Football. We had survived Camp Hamilton and looked forward to the up coming season with much enthusiasm.

As a senior, your thoughts at this time are memories of past camps and knowing this is probably the last time you will have this experience. You had anxiously waited for this moment, the end of "camp", but now move slowly, as nostalgia wells up and you recall the good and bad experiences from previous years. The underclassmen look at you with a perplexed stare and can't comprehend why you aren't as excited as they are. You come out of your trance and head for the bus, ready now to accept the role of a Windber "Rambler."

12

Nicknames

Crazy Legs---White Shoes---Refrigerator, the football world is loaded with nicknames. Windber High School football also shares this same phenomena. Throughout this research I found numerous nicknames attached to many of the players, coaches, and managers. The origin of most of these nicknames remains a mystery. Some were directly attached because of the individuals accomplishments on the gridiron while others possibly due to a physical feature or particular incident. The most unique aspect of these nicknames is that most of them are still used today and many people would not recognize the given name of these players, coaches, and managers.

During my research I contacted a number of former "Rambler" football players from the time period I played and asked if they could recall any nicknames and possibly how these nicknames were derived. Terry Heckler, quarterback of the 1959 team and artist of the caricatures in this book shared with me how his nickname "Fern" came into existence.

Fernnnnnnn

"We practiced football year-round. In the winter we'd be hitting dummies in the wrestling room and running plays in the gym. On the first day of summer vacation we started full bore team practices every week day evening up on Sunset Field tucked away behind the Polish cemetery on top of 4th Street Hill. It was getting in shape, running our plays, and fundamentals all done in street clothes waiting for the day in August when "Big John" (Coach Kawchak) would call the names of the boys who made the team to camp. It was the summer of 1958.

I was a junior playing second team quarterback. A bunch of the seniors, "Mouse" Marron, "Bones" Depolo, "Eggs" Minitti, "Jess" Heeter, "Mooney" Csordas, and John Repko were given a special paying job by Assistant Coach Atty to do hard labor for an evangelist setting up a big tent over by the stadium. Every evening up at Sunset, before practice, Bones and Mouse started to yell out odd things picked up on their evangelist day job. One of the jobs they did was pulling the big tent canvas around for some old sinner sitting at a sewing machine patching tears and holes. Bones liked to mimic anybody he took an interest in, like, Little Richard and Jerry Lee Lewis. He took a big interest in the sewing machine guy. Bones would pretend like he was sewing and yell out, "ya yoballs get off my canvas Fernnnnnnn!" Then he'd say, "He comes up with some good shit ... Gumnuts! Get off my canvas Fernnnnnnn!" So bones would yell this stuff out while everyone was restless wondering what first team player was going to start throwing around some underclassman who never had a chance of going to camp.

As the days went on, Bones started to call his canvas crew teammates Fernnnnnnn during practice. Then everyone started calling each other Fernnnnnnn but only carefully. Those outside the canvas crew couldn't use it loud or they got thrown around. Downtown one night, outside Reno's Pool Room, I saw Mouse grab "Little Hitler" when he asked about all the Fernnnnnnn shit. Mouse made it clear that no one but the team could use the name or know where it came from. You never knew what rules Mouse would enforce. That was 1958.

In 1959, my senior year at the first summer Sunset practice, things were somber. Many of the positions were up for grabs and everyone was on edge waiting for Big John to set the teams for running plays. After "Budder" (John Bourch) caught my first pass I yelled out, "way to go Fernnnnnnn!" Like a flash I realized I picked up where Bones left off. We all called each other Fernnnnnnn up at Sunset. Then at camp, maybe because I re-started it at Sunset, everyone called me "Fern".... without the machine gun ending. I found myself quietly responding with a recognition Fern but included the machine gun N's. This particular exchange seemed to be strictly followed throughout the season. Even the coaches called me Fern which I responded to as if it was my name, never uttering Fernnnnnnn to them. When the season was over, so was the name Fern. So I thought. Over the years the name has become almost spiritual to me. After all it did sort of come from an evangelist. When I saw it in your e-mail address my heart soared. "Fern" I thought was adopted once again by later teams. But I guess it's just a street name. What intrigues me is how your street name has stimulated an elaborate explanation that probably would have never been shared. I mean what's in a name, Fernnnnnnn".

It would be impossible to compile a complete list of all nicknames attached to individuals over this 94 year history of Windber High School Football. The following list is a sample of nicknames found during the research. It is the authors' hope that these names will rekindle memories and help anyone who did not know the given name of these players.

A Reflection on Windber High School Football

John "Jada" Lloyd-1922	James "Whitey" Hagan-1923	Gerald "Snitz" Snyder-1924
Nick "Kelly Kat" Costa (Manager)-1926	John "Scare" Torquato-1926	Jim "Scoop" Camile-1926
J. Harold "Duke" Weigle-1927	Niles "Stud" Dalberg-1930	Tom "Boz" Marron-1933
Arthur "Arpy" Garlathy-1934	William "Cooney" Farkas-1935	George "Leo" Bokinsky-1937
Edward "Bud" Bossick-1937	Joe "Gump" Polansky-1941	Jack "Tish" Lochrie-1942
George "Grundy" Solomon-1942	Andy "Guthead" Boyko-1942	Ray "Scare" Torquato-1942
Charles "Bebs" Popelich-1942	Carl "Hog Call" Geisel-1943	Nunzio "Touchdown" Marino-1943
Anthony "Mex" DeMuzio-1944	William "Bela" Laslo-1944	Frank "Pussy" Kush-1947
Ronald "Link" Younker-1949	Lou "The Toe" Sam-1949	Bernard "Wimpy" Washko-1950
George "Scotty" McKelvie-1952	Joe "Gunda" Kush-1954	Gwynn "Gatch" Gahagen-1955
Roy "Pete" Seese-1955	Harold "Carbide" Klemick-1956	Henry "Herke" Polasko-1956
Alysous "Hoko" Tavalsky-1957	John "Mooney" Csordas-1958	Tom "Mouse" Marron-1958
Bob "Eggs" Minitti-1958	Tom "Bones" Depolo-1958	Gene "Jess" Heeter-1958
Terry "Fern" Heckler-1959	Ed. "Ridge Runner" Hadix-1959	Robert "Mick" Seese-1960
Robert "Moose" Oyler-1960	Joe "Church Mouse" Pachella-1960	Joe "Hunchy" Hancharick-1960
Steve "Smega" Kush-1961	Dennis "Zerk" Zahurak (Manager)-1961	Tom "Mustard" Rosa-1962
Joe "Red" Decewicz-1965	Richard "Rico" Shark-1966	Tom "Toma" Voytko-1967
Tim "Bass" Voytko-1967	Pat "Tish" Lochrie-1967	James "Peachy" Miller-(Manager)-1967
Steve "Beak" Robatin-1972	Jim "Dough Boy" Lamonca-1972	Jim "Ears" Hudack-1973
Jason "Jake" Oyler-1988	Mike "Fish" Facciani-1988	Tom "Bo" Toomey-1989
Cory "Toby" Gaye-1991	Charles "C.W." Beckley-2005	Patrick "Vito" Ferrante-2006

13

On to College

It is very difficult to determine exactly how many boys have played football for Windber High School and that number is required to determine the percentage of boys who continued their career at the college level. Records from the very early years are difficult to find and the rosters from those early years indicate only the starting lineups. I made an estimate of approximately 3700 boys who have played football for Windber High School. This was based on using 40 members on each team for the 94 plus years covered in this document. I factored in a small number for the early teams and increased this number in the later years. This obviously is a guess since there is no way of getting an exact total. From this estimate of total players and the number of players who have played at least one year at the college level I have concluded that four percent of Windber High School football players have had the opportunity to continue their playing career at the college level.

In researching this area of individuals who continued their football career at the college level, I found over a 165 boys with documentation indicating at least one year of playing collegiate football. Many of these boys completed four years of college football and some played for more than one school. The list of players located can be seen in Appendix IV beginning on page 289. I can not be one hundred percent accurate because of records and apologize if I have missed any players. Please inform me of any mistakes or names that need to be added.

Who was the first Windber High School football player that continued his playing career in college? I was very surprised when I came across an article in the January 21, 1915 issue of the *Windber Era* as copied from the *Syracuse Herald*. It reports:

> "William J. Farber of Windber has been greatly honored by the award of the Monx Head Trophy. The trophy is presented each year to the most representative man in the junior class, who has measured up to certain standards both in scholarship, athletics and other college activities. Farber is the third man to receive the trophy. Besides the trophy, the winner has his name engraved on a bronze tablet in the trophy room of the gymnasium, which is to be maintained permanently."
>
> "Farber has been unusually active in athletics ever since he came to Syracuse. His home is Windber, Pennsylvania and he prepared for college at the Bethlehem Preparatory School at Bethlehem, Pennsylvania. While in the preparatory school he played on the football, basketball and baseball teams."
>
> "In 1911 he entered Syracuse and his freshman year played on the freshman football, basketball and baseball teams. Since that time he has earned his letter in football and baseball. He is also a member of the athletic governing board, senior council and is president of the student body."

Although Bill Farber is not included in the official roster of Windber High School football because of playing prior to 1914 he still must be deserving of being the first Windber High School football player to continue his career at the college level. Bill was the starting fullback on the 1908 Windber High School team, however this team is not recognized as the first official team because a number of boys on this team were out of high school.

After finishing his college career, Bill Farber, continued on as an assistant football coach at Syracuse. As of this time I have not been able to locate any other information concerning the career of William J. Farber.

College football is demanding and I feel sure any Windber High School football player who participated at the college level was well prepared.

14

Reflections on Windber High School Football

The reason for selecting the title of this chapter and the book stems from the research I have conducted concerning football fever which is rampant in Windber during the late summer when football camp begins and lingers on after the last game of the season. The title is derived from two essays I was fortunate to find. Both of which convey a message that helps explain why the history of Windber football is so stepped in tradition.

The first essay was written by Jack Gallagher, a retired Foreign Service officer, WWII veteran, teacher, basketball coach and former resident of Windber from the age of two until the age of ten. After reading Jack's essay, I reached him by phone and explained the objectives of my research. He said I could use his essay as I saw fit.

I decided that the entire essay should be included in order to look at how an individual can be influenced by family, community, and high school football. Jack Gallagher has given a very real insight into the tradition of Windber High School Football.

A Boy's Life in Football, Pennsylvania
by
Jack Gallagher

My wife keeps telling me how lucky I was to have had an incredibly happy childhood. Before she commented about those long ago days, I had never given much thought to evaluating my childhood in Windber, Pennsylvania; but now, as I look back at those younger times, I realize that she knows what she's talking about. Yes, fate put me in the right place as a boy, and my spouse's assessment of my boyhood is right on the mark. In Windber my childhood buddies would say that her observation scored a "touchdown." That Windberite way of summing up her remarks should clue the reader as to what was different about that little coal town of some 9,000 inhabitants in the 1930's and 40's. It was football!

Oh, yes, we had other reasons besides football for feeling happy, not the least of which were loving parents and caring neighbors. With such strong supports behind us we took a happy frame of mind into our boyhood activities like playing Cowboys-and-Indians or running all over town playing Blacksmith Tag, and on Saturdays we never missed the weekly episode of whatever western serial was showing at Dan Kough's old Opera House (Now part of First Commonwealth's Bank drive through service area), where we paid the exorbitant sum of one nickel for two balcony tickets each Saturday. Sometimes we took a break from the action to invade a neighbor's yard and snare a forbidden fruit from one of the trees that bore the most delicious miniature green apples that any boy ever tasted. On Sundays we slowed down long enough to put our "Sunday-go to-meetin" clothes on and went to Sunday school and church. We learned about God and were especially relieved to find out that by praying to Him we could get our sins-such as apple theft-forgiven.

On Mondays we returned to action for another week that might include kite flying, wiener roasts, and "bucketball." No one owned a backboard or even a basketball, so my brother Charlie and I would use any rubber ball we could find and try to shoot it into the bottomless old rusty bucket we had nailed onto the garage. In the winter, Cambria Avenue, where our family lived, became our sled-ridding slope, and my brother Ed and I would pour out our snow-inspired energies there until nine o'clock at night. That's when Officer Quinn would show up and tell us it was time to go home. Our greatest delight came on the Saturday's during the football season. We all had season tickets that cost us a dollar apiece, and no one would think of ever missing a game at old Delaney Field, where our high school team always won. Come to think of it, I never saw our heroes ever lose a game, even when they played in another town. If I was unable to go to a road game, I would join my buddies on the long walk down to Shaffer's Drugstore, where we would wait patiently for the manager (who maintained telephone contact with someone at the game) to post the updated score on the storefront window at the end of each quarter.

Of course, along with all of that wonderful childhood activity, we went to school every weekday, even liked our teachers and generally stayed out of trouble-but during football season we were counting the minutes until the final bell rang so that we could dash home, change clothes, and run to the nearest vacant lot, usually the Methodist churchyard to play football.

As you can see, football had become a Windber tradition. No boy could, or wanted to, ignore that tradition. The high school's alma mater even played a role in fostering it: *Hail dear old Windber High. Hail to her name, her fame, her deeds in the days gone by.* I'm an old man now, many years removed from Windber, but as you can see, I still remember those words.

Berwind White Coal Company provided the economic base of the community. The town lived materially on coal, but spiritually it lived on football, so much so its name might have been Football, Pennsylvania. In Windber, man did not live by coal alone but by every gridiron deed that came out of Windber High School!

My dad, the town's Methodist minister, moved to Windber when I was two years old. By the time I entered grade school my playmates and I had already come to know that the goal of any boy was to play on a Windber High football team that would beat Johnstown, a mighty metropolis of some 60,000 people who even had an escalator in one of their department stores! As youngsters we had learned that Johnstown was known across the nation because of a famous flood that had inundated the city, but we preferred to think of it as the site of a giant's stronghold where we hoped to do battle in our high school days. I recall visiting in a neighbor's home where a baby boy had just been born. In his crib I saw-you guessed it-a new football. It was never too early to set a boy on the right path!

While I was attending elementary school, my oldest brother, Gil, was a high school student; but, much to his sorrow, he wasn't cut out to be a football player, a shortcoming that he overcame in a most logical way-he became the sports editor of the school newspaper and also joined the band so that he would be assured of a seat at the stadium. Thus he not only witnessed Windber's 1933 victory over John Harris High School of our state's capital but also had the satisfaction of writing about that contest. He probably had even greater satisfaction in writing about Windber's win over Johnstown in front of some 20,000 fans in a game that qualified our "Coaltowners" for the showdown against John Harris. Today Gil talks about Jim Cavacini's 76-yard punt that saved the championship and Bill Farkas's extra point kick that was the margin of victory over John Harris.

That championship game even altered the behavior of my preacher dad. A Sunday evening service following that splendid triumph featured not only prayers of thanksgiving but also a play-by-play movie of the entire four quarters. Windber mania had peaked, and Dad had no trouble in relating *prayers* and *players*. After all, there is only a one-letter difference. Fortunately for Dad, his bishop did not live in Harrisburg!

It was not surprising that Cavacini went on to play football for the renowned Bo McMillan's Indiana Hoosiers, and Farkas became a Pitt Panther under the tutelage of the legendary Jock Sutherland, while fullback John Carliss continued his career by playing for the West Virginia University Mountaineers. Even before members of that championship team had joined the college ranks, former Windber players such as Joe Gates, a brainy quarterback who starred at Duquesne when the Dukes enjoyed status as a major Eastern power, were already making names for themselves in college football. As the focus grew on subsequent Windber gridders who enhanced the tradition by compiling four consecutive undefeated seasons and other fabulous records in the 30's and 40's. Windber footballers were adding to their achievements at schools like Notre Dame, Michigan State, West Virginia, and many of the smaller Pennsylvania colleges such as St. Vincent and Muhlenberg. One Windber standout, Frank Kush, won All-American honors in college, later coached at Arizona State University, then moved on to Baltimore to coach the Colts of the National Football League. Another Windber player, Nunzio Marino, an All-Pennsylvania high school star, played quarterback at Notre Dame. Windber sports buffs still recall that the first time he carried the ball for the Fighting Irish he ran 58 yards for a touchdown! Yes, football stars stand at the top of the little coal town's list of heroes-even outranking Johnny Weissmuller, the Windber native who won international acclaim as an Olympic swimmer and as Hollywood's most famous Tarzan.

In the early 40's I attended a sport's banquet at which the featured speaker was Regis McKnight, a high school coach at the time but now remembered as the highly regarded mentor of successful football teams at Indiana University of Pennsylvania. In his banquet remarks, Coach McKnight said, "Windber had the best high school team I ever saw."

No one in Windber would dare dispute his observation.

(The author would like to interject a note at this time regarding Regis "Peck" McKnight. I had the pleasure of having Coach McKnight as a professor while attending Indiana University of Pennsylvania and after he found out that I was from Windber and was playing football for the university, he and I became very good friends. He invited me over to his house a few times for a home cooked meal and his son, Barry, who I played against in high school and went on to play college football at Pitt, would talk about the games between Indiana High School and Windber High School. Barry was a three year starter for Indiana High School and never won a game against Windber.)

What made Windber so successful in football? First of all, it was each player's duty to continue the tradition of winning. Secondly, all the gridders knew that the whole town supported them, so much so that when they traveled to play Johnstown, everyone in Windber-well, not the hospital patients-went with them. Windber would then appear deserted, a ghost town. It seemed that every Windber car must have been parked outside Johnstown's Point Stadium. Anyone who lacked an automobile ride to the game simply hopped on the old "Toonerville Trolley" which, despite being overloaded, would manage to make the 7-mile trek into the lair of the giant foe. In addition to tradition and support of the citizenry, the players benefited from coaching that was decades ahead of that in other towns. The Windber coaches had masterminded game plans that went far beyond the conservative running game that reigned in other communities. The Ramblers, as the Windber teams came to be known, not only ran the ball but also threw dozens of passes, used trick plays, and had no fear of tossing laterals all over the field, a razzle-dazzle football new to their opponents, who simply did not know how to stop it. The old *Pittsburgh Sun-Telegraph* may have been the first big city newspaper to recognize that something different was going on in Windber. The sports page carried a banner headline about little Windber beating another giant, Bethlehem, a city eight times larger than Windber in population. The news account told how Windber had filled the air with 30 passes, almost unheard of in those days, and had overwhelmed the bigger city team by a score of 75-12. (You can be sure the Windber coaches were perplexed that their defense had allowed 12 points!) Yes, other teams came from more populous communities and often boasted bigger boys than Windber, but the "Coaltowners" had the coaching, the tradition, and the whole community's support-a civic "togetherness" that endowed its young men with an unbelievable desire to win and to bring pride to the community.

As a youngster I was part of that magic, and life almost seemed to end when I was a Fifth Grader, for that's when the bishop transferred Dad to another charge, which meant that I would no longer be seeing Windber football games and that I would be separated from my boyhood pal, Pat Walker. Eventually, in another town, I became a high school BASKETBALL player. If I had still lived in Windber, my boyhood friends would have wondered what went wrong with me; but I never forgot Windber in my high school days and would on occasion return there and go with my friend Pat to see a game, the most memorable of which was a Windber victory in 1942 over-you guessed right again-Johnstown!

I suppose that an outsider would say that Windber's citizens, with their emphasis on football, had their priorities wrong. I disagree. Football was a unifying glue in a multiethnic community, a spiritual energizer that, I would bet, proved a lifelong force in the development of many a young man once he left life between the goal posts. Windber football had taught them to cooperate with their fellowman, to set lofty goals and work toward their achievement, while never fearing any giants that might stand in their way.

Recently my wife and I drove through Windber and were attracted to a display on the outside wall of a shoe repair shop on Graham Avenue, Windber's main thoroughfare. That display featured the glory days of Windber football. We stopped, and I went inside, where I met Gino Stevens, who is an historian of those wonderful times of the 30's and 40's. He generously gave me a video of Windber's great 1942 victory over Johnstown-the same game I had seen with Pat Walker. Geno also phoned my old friend, Jack Lochrie, who invited my wife and me to stop by his house to talk over old times. How could I refuse? After all, Jack ran 80 yards, after picking up a fumble, for a touchdown against Johnstown in that 1942 game.

During the ensuing visit with Jack I happened to mention how the "Toonerville Trolley" had played a part in the football rivalry with Johnstown, a bit of Windber lore rattled around in Jack's own bag of nostalgia and suddenly shook loose one of his persistent boyhood memories. "I remember," said Jack, "how people who didn't have a ride to an Altoona game traveled there by train."

Windber, as we both recalled, had no railroad passenger service, but there was a spur line for the freight trains that transported Windber coal to market. Coal shipments-obviously less important than a game with Altoona, a city of some 80,000 and a rival every bit as tough as Johnstown-simply had to be rescheduled so that the Pennsylvania Railroad could dispatch a special train to pick up the huge throng of students and townspeople anxious to board the coaches and head to Altoona. (I have little doubt that every coal company executive in Windber not only cooperated in opening the tracks but also journeyed to Altoona to root for the coaltown eleven.) Enroute the train, probably overloaded, would huff-and-puff its way around the railroad's famous Horseshoe Curve, then gradually chug its way through the mountains to its destination, where the Windber fans would jump out and rush like an invading army to the football stadium. Meanwhile, back in Windber the streets were deserted again!

Yes, our visit with Jack had found us continuing to reflect on the good old days of Windber's glory, but I now have to admit, albeit ever so sadly, that times have changed. Coal no longer fuels the economy, population has plummeted, and so too has Windber's statewide football dominance; but memories linger, so much that in my imagination I'm still listening to the 1933 band playing the alma mater, and I'm still singing along: *Hail to ....her deeds in the days gone by!*

This reflection of Windber's football history, by Jack Gallagher, I'm sure will invoke many memories, especially for anyone who lived during this time period. Yes, times have changed, but the tradition of Windber football lives on. This unrivaled tradition can't always be seen but is felt by Windber players and fans.

The following essay by Larry Betcher, a member of the 1985 Windber High School football team and a 1986 graduate, was composed as an assignment for an English class during his senior year. The essay was provided to me by Ralph DeMarco, current Middle School Principal and First Assistant Football Coach. Ralph remembered he had the essay in his file cabinet when I mentioned I was looking for material concerning the tradition of Windber High School Football.

My Home Town
by
Larry Betcher

Larry Betcher-1985

The four o'clock horn echoes through the mountainside and the mysterious black hole that disappears into the face of the hill is illuminated by a single blinding light. The one-eyed monster appears to be coming out of the darkness to silence the annoying horn. He finally shows himself to be a train about four feet high with a steel canopy covering its entirety. It is packed full of weary, helmeted men of different sizes and shapes who look as if they've been spray painted black. The train proceeds up the track to the shower room where it is quickly deserted. It is lonely not for long, though, because the evening shift then fills the seats as quickly as the daylight shift emptied them. Until recently, such was life for more than half of the working population of Windber, Pennsylvania. The name itself was derived from the Berwind Coal Company which still runs the mines today. The mines have almost all been closed down by the decline in the steel industry as of late. However, a string of trucks loaded with coal, winding its way through the streets of town is still a common site.

The town lies in a small valley, separated from neighboring peoples by the surrounding hills. While approaching the town from the hills, one first notices St. John's Catholic Church, the tallest structure in town and just one of the more than ten churches that serve the tiny community. The religions and nationalities of the people divide the village into a drastically scaled down version of New York City's boroughs and districts. The West end of town is home for the Polish, Hungarian, and Slovakian people, all of which patronize their own respective churches. On the other hand, the East end, made up of Italians, is jokingly referred to as "Little Italy" by its inhabitants. In addition to the nationality divisions of the people, employment and financial separations do exist. Mine 40, Mine 37, and Mine 35 are all developments constructed to house the families of the men who earn their living as coal miners. The term "development" is used loosely, though, because all they consist of are rows of double houses covered with coal dust. Even with these minor segregations, Windber remains one big, hard-working, middle class family.

Being such a society, the individuals receive little respect from and get very little attention from near by communities. The people need someone or something to bring notice to the town- they need something to support to make themselves feel important. That something is the town's high school football team. The pulse of the entire community can be measured by the team's success over the season. And like the town itself; the team has felt it's share of disappointment lately.

In the late 1930's, when the town was a bustling, growing community- the team was the state champion. The nickname "Ramblers" was later adopted because of the distances the team had to travel to find opponents who were willing and brave enough to take the field against the young coal miners. The word football was synonymous with Windber throughout the state and parts of others. The supremacy of Windber has changed though. The field where the old Ramblers played their home games now supports a home for the sick and elderly, the new Ramblers no longer travel to Pittsburgh and Maryland to find competition, and there hasn't been a state championship team since 1937. However, there is one thing in the town of Windber that has not changed and never will change- the deep, deep; love, admiration and respect the people have for their Ramblers.

Remembering the past is what keeps Windber alive and prospering. The pride these people and anyone who was ever associated with Windber- possess, separates Windber from any other town. The pressure to develop and display this pride that confronts the younger generations may seem staggering; but, then again, not everyone is born with the unteachable understanding of what it takes to be from Windber- not everyone can be a Rambler. This is what makes Windber my only true love.

15

Most Notable Windber High School Football Player

My original plan in putting this document together was not to dwell on or highlight any particular player or players because Windber High School has produced many very good football players. These high school gridiron stars could not have attained the fame many are noted for without the help of their teammates. Yes, even down to the lowly underclassman who held the tackling dummies during practice, everyone contributed. They were part of a team, a group of players, coaches, and managers working together to obtain an objective.

However, there is one name that is always mentioned when the topic of Windber High School Football is brought up: **Frank Kush**, the most celebrated alumnus of Windber football. Frank was inducted into the Cambria County War Memorial Hall of Fame in 1967 and in the first Windber Hall of Fame in 1979. He was inducted into the College Football Hall of Fame in 1994.

Because Frank has gained notoriety on a national level for his coaching exploits and has not forgotten to mention how his home town provided inspiration, I felt an obligation to expand on this most notable football alumnus. I apologize to anyone who feels slighted in anyway because of this decision.

Frank Kush played for the Ramblers from 1944-47 and was a stalwart on the line, playing left guard for two seasons and left tackle his senior year. I never saw Frank play, as I was just a toddler at the time. However, I have been very fortunate to meet Frank on a number of occasions; the first was in Pittsburgh, at a national football coach's clinic, during the early 1970's, where he was one of the featured speakers. A group of high school coaches from this area were invited up to his hotel suite following the clinic and we got to socialize with Frank and some of his Arizona State University coaching staff. When I introduced myself, I told Frank that I had been a teammate of his youngest brother, Steve, at Windber, and, in fact, played next to him on the offensive line during the 1961 football season. I asked about Steve and we chatted about the clinic.

My second encounter with Frank was at a Fourth of July picnic in 1988, at my cousin Howard Lochrie's house. My cousin is the son of Gilbert Lochrie, now deceased, who had been a teammate of Frank's in high school. Gilbert had invited Frank to the party as they both were visiting Windber for their 40 year high school class reunion. I was introduced to Frank by my Uncle Gilbert and mentioned to him that I had met him a number of years earlier in Pittsburgh. We talked about his brother, Steve, whose nickname is "Smega". Upon hearing this nickname, my uncle started to laugh. He was reminded of an incident involving himself and Frank some years earlier at a swank hotel in Washington, D.C. Gilbert and Frank had made arrangements to meet at this hotel since "Gib," Gilbert's nickname, lived in McLean, Virginia, and Frank was in Washington for a speaking engagement. Upon entering the lobby of this posh hotel, Frank, was greeted by "Gib," shouting at the top of his lungs "Pussy," Frank's nickname in high school. After Gilbert told the story, which was accompanied by much laughter, Frank said "I was ready to melt into the marble floor".

The third time I met Frank was in Tempe, Arizona in 1996. I had made arrangements to visit his brother, Steve, and was invited to play in a golf tournament sponsored by Frank for the benefit of the Arizona Boys Ranch. This ranch had been established to help delinquent youths who had reached a point in their lives where the only choice they had was prison or the Ranch to help in rehabilitation. I took the opportunity to purchase a book entitled **The Last Chance Ranch** by Mark Emmons; This is a story about football, gang members, and learning to live by the rules. (This book can be found in the library at Windber Area High School) On the plane ride home I began reading this book and came across a chapter titled, The Man, The Myth, The Legend. This chapter was entirely devoted to Frank Kush, who was serving in an executive administrative position at the ranch and had been hired to help spread the word about what the ranch was doing in the community. Although not directly involved in coaching, Frank did help field the first ever high school football team at the ranch.

I would like at this time to share some of this chapter material concerning Frank.

"Kush had one thing in common with most of the kids at the ranch: He had grown up with next to nothing. The son of a Polish coal miner, he had been born on January 20, 1929, in the company town of Windber, Pennsylvania. Kush remembered Windber as a bleak place where all the houses were painted either yellow, green or gray. To this day he could still recall that the town had thirteen churches and fifty bars while he was growing up."

"The fifth of fifteen kids, he lived in a house located above Mine No. 35. The place had no hot water and no telephone. There were six children sleeping in his bed. Kush said the biggest paycheck he could ever remember his dad bringing home, after food and rent had been deducted, was $2.62 for two weeks' work. Such was life in the coal fields. While Kush never lacked for discipline, most everything else was in short supply-----College was the first time he ever got three meals a day or was introduced to steak. But if there was a saving grace for the Kush clan, it was that ignorance was blis."

"The Kush kids just assumed that everybody lived as they did----"We were as poor as some of these kids at the ranch," Kush said. "We didn't have a pot to piss in when my dad died. But the difference was my family, my teachers, my community. They wouldn't give up on me." And he had football. In the coal-mining towns of western Pennsylvania, the game is a way of life. "I'd be dead by now if it weren't for football," Kush said. "I'd be a dead coal miner. Football saved me. The game gave me opportunities that I never thought I would have, and I took advantage of the opportunities -------Kush was demon on the field. He was a star lineman who routinely put much bigger players flat on their backs. He was named to Pennsylvania's all-state team and ended up receiving about fifteen scholarship offers. Many schools, though, weren't aware of his small stature. For instance, Kush took a recruiting trip to the University of Georgia. The Bulldog coaches had read about him in the newspapers, so they invited him down for a look, sight unseen. When Kush got off the plane, the assistant coach who was there to meet him didn't recognize him because he was looking for a big, strapping fellow. When they finally did hook up, the assistant took him to meet the head coach, Wally Butts. Butts took one look at Kush and, with a deep southern drawl, offered Kush some free advice. "Son, I think you're kinda small to be playing college football, especially at Georgia," he said."

"That got Kush to thinking that maybe he was too little, although he was still determined to use the game as his escape hatch from the coal mines."

"He attended Washington & Lee College in Virginia as a freshman and then transferred to Michigan State. During his three Years at Michigan State he was a two-way starter, the team lost one game, the school won a national title, and Kush was named All-American as a guard. He thought of pursuing a career in professional football but was told by Paul Brown, a coach for the Senior Bowl, that he just didn't have the size to play professionally. He recommended that Kush pursue another career. And for awhile, Kush did try something else: the Army. And, once again, football saved him. The way he remembered it, his class of second lieutenants was about to be shipped out of Fort Benning, Georgia, to the conflict in Korea. Instead, he was told to stay and coach one of the bases' football squads. Kush said he later learned that thirty-nine of his seventy classmates were killed in the fighting."

"A coaching career was born. In 1955, Dan Devine, an assistant coach at Michigan State, was named head coach at Arizona State University. He selected Frank as an assistant because of his playing and coaching experience. Dan Devine left after three years and Frank became head coach at the age of 28."

"His record over a span of 22 seasons, 176 wins, 54 losses and one tie. Between 1970 and 1975 the "sun devils" were 62-9 with many players moving on to play in the NFL."

"Frank was a demanding coach. He decided that a secluded location with no distractions would be a perfect place for the football team to prepare for the season and developed Camp Tontozona, on Tonto Creek, 100 miles north of Phoenix." Could this idea of a camp come from Frank's experience at Camp Hamilton? "This was not a mountain retreat and as the years passed a mythology grew around Kush's Tontozona practices. Like many myths, these had a basis in truth. The players had two beliefs: If they could play for that man, they could play for anybody and hell would be a piece of cake after surviving four years with him"

"Following an alleged punching incident of punter Kevin Rutledge, due to a shanked punt, in a 1979 game with Washington, he was fired in January 1980. Two juries ruled in Kush's favor following a $2.2 million law suit filed by Rutledge."

"After the 1982-83 Canadian Football League season, in which he piloted the Hamilton Tiger Cats to the Eastern Conference championship, he replaced Mike McCormick in 1984 as head coach of the Baltimore Colts of the National Football League. He spent three years as the head coach of the Baltimore Colts in Baltimore and coached the Colts in 1987 after they moved to Indianapolis."

"1987 would be the last year Frank Kush would coach football; however, he helped organize the football team at Arizona Boys Ranch by recruiting a top notch high school coach and would often stop by practices to see how the kids were doing."

A quote from Frank, taken from the book **Last Chance Ranch**; "football taught me determination, how to deal with adversity and the importance of refusing to quit. These kids aren't going to get anywhere in life if they don't learn those basics". To Frank, football was as good as any to deliver life's lessons.

Frank Kush talks to offensive lineman during practice at Arizona Boys Ranch.

Photograph taken from the book **Last Chance Ranch** by Mark Emmons

My fourth opportunity to talk with Frank Kush occurred during the centennial celebration of Windber in 1997. Frank had been selected to be the grand marshal for the centennial parade. I had invited his brother Steve to stay at my house, as he was going to be in attendance, for the week long event and extended an invitation to Frank for dinner on Monday of that week. He said he would join my wife and myself along with Steve if he could bring a boyhood friend, Rudy Matecic. I told him that would be great because I knew Rudy and would enjoy talking about his family since I had taught some of his children in school.

We all enjoyed a delicious meal prepared by my wife, Carol. Frank, Rudy, and Steve all commented on how lucky I was to have a wife who could prepare such good ethnic food. Being of Polish heritage, my wife sure impressed these three voracious eaters who are also of Polish heritage.

Following dinner I showed Frank, Rudy, and Steve some of the material I had put together on the starting lineups of Windber High School football from 1914 thru 1996. This promoted discussion of former teammates and reminiscing about Windber High School football. The stories were numerous, with both Frank and Rudy sharing memories of boyhood experiences growing up in Mine 35 and Rambler football teams of the early 1940's. I wished I could have recorded some of the stories.

The last opportunity I had to speak with Frank was at the Coal Kids Reunion held during the summer of 2005. This reunion is held almost every year and is limited to the former kids of coal miners who grew up in Mines 35 and 36. I was very fortunate to be invited by a close friend, Andy Pipon, who had lived in Mine 35. He told me that since I had worked in the mines and that my father was a coal miner, the only thing missing was that I didn't grow up there. I felt very privileged to be asked and was even challenged as to why I was there. Andy Pipon and Steve Kush responded to the individual with "we adopted him."

Football was not discussed in any detail. The topics of conversation revolved around family, childhood experiences, and the close knit unity established growing up in the coal fields. Frank Kush did not put any air on because of his notoriety and was just one of the coal kids back to enjoy socializing with some of his boyhood friends. He had come back to his roots. He had not forgotten his home town and the people who make it up.

16

Myths, Incidents, and Circumstances

Throughout this 90 year plus history of Windber High School football there have been countless stories generated as a result of incidents involving such things as: eligibility, game highlights, football camp, half-time talks, and even physical exams. Some of these stories have been told and retold so many times that some appear to have taken on a mythical flavor. Yes, some are mythical, but many do have a basis in fact. It is the intention of the author, as you read these myths and stories, that they will provide some amusement and conjure up some of your favorite high school football memories.

From the Mines to the Gridiron

One of the most circulated stories concerning high school football at Windber during the decades of the 20's, 30's and 40's is that the players would toil in the coal mines during the week and then show up at Delaney Field on Saturday afternoons to vanquish their opponents.

This rumor possibly does hold some truth because high school age boys did work in the coal mines. In fact, many boys did not complete high school during those decades, the need to help with family income was more important than an education. Some of these boys who participated in high school football did work with their fathers during the summer months which could have perpetuated this rumor.

Also, record keeping in the past was not what it is today and the possibility of an older boy participating in high school football does exist. However, much to the dismay of Windber opponents, these tenacious, mostly undersized, boys were not the coal miners, but the sons of coal miners who had inherited good work ethics, were well prepared because of excellent coaching, and the determination to carry on the winning tradition of Windber High School Football.

Born with a Football in Their Hands

Another widely circulated rumor, even to this day, is that all males born in Windber are born with a football in their hand. This myth of course is obliviously a true myth. It was rather amusing as I researched the micro-film of the *Windber Era* and came across a picture of an infant holding a football. The caption underneath made reference to this myth about every male born in Windber. Unfortunately I did not have the technology to reproduce that picture and caption. However, I took it upon myself to try and give the reader the same reaction I had when looking at that article. The following pictures are my two sons as infants and as you can see with the technology of today it does appear as if they were born with a football in their hand.

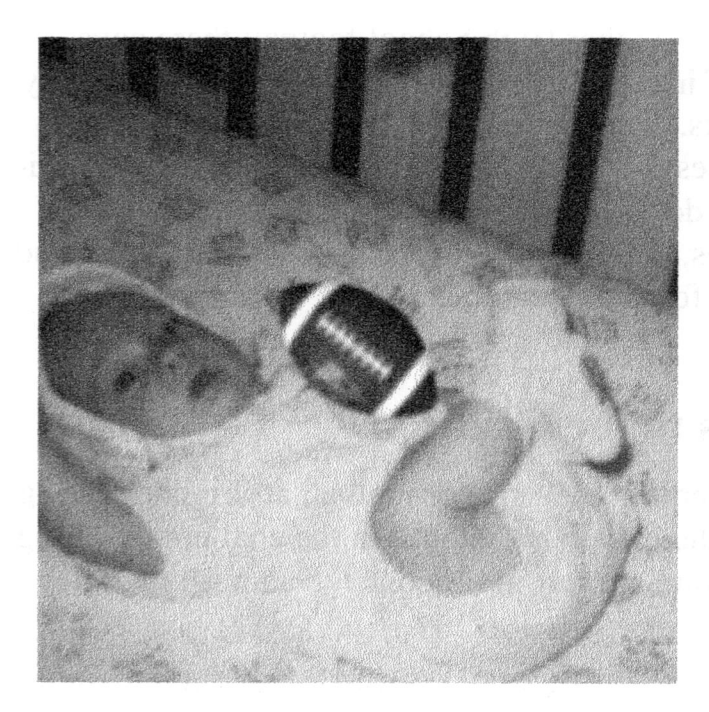

Charles Joseph Mayer

Curtis Lee Mayer

Pictures like these could have been used by a sportswriter prior to a big game with the intention of possibly intimidating the upcoming opponent or just as a ruse to help perpetuate this myth.

9:30, Time to Go Home

During my freshman year at Camp Hamilton, I was assigned to Cabin Nine. Gene Heeter, a senior, who went on to play football for the University of West Virginia and at the professional level with the New York Jets, (Gene has the distinction of catching the first touchdown pass in Shea Stadium history),was captain of the cabin.

One night after lights out, the discussion in cabin nine was about girls, a frequent topic. Gene proceeded to relate a story about a date he had been on during his junior season. This date took place during September of that year and players had to adhere to training rules. One rule was being in the house at 9:30 pm when the curfew whistle blew at the fire hall. If the coaches caught you out after curfew, and they did on occasion, the resulting discipline would be countless laps around the practice field following practice.

The story began with Gene telling us the name of his date, followed by a number of whistles from the intense listeners and all of us agreeing he was a very lucky guy. I forget, exactly, where Gene told us he went on this date but it ended up at a secluded parking spot. The action steamed up the windows and before Gene could give the proper good night, the curfew whistle blew. Gene stopped immediately and said to his date, "9:30, time to go home."

The next day, during the scheduled water break of morning practice, Gene approached the water bucket and was about to quench his thirst when Jack Lochrie, assistant coach, said "9:30, time to go home." All members of cabin nine, excluding Gene of course, began to laugh hysterically. Obviously, Coach Lochrie had been standing outside the cabin and had over heard the entire story.

Following a brief explanation of "9:30, time to go home" to the team by Coach Lochrie, Gene, felt like crawling under the turf. The ensuing teasing of Gene by teammates lasted the rest of morning practice and everyone thanked him for providing the longer water break. I just wonder how many times Gene Heeter was reminded of this incident when he heard the curfew whistle blow?

The Phantom Double Team

The opening game of the 1961 season was an away game with the "Little Presidents" of Washington, Pennsylvania. Windber had played them the previous year at home and defeated them. This would also be my very first game as a starter. I do not remember much of the actual game except for the pummeling we received at the hands of very good football team. Dennis Zahurak, then a student manager, reminded me of a very humorous incident that occurred in our locker room at halftime.

Halftime is a brief respite from the gridiron battlefield and time is usually spent by the coaches analyzing why things were or were not working. In this particular game, the were not working phrase came into play.

Head coach Jack Lochrie, standing in front of a chalkboard, with chalk in hand, asked each defensive lineman who was blocking them. As each lineman responded, coach Lochrie drew the representative circle for an opposing offensive lineman opposite an X for our defensive player. After all responses were made and the corresponding X's and O's inserted, there appeared the most unusual alignment in the history of football. It looked as if everyone on the defensive line was being double teamed and the alignment indicated the "Little Presidents" were playing with an illegal number of players. Coach Lochrie's reaction was to throw a piece of chalk at the board and shout "How and the hell can all of you be doubled teamed at the same time?" "They only have 11 players!"

The second half of the game continued as the first, we couldn't defend the phantom double team and Washington defeated us 36-0. It is a shame that no picture of the most unusual offensive alignment in football history was taken of that chalkboard in Washington, Pennsylvania on that September evening in 1961.

Football Physical

One of the most amusing stories I was involved with during my three years of playing varsity football at Windber occurred during the summer of 1960. It was approximately three weeks before pre-season camp started and the varsity football players were scheduled for their annual physical exam. Dr. Aron Rosenbaum, whose office was located on the second floor of the Reno Building on 15th Street, was the doctor hired by the school district to perform these physicals.

Dr. Rosenbaum, who spoke with an accent, was a very patient individual. He examined over 90 varsity and junior high football players over a three day period. It was day three of this examination period and Dr. Rosenbaum's patience was growing thin. He stepped out of the exam room into the waiting room on two occasions that morning. His first appearance occurred because of the noise generated by some of the players for horseplay, something that teenage boys were accused of very often. His accent, weighing very heavy, was directed at no one in particular as he reprimanded everyone in the waiting room. Upon his return to the exam room a number of boys began mimicking Dr. Rosenbaum's accent. Pete Roscetti, a very skilled athlete and offensive end on the 1960 team, was imitating Dr. Rosenbaum much to the pleasure of everyone, when Dr. Rosenbaum appeared for the second time. Again, with a much deeper accented growl with irritation attached, he asked that everyone calm down and be quiet.

Pete Roscetti and I were called into the exam room after two players had exited. The typical procedure was that one individual would disrobe down to their underwear while the other waited behind a screen. Pete was the first to be examined as I sat behind the screen.

Dr. Rosenbaum began to examine Pete and things were proceeding normally until the doctor asked Pete to drop his underwear in order to check for hernia. As Dr. Rosenbaum placed his hands in the proper location, Pete, with an accent similar to Dr. Rosenbaum's said "Oh! doctor your hands are cold." I immediately lost it and started to laugh out of control. Dr. Rosenbaum with a very deep accented agitated voice said "Out, Out, Out." Pete exited the room laughing with me following close behind. As we entered the waiting room everyone had a bewildered look on their face because of the two laughing hyenas. It didn't take long for Dr. Rosenbaum to appear and usher everyone out of the waiting room.

I can't recall if Pete ever apologized to Dr. Rosenbaum for the escapade, but we did eventually get physicals and from that day on Dr. Rosenbaum was called Dr. Cough, Cough. Which would have been his next directive to Pete if his hands had not been cold.

Spring Loaded Toilets

The restroom at Camp Hamilton, for the players, was located behind Cabin One next to the shower room with a narrow path separating the two structures. The building itself was a relatively narrow structure approximately ten feet wide and 20 feet long. Along the wall facing Shade Creek was a long raised urinal and on the opposite side, separated by three feet, were eight toilets raised above the floor on a platform about a foot high.

The facility could accommodate 10 or 15 people very easily, depending on what biological transaction was taking place. Privacy did not exist, as the eight toilets perched on the raised platform did not have any partitions separating them. You tried to take care of business in privacy when using the toilet, but invariably along came a teammate hoping the same thing. Pleasantries were discussed and business taken care of.

Most people would think that the task of pulling up your pants and stepping away from the toilet could be easily accomplished by a teenage boy. Wrong! It was a daunting exercise, executed by grasping your pants or shorts and jumping off the foot high platform on which the toilet was attached before your back side was covered with water. Why, do you ask? The modern day toilet seats, at Camp Hamilton, were spring loaded and upon an individual standing up they released the mechanism to begin the flushing process.

After your first or second attempt using these modern porcelain fountains, you got the timing down and managed a perfect jump with pants or shorts in hand as the water missed your butt. Of course you could not propel yourself too far because of the raised urinal on the opposite wall. Practice and more practice, just like on the football field, enabled you to master the spring loaded toilets.

You never instructed a new camp arrival on the necessary maneuvers required to use the toilets because the delight you received in watching their soaking and hearing the tirade of expletives from their mouth was unforgettable.

The Wait

The last game of the 1961 season had the Ramblers traveling to Harrisburg to play Bishop McDevit. This team was highly touted with a number of boys destined to play Division I football. The Ramblers had only won two games up to this point in the season and were determined to win this game. All of the seniors, of which I was one, had made a pact that we would give everything from the opening kickoff to the last second of the game. We had to win this game. The game was very hard fought; both teams battled back and forth, but, when the final second ticked off the clock the score read Bishop McDevit 27, Windber 20.

As seniors, we all realized that we had played our last game together and had given every ounce of effort to try and win the game. We slowly trudged to the locker room with our heads down, undressed, showered, and prepared for the two and a half hour bus ride back to Windber.

The most memorable event, aside from this being our last game as high school football players, occurred in the parking lot as a player walked toward the waiting bus. This player collapsed, became unconscious and was rushed to a hospital. Upon awakening he noticed IV lines attached to both arms. It was explained to him that because of fluid loss during the course of the game, a chemical imbalance had taken place and the IV solution of saline being administered would bring things back into balance.

Fortunately, the situation was not as serious as first thought and a wait of an hour was all that was required before this player could return to the bus for the ride home. Unfortunately, for the rest of the team, the hour long wait had delayed their scheduled restaurant stop. The coaches were hard pressed to keep this hungry, battered team from taking the bus to the anticipated eating stop. After a quick explanation by the coaches of the player's situation, order was established and the restaurant stop was made.

To this day, however, that former player is often reminded of how he made the 1961 team "wait" and should have been more concerned about his teammate's stomachs. Yes, you have guessed correctly, I was that 1961 player who delayed his teammates.

We Need Some Fire

While discussing some of the research I had completed with James "Peachy" Miller, a student manager on the 1966 and 1967 teams, he was reminded of an amusing incident that took place during halftime of the Windber vs Bishop McCort game in 1966. The game was played at Point Stadium in Johnstown with Bishop McCort outplaying Windber in the first half.

During the halftime break Coach Younker attempted to motivate the team. The method used was very unorthodox. Instead of yelling in ear holes or picking on individual players, Coach Younker, casually pulled a lighter from his jacket and proceeded to ignite the playbook he was holding. As the playbook went up in flames on the floor of the locker room, Coach Younker yelled, "We need some fire."

Needless to say this motivational tool proved inadequate as Bishop McCort extinguished the "fire" during the second half and went on to defeat the Ramblers by a score of 34 to 14.

Camera Flashes

I had the pleasure of talking with Nick Beckey, starting guard on the 1954 team, during a program about the origin of the single wing at the high school cafeteria in October of 2006. Nick was in attendance because his grandson Josh Kotula, an All State selection during his junior year in 2005, and the 2006 team along with parents, grandparents, and friends were present for this program.

Following this program on the single wing, Nick introduced himself and told me that his grandson, Josh, suggested he talk with me about some of the research I had done on the history of Windber High School football. I could tell as we talked about the past that Nick still had the passion for playing Windber football and probably helped instill this tradition in his grandson. He related to me about watching the football heroes from Mine 35 and 36 playing for the Ramblers while he was a youngster and was inspired to carry on this tradition when he played.

He then related a story to me about an incident that occurred during a game in 1954. Roy "Pete" Seese the starting fullback on that 1954 team had just taken a handoff and broken through left guard into the open on the way to a 40 yard run resulting in a touchdown. The most unusual part of the run took place at about the five or ten yard line when "Pete" slowed up and turned to the sideline, almost getting tackled before crossing the goal line.

Following the game, as everyone was showering, Nick asked "Pete" "Why did you slow up and turn toward the sideline instead of running straight ahead?" "Pete" responded, "That's where all the **camera flashes** were coming from."

17

Student Managers

Student managers are an integral part of a football team. You see them in most team pictures, helping out on the sidelines during games, or running out on the field to get the kicking tee. They receive no mention when the team is introduced nor any recognition following a victory. Who are these unsung members of the team and what role do they play?

Throughout this 94 year history of Windber High School football, many boys have served as student managers. During the early days of W.H.S. football there was usually a student selected by the head coach to handle equipment, line the field, and even schedule games. It was considered an honor to be selected for this position. When the position of athletic director was established, the role of the student manager became one of being responsible for equipment.

Handing out uniforms at practice, hanging up uniforms following practice, accounting for footballs, making sure water buckets were filled, and placing pads on sleds were some of the every day jobs performed during pre-season camp and football season. They are the first to arrive at practice and the last to leave. They locate the lost clipboard for the coach, dry wet balls during practice and games, help locate a teammates misplaced helmet, and receive no accolades. The student manager plays a very important role. Unless you have observed the student manager as a player or coach or served as a student manager, it is difficult to understand this very important role.

Throughout the history of W.H.S. football, students, serving in the capacity of student manager, performed during rain, sleet, and snow. Why did they participate? This question has a multitude of answers. I am not going to attempt to answer this question, but I would like to say Thank You!! Job well done!!

The following pictures of various student managers is a tribute to the arduous workers and unsung members of all of the Windber High School football teams.

"The Windber football team this year (1925) was fortunate indeed to have two capable students to help in the management of the team. Warren "Holke" Schafer (No photograph available) and Nick "Kelly Kat" Costa were the two fellows who should not be forgotten for their services to the team."

"It isn't everybody who will be found ready to assist when the weather isn't altogether as it should be. But rain or shine the two student managers were on hand Saturday mornings to line off the field and do other odds and ends to prepare for the game the same afternoon. These things, and many others were done without a whimper from them."

Taken from the 1926 *Stylus*.

Nick Costa

1937
L-R: Ben Bossi,
Steve Izing,
Mace Baranik,
Angelo Stevens.

1941
Row 1, L-R: "Smuff" Pierre, Nick Jordan.
Row 2, L-R: "Skip" Wirick, Mike Valent, Frank Bertino.

1952
L to R: E. Wargo, G. Stefan, R. Statler, H. Clark, J. Novak.

1960
Row 1: L-R: Steve Skillman Richard Opett, Joe Molnar Ray Wozny.
Row 2: L-R: Dennis Zahurak Dennis Peterman, Charles Heggi.

1975
L-R: Jim Byrne, Byran McCuch, Matt DiNinno, Randy Livingston.

18

Songs, Cheers, and Yells

Windber High School football has produced a number of songs, cheers, and yells, unique to the football team and community, many of which continue to be used today. Some were found during research and others have been used for numerous years. I am sure one or two can be recited from memory and bring back recollections of gridiron battles years ago. The majority of these songs, cheers, and yells were found in various issues of the *Hi-Times*, Windber High School's newspaper.

Many cheerleaders over the course of this 94 year history of Windber High School football have contributed their time and talent in performing these songs, cheers, and yells. They are an integral part of this history because they stood in the rain and snow on the sidelines and inspired the players, coaches and fans. The cheering squad photographs throughout this chapter were selected at random and represent a cross-section of cheering squads over this 94 year history. I apolgize for not including all squads.

Songs

#1

Windber will shine tonight,

Windber will shine,

Windber will shine tonight,

All down the line,

Windber will shine tonight,

Windber will shine,

When the sun goes down, and the moon comes up,

Windber will shine.

1925-1926
Front: Joseph Magazzu, Howard Kimmel
Back: Genevieve Hoffer, Margaret Delehunt.

In the October 14, 1930 issue of the *Hi-Times*, two songs appear that were written by Dorothy Claycomb and Olga Harris. The article goes on to say that all students are requested by the cheerleaders to learn these new songs and to bring their papers with them to pep meetings when asked to do so.

#2
Written by Dorothy Claycomb and Olga Harris
Tune-"On Wisconsin"
Windber High School, Windber High School,
Play up to that team.
Show them that the Blue and White
Shall ever be supreme,
On to victory, on to victory
Make for us a name,
Fight fellows, fight, fight, fight.
And win this game

1935-1936
L. to R. F. King, Faust, Palovich
Redfoot, M. King, Seese.

#3
Written by Dorothy Claycomb and Olga Harris
Tune-"The Quilting Party"
Stanza 1:
All with mud our heroes splattered,
Some as dark as chestnut brown;
But they never stopped and ne'er did falter
Till they held the last man down.
Chorus:
Always fighting for a victory,
Always getting up new steam;
Giving Windber Hi that longed for glory
That's our Windber gridiron team!
Stanza 2
Sometimes when they miss their footing
And they land in mud-pell-mell!
With a grit of teeth, they're up and onward
On the victory-ne'er to fail!
Chorus:
Always fighting for a victory,
Always getting up new steam;
Giving Windber Hi that longed for glory
That's our Windber gridiron team!

1939-1940

Kneeling, Left to Right:
A. Kitcho, M. Ruffner
Z. Dyke, E. Deyarmin.

Standing, Left to Right:
M. Beckley, E. McNulty,
M. Gilban.

#4
When Windber's football men all fall in line,
We're going to win again another time
And for the players we will yell, yell, yell
And for the dear old school we love so well, so well
And then we'll fight, fight, fight for every yard,
We'll circle the end and hit that right hard
And then we'll roll old (name of opponent school) in the mud,
in the mud,
Windber High!

1954-1955

Row 1, L-R: J. Stoy, J. Mickey, J. Cunsolo, M. Keirn.

Row 2, L-R: V. Campitell, M. Findish, H. Makuch, B. Paul, P. Potts, P. Horvath.

#5
Here's to our high school, ever so dear.
Always victorious, year after year,
Three cheers forever, three cheers together,
Three cheers for Windber High,
Rah---Rah---Rah.

#6
From the hills of old Mine 40, into 35
There's an old abandon shit house
Known as Windber High.

There she stands in all her glory
High up in the sky
Smelling like a lavatory
Onward Windber High.

1965-1966

Row 1, **L-R**: L. D'Arcangelo, C. Berkey, Co. Capt. K. Hajnos, Capt. P. Phillips.

Row 2, **L-R**: C. Koot, C. Palumbo, B. Stoy, K. Rogel, C. Mandel.

#7
Song of the Ramblers
(Written by Mary Elizabeth Solomon Class of 1941)
Tune--"Notre Dame Fight Song"

Cheer, Cheer for Old Windber High,
We are the Ramblers, we're riding high,
We can pass and we can kick,
To make a touchdown, we'll pull a trick,
Whether they're big or whether they're small,
Old Windber High will win overall,
While our team goes marching forward,
Onward to victory.

1975-1976
Row 1, **L-R**: Sue Holden, Patty Spinos. **Row 2**, **L-R**: Mary Ann Lapinsky, Sandy D'Arcangelo, Nettie Kadar, Debbie Tengeres, Anna Yauneridge, Kathy Campitelli.
Row 3, **L-R**: Barb Cunsolo, Linda Sutor.

#8
Oh Sassa, Oh Sassa
Hit'em in the Belly with a Big Kielbasa

1984-1985
Left to Right: Kerri Campitelli, Heather Kalmanir, Judy Gosnell, Cheryl Leonardis, Stef Hlatky, Laura Papinchak, Lorrie Pierce, Karen Toki, Kris Micari, Ellen Cover.

1995-1996
Row 1, **L-R**: C.Czajkowski, L. Voytko, K. Lybarger. **Row 2**: M. Gula, K. Baldwin, P. Sellers, S. Palumbo. **Row 3**: K. Kohler, J. Peters, C. Yonish, J. Rizzo, K. Kaiser. **Row 4**: D. Gibson, L. Cameron, M. Suto, E. Fodor, A. Miller, M. Newcomer, A. Naughton.

Yells and Cheers

#1
Written by Delores (DiGuilio) Hobba in 1964, first words are spelled out by letters and then verbally shouted.
M-I-G-H-T-Y
R-A-M-B-L-E-R-S
F-I-G-H-T
Mighty Ramblers Fight.

#2
1-2-3-4
3-2-1-4
Who for, what for?
Who're you going to yell for?
W-I-N-D-B-E-R
That's the way you spell it,
This is the way you yell it:
Windber, Windber, Windber.

2000-2001
Row 1, **L-R**: S. Pinelli, K. Conrad, C. Thompson. **Row 2**: A. Curry, J. Gula, J. Swiokla, C. Wojcicki. **Row 3**: L. Conrad, C. Berardi, M. Miller, K. Ferante, K. Moschgat. **Row 4**: H. Farbo, A. Charney, E. Hanley, K. Ola, L. Stem, K. Zankey. **Row 5**: A. Benton, A. Carter, S. Horner, J. Helman, Coach-J. Peters. **Row 6**: M. Chippie, C. Clark.

#3
Strawberry shortcake, huckleberry pie,
V-I-C-T-O-R-Y
Are we in it?
Well, I guess,
We belong to W.H.S.

#4
T-E-A-M
T-E-A-M
T-E-A-M
Fight---Win
Fight---Win
Fight---Win
Windber

#5
Hit Em High!
Hit Em Low!
Come On Windber
Let's Go!!!

19

Impact Individuals

Many individuals have impacted the development of this 94 year history of Windber H.S. football. They include headcoaches, assistant coaches, athletic directors, principals, players, managers, and even members of the custodial staff. I have selected six individuals who I feel have played major roles in the development of this history. Some people may disagree with my selection, but as I expand on each individual, it is my hope that you as a reader may see why these six people were selected. The basis of my selection revolved around an individual's tenure, win vs loss record, an important point in Windber's football history, impact on program, and influence on players.

Jim Hyde

Jim Hyde, the first player to return to his alma mater and serve as head football coach, was instrumental in providing W.H.S. Football during its infancy with the foundation required for competitive football teams. His record of 16 wins, 14 loses, and 6 ties doesn't sound real impressive. But, if you look at the competition played, teams like Altoona, Somerset, Indiana Normal School, Huntingdon, Clearfield, Turtle Creek, St. Francis College, and Greensburg, this record is impressive.

Hyde played left end on the very first W.H.S. Football team in 1914, and again on the 1915 team before attending Indiana Normal School, now Indiana University of Pennsylvania, where he also played football. After earning a teaching certificate, which required only two years at that time, he returned to Windber and coached for five years, 1918 thru 1922. Leaving Windber in 1923, he moved to the Erie, Pennsylvania area and according to information I found in the book *Ramblers, The History of Cathedral Prep* by Daniel J. Brabender on page 252. " Hyde served as an assistant coach at Erie Central before becoming Central's head coach in 1926 and remained there for three years, compiling a record of 7 wins, 19 losses and three ties. After sitting out of football during the 1929 season he was hired at Erie East in 1930 as head coach and remained there until 1947, compiling a record of 114 wins, 54 losses, and 16 ties. In 1948, Hyde was hired by Erie Academy, and in 1951 he completed his last season coaching. While at Erie Academy he compiled a record of 11 wins, 24 losses and four ties. His over all record in the Erie area was 132-97-23. He retired from the Erie grid scene ranked first in years coached (25) and games coached (252); tied for second in wins; and first in losses and ties. Hyde was inducted posthumously into the Metropolitan Erie, Pennsylvania Sports Hall of Fame in 1991."

Jim Hyde is probably more well know by Windber football followers as the coach of Erie East, when his 1937 team defeated Windber by a score of 6-0, ending Windber's 41 game winning streak, the third longest in the nation at that time. Taking into account the 25 years Hyde coached in the Erie area, coupled with the five years as head coach at Windber, 30 years of coaching high school football is certainly impressive.

J. Harold "Duke" Weigle

J. Harold "Duke" Weigle, the second former player to return to his alma mater and serve as head football coach, played for Windber as a fullback in 1926 and as the quarterback in 1927. He attended Schuylkill College, now a part of Albright, where he also played football. Weigle returned to Windber in 1932 as an assistant coach to T.T. "Tubby" Allen and helped Allen guide the 1933 team to Windber's first State Championship. His first year as head coach at Windber in 1934, produced the school's second undefeated season. "Duke" followed this up with undefeated teams in 1935 and 1936. His record of 31 wins, 0 losses and 6 ties stands alone in this 94-year history of Windber High School football.

Weigle moved on to Tamaqua High School in 1937, little did he know, that his brother, Ralph Weigle, who replaced him as head coach would produce Windber's second State Championship in 1937. "Duke" then coached at Phillpsburg High School in New Jersey and then returned to Western Pennsylvania to coach Windber's arch rival, Johnstown. He coached Johnstown to a State Championship in 1941. Following his Johnstown experience, "Duke" moved on to McKeesport where he finished his coaching career in 1966.

Joe "Pearly, Razzle-Dazzle" Gates

Joe Gates, the fourth former player to return to his alma mater and serve as head coach, played halfback his freshman year in 1927 and then quarterback in 1928 thru 1930. Gates has the distinction of being only one of eight players to have started on the varsity football team for four years in this 94 year history of W.H.S. football. He enrolled at St. Francis College in 1931, but left school to help coach at Windber when T.T. "Tubby" Allen was sidelined most of the season by pneumonia. After remaining out of school for one year, he transferred to Duquesne, where he received his degree in 1936.

During the 1934 and 1935 seasons he was the regular quarterback for Duquesne under Elmer Layden, one of Notre Dame's famous "Four Hosreman." Gates then served as the Duquesne freshman head coach for two years before taking the head football coaching job at Wheeling Central Catholic, posting a record of seven wins, one loss, and one tie. In 1938 he became an assistant to Don Fletcher, then head football coach at Windber. Gates became Windber's 13th head coach in 1939 and lost only one game. That lone loss was to Pottsville, coached by T.T. "Tubby" Allen, Gate's mentor at Windber, by a 12-0 score. In 1942, Gates led the "Ramblers" to an undefeated season, the biggest win being a defeat of Johnstown by a score of 20-13. Johnstown was coached that year by Harold "Duke" Weigle a teammate of Joe Gates on the 1927 Windber eleven.

Leaving Windber in 1943 for Greensburg, Gate's led the school to a 7-1-2 mark and then served a two year tour of duty with the U.S. Army and was wounded in action in France. He was the holder of the Combat Infantryman's Badge and the Purple Heart. Gates returned to Greensburg in 1946, only to suffer a losing season with a 4-5-1 record. Joe Gates then moved on to his fifth and last head football coaching position at the former Nanty Glo-Vintondale High School. He remained at Nanty-Glo for 19 years and became the first coach at Blacklick Valley, a jointure of Nanty Glo-Vintondale and Black Lick Township in 1965. Gates compiled a 107-91-13 record in his 28 year high school coaching career.

This impressive former player and coach of some of Windber High School's outstanding football teams died in 1968.

John Kawchak

John Kawchak was the first W.H.S. head football coach to have tenure of more than five years. In the first 35 years of W.H.S. football history, there had been only one coach with five years of tenure, Jim Hyde, the first player/coach. During Kawchak's tenure from 1948 thru 1960, many Quad A and Triple A ranked schools dominated the schedule. Many followers of W.H.S. football feel this was the most difficult schedule in the history of W.H.S. Football. Even with this difficult schedule, Kawchak coached teams produced 82 wins, while losing only 36 with 5 ties.

Kawchak grew up in the Woodvale section of Johnstown and played football at Joseph Johns Junior High School and Johnstown High School. He was first introduced to Windber football while playing left tackle for Johnstown during the 1930 season when Windber and Johnstown played two games. The first, a regular season game ended in a 0 - 0 tie, the second, a post season charity game, with Windber defeating Johnstown 7 - 0. John Kawchak did not know at that time he would become one of Johnstown's biggest coaching adversaries.

His football experience continued while playing college football for Carnegie Tech, in Pittsburgh, where he earned the annual Walter H. Burns Trophy, which is awarded to the most valuable player on the Carnegie Tech squad during his senior year. Kawchak's first coaching experience was at Johnstown Catholic High School in 1938. He entered the public school system, in 1940, as a coach at Garfield Junior High School, Johnstown. In 1941 he moved up to the Johnstown senior high school staff as an assistant to Harold "Duke" Weigle, former Windber player and head coach.

In 1945, Kawchak joined the WHS football staff, where Steve Terebus, a boyhood friend, high school teammate, and college teammate was head coach. He continued as an assistant coach until 1948 when Steve Terebus moved to Conemaugh Twp. High School. Kawchak was named head coach and continued in this capacity for 13 years. He was the first Windber coach to lead the "Ramblers" on to the gridiron at the new Windber Stadium in 1949. During his tenure, a winning percentage of 68 percent was achieved against many teams out of Windber's class in size, teams such as Aliquippa, Allentown, Beaver Falls, Meadville, Turtle Creek, Ambridge, Altoona, Johnstown, Pittsburgh North Catholic, Har-Brack, Bradford, McKeesport, Monessen, Chambersburg, Indiana, Westinghouse, and Washington.

John Kawchak was inducted into the Pennsylvania Scholastic Football Coaches Association Hall of Fame in 1988, the Cambria County War Memorial Sports Hall of Fame in 1978 and the Windber Hall of Fame in 1979.

I had the opportunity of playing for Coach Kawchak during my sophomore and junior years in high school. He had a unique style of coaching, at least in the twilight of his career, during practice you would observe him walking around the field with his cigarette holder in mouth, hands in pockets, the time worn brown hat on his head, and a piece of rope holding up his khaki or navy blue pants. He didn't add much verbally and appeared to be deep in thought. His assistant coaches would do all the instructing, with yells or screams, when things needed addressed. On rare occasions he might stop a drill in order to correct a problem and each player watched and listened as this imposing figure worked out the problem.

His biggest pleasure in coaching was not his winning record nor his near perfect teams, but seeing over 60 of his former players accepted by various colleges and universities in the country, as reported by a *Tribune-Democrat* sportswriter in 1978 during Kawchak's induction into the Cambria County War Memorial Sports Hall of Fame.

Coach Kawchak missed undefeated teams in 1949, 1950, 1953 and 1954, each time by an upset. Although he never had an undefeated team during his 13 year tenure, there was only one losing season. The 82 wins, 36 losses and 5 ties is an impressive record.

This icon of Windber Football during the late 1940's through 1960 was also a tremendous math teacher, his disciplined coaching carried over to the class room and I can honestly say he was the best mathematics teacher I ever had.

In the classroom and on the football field, Coach Kawchak in his own quiet way, with a few emotional outbursts, would motivate and direct both students and players with uncanny skill.

Joe "Gump" Polansky

"Gump", a nickname, of which I have not a clue to its origin, was not a head coach as the other members of this impressive list. No, he was just a janitor. Many people might think, how could a janitor have an impact on a football program?

Joseph "Gump" Polansky was born in 1922 in Windber, son of the late Felix and Anna Plonski. His father was a coal miner and the family lived in Mine 35. Life in the coal fields at that time was not easy and I'm sure Joe's childhood, like many of the children of coal miners, was a hardship. Around the age of 11 or 12, when Windber High School won its first state championship, Joe Polansky, probably was dreaming of becoming a high school football star. He achieved that dream. He was one of only eight four year letter winners in the history of Windber High School football.

Joe was a starting fullback or halfback from 1938 through 1941 and was a highly talented punter. He was injured much of his senior year, which prevented him from earning local or state acolades. Gump, had intentions of continuning his football career at the college level but an unfortunate accident caused him to lose sight in his left eye. Due to this accident, Gump, couldn't pursue his college plans and the Army would not accept him because of the disability.

He joined the janitorial staff at Windber High School in 1943 and also helped coach the freshman football team. For 35 years, Joe performed his jobs as janitor, coach, equipment manager, and golf coach. He became an icon at Windber High School.

I will never forget the pose of Gump standing in the hallway next to the boiler room on the first floor, slamming the shutters on cabins at Camp hamilton for wake up call, helping aspiring punters with technique, and berating you if you complained about an injury. He would give you pointers about blocking and tackling with a kick in the pants, if needed, and you would understand because you knew he loved football.

Being an avid golfer, Gump, could be seen at Windber Country Club, following his retirement, helping anybody with their game. One day, as he observed my swing, he said, "Mayer, swing the club down the line." I almost thought a kick in the pants would follow.

Joe "Gump" Polansky died August 25, 2002 at the age of 79, yes, a janitor, but an impact individual who provided inspiration for Windber High School athletes.

Phil DeMarco

Phil DeMarco is the ninth former player to return to his alma mater and serve as head coach. He has the unique distinction of having the longest tenure, 23 years, with a record of 170 wins 74 defeats and five ties.

He was born in Windber in 1949, son of the late Ralph S. and Dorothy R. DeMarco. He and his wife, Donna, have one son, Philip. Phil's brother, Ralph, is the current Windber Middle School principal and helps coach the varisty football team.

Phil played varsity football for Windber High School from 1964 through 1966 and was selected as a first team offensive guard on the 1966 *Tribune Democrat* All Star Team. Phil graduated from Windber Area High School in 1967 and attended Valley Forge Military Academy where he graduated in 1969. After graduation from the University of Pittsburgh at Johnstown in 1974, with a degree in education, he taught in the Westmont School District until 1980. While at Westmont, he coached junior high football for two years and then moved up as an assistant coach on the varsity for seven years.

In 1985, Phil, was hired by the Windber Area School District as head varsity football coach and began teaching Reading at the middle school in 1987.

On January 15, 2008 I interviewed him for the purpose of this book and found him concerned over the change in the varsity football program. The change I make reference to, is the moving of the freshman up to the varsity, due to the fact that most schools in the area have eliminated their freshman programs and Windber no longer can find opponents to play. Coach DeMarco had a meeting with Superintendent of Schools, Rick Huffman, the day before our interview in order to work out some of the problems in this change. I could tell from his demeanor things were going to work out, however, he was concerned how the freshman boys were going to handle the varsity level competition.

In planning for the interview with Coach DeMarco I designed a few questions to help give me a better perspective on this very impressive coach. The first question I asked was: "What is your basic coaching philosophy?" He responded, "From day one, back in 1974, as an assistant coach, until now, I have only one philosophy; be yourself. Take in all the advice available, but in the end, you have to coach from within and the team will take on your personalty."

The second question I asked him: "In your 23 years as head varsity football coach at Windber, what year or years stands out as the most memorable?" His response; "The 49 game regular season winning streak from 1997 through 2001 has to be at the top of the list. However, the one game that is most memorable was the 2001 District V and VI Regional Championship against Bishop Carroll. We lost that game in overtime. It was the most heart breaking loss I have ever experienced."

Question three was somewhat of a loaded question and Coach DeMarco affirmed my respect for him with his response. I asked: "To what do you attribute your success?" He answered, "Great kids willing to do whatever is asked and an outstanding coaching staff who epitomizes hard work, dedication, and loyalty."

The fourth question was answered very quickly. "Why have you stayed at Windber? With your success, you could have moved on to bigger schools." Without hesitating he answered; "I have found over the years that it is not always greener on the other side. Small School high school football is the best coaching experience you could ask for. The atmosphere of Windber's tradition exceeds none."

Question five: "In your 23 years as head coach, how have you changed as a coach?" Phil answered; "When I first started I didn't compromise, I was the man in charge! Over the years I have learned to compromise. I still expect discipline and hard work, but, at times there has to be some give and take."

I was very hesitant to ask question six, because of the radical change to a very sucessful program. I asked: "What prompted you to change to a Single Wing Offensive Formation?" Phil responded; "We needed a new identity. Nothing broken, just decided to go in a different direction."

Question seven: "What keeps you motivated?" He emphatically stated; "The Love of the game of football!"

I then asked; "Is there any one person, such as a coach or individual, who has provided inspiration?" He responded; "My dad, Ralph "Grandy" DeMarco, my best friend and supporter until his death in 1998. Two former coaches were very inspirational. Jack Yoder, former Westmont Hilltop head football coach, with whom I had my first coaching experience and Nick Campitelli, former Richland High School coach, who in my formative years would take time to explain things. They both helped me to develop."

The 2008 season, will be the start of Coach DeMarco's 24th year as head varsity football coach at Windber High School. He will be presented with a new challenge due to the addition of freshman to the varsity program. I feel confident he will meet this challenge. His coaching staff and dedicated players will continue to carry on the tradition of the Windber High School "Ramblers."

20

Tidbits of Information

This chapter provides some informative material, pertinent in this reflection of Windber High School football, that was not included in preceeding chapters. Most of these tidbits have a special place in the history of Windber H.S. football and help tell the story about the players, coaches and fans.

Kawchak's Letter

A copy of a letter, written by Coach John Kawchak, was provided to me by Pat Freeman, the author of the "Monster" which appeared in an earlier chapter. Pat explained to me that each senior player on the 1950 team received a hand written letter from Coach Kawchak imploring them of the important rivalry between Windber and Johnstown, the next game on their schedule in 1950.

Pat also stated, "I still get a tear in my eye when I read this letter. Coach Kawchak was a great coach and math teacher."

The following is that copy of the letter sent to Pat Freeman in 1950 prior to the game with Johnstown. Windber defeated Johnstown 12 -6.

Dear Pat,

This is it! The game of games! Let's beat Johnstown Saturday.

Pat, this game means everything to the people of Windber. They have a great faith in the ball players. Let's live up to that faith by giving everything that you have against Johnstown. Be mean, vicious and deadly Saturday. Be wide awake, and fight for every inch!

We have worked hard in preparing for this game. At times the work was both monotonous and tedious, but it had to be done. Let's make that hard work pay off against Johnstown.

Pat, this is your last chance to play against Johnstown. You'll soon be through. There is nothing that you shall remember as a Johnstown victory. The reason that I keep coaching against my doctor's orders is that I want to beat Johnstown. I shall always cherish the memory of beating Johnstown. This may also be my last chance.

Let's beat Johnstown Saturday, nite.

Your Coach,
Gustave Nawrocki

Only in Football, Pennsylvania

I would be willing to bet that even in Odessa, Texas, the town brought into prominence by the book *Friday Night Lights*, lacks a shrine to it's high school football heroes unlike what is found in Windber, Pennsylvania. This shrine, I make reference to, is located near the corner of 21st Street and Graham Avenue in the east end of town.

Yes, a shoe repair shop. A highly unlikely location for a shrine to high school football heroes. The shop is operated by Geno Stevens, the son of the founder Sam Stevens, and could be considered the prime historian of the Glory Days of Windber High School football during the 30's and 40's. He has collected a great deal of information pertaining to this glory day time period. Most of this information includes: Newspaper articles, photographs, memorabilia, and videos of the 1937 State Championship game, Windber-vs-Steelton and the 1942 Windber-vs-Johnstown game, both of which were played at Point Stadium in Johnstown.

Geno is willing to share this information with anyone having the time to listen. He will also share his coaching view points on football and basketball. Geno gained much of his information on football as a member of the high school band which was in attendance at all games.

The front of the shoe repair shop is adorned with illuminated displays of some of the most noteworthy Windber High School football players from this 30's and 40's time period. Geno has provided this shrine, I'm sure, because of his enduring memories during the glory days of Windber High School football and he has provided us with a way of keeping alive the memories of Windber's razzle-dazzle football of the 30's and 40's. **Only in Football, Pennsylvania!!!**

Poem

"Do You Agree"
by
John Alex, following Windber's victory over Johnstown in 1942

What makes Windber love their friendly little rival?
Who, what, when, where and why is all this so vital?
Yes, those are the questions in both towns that are asked.
Which the miners answered while the Trojans just gasped.
But gasped for what? ----- They'll never say.
They gasped; we celebrated till the break of day.
On Sunday, in church, the good Father, he said,
"Today we rejoice for the Trojans are dead."
What is the object of a game such as this?
Recalls the caveman's way of throwing a kiss.
They run so hard, the turf it just rocks,
What makes it bloody are those dirty socks.
The ends and tackles, those centers and guards,
Each gets his man and socks him hard.
The backs, they run for good old glory,
The reward they get is a newspaper story.
But that to me is water over the dam,
The thing I want---Beat Johnstown---Be Damned.
When the question that will be answered first
The others will follow with exploding spurts.
For Saturday night was really the night
Cause our team played to everyone's delight.
A beautiful night-and how lovely it was,
Could only be seen by that clamoring fuss.
The field was dry and the weather was cool
And our team showed they were no one's fool.
It was a year ago when home we went blue
But tonight it would be different---that much we knew.
The place was the Point Stadium-it bulged at the walls.
With 18,000 screaming their various delirious calls.
They came by motor, by plane and boat.
And saw the Trojans turn out to be the goat.
The fans were excited which readily was seen.

A Reflection on Windber High School Football

But for the Windber boys their eyes shone green.
Ball hawks they were, they held on for dear life,
The Trojans were doomed, like a drunkard's wife.
Who were the actors and what did they do?
The miners from Windber knew victory was due.
The Trojans came out and played like H_ _ _.
But couldn't stop the miners from ring'n the bell.
The Johnstown backs thought things were fine,
But changed their minds when they hit our line.
We hit'em so hard, the ball they couldn't hold.
Lucky breaks, the miners by Johnstowners are told.
Breaks they may be, but not as you say,
Our vicious tackling made their fumble pay.
Pay they did, and how dear it was-
To the folks in Windber it was interest plus.
To get revenge, it was sweeter than sweet,
For we smile so pretty when a Johnstowner we meet.
Cause ours are the boys who can really play ball.
They really sock'em whether they're big or small.
They played like demons and strutted their stuff-
The thing Johnstown forgot was their powder puff.
Why they were playing could easily be seen,
Beating Johnstown is the fulfillment of a dream.
The instinct is in us and little can we do,
We had them corralled, which they all knew.
They thought we were boys like some husbands we know,
When payday comes, just hand over the dough.
Payday was Saturday-But no payday for them,
Payday for our miners-Every one a little gem.
Why do we delight in winning this game?
Just listen to this-You'll think the same.
Our town number one thousand times ten,
And we're all fine specimens of good men,
And your fair city numbers 70,000 strong,
Instead of football, you should play ping-pong.
You have a few good boys-But not enough
To beat our miners who are rough and tough.
Too much pie and, yes, maybe too much cake
From this two a football player you'll never make.
But behold the day when we'll meet again,
I feel sure that you won't even win.

Windber American Legion, Post 137
1959 Football Hall of Fame Project

In the October 30, 1958 issue of the *Windber Era* there was an announcement of a discussion at the Windber American Legion, Post 137 pertaining to the selection of a Windber football player hall of fame. In 1959, Windber American Legion, Post 137 sponsored a project to identify the most outstanding players and coach for a Windber High School Football Hall of Fame. A committee of twelve members, chaired by R.E. Leach primarily confined their selections to the period Windber High School was recognized throughout the state of Pennsylvania as a major power in high school football, the 1920s and 1930s. The period before 1920 was not considered because authentic records were not available.

William "Bill" Zepka, a member of this committee, compiled a roster of offensive starting lineups from 1914 thru 1959. As indicated on the original roster, it is the most complete roster in existence. However, there may be errors in the correct spelling of names and errors in regards to the positions of the players since record keeping in the early years was not good. Most of the names during those early years were obtained from the memory of those individuals who had played or from family and friends of those players.

The choice's made by the committee:

Ends: Louis Fruhlinger (1922-23) and William "Cooney" Farkas (1933-35)

Tackles: Niles "Stud" Dalberg (1927-30) and Arthur "Arpy" Garlathy (1933-34)

Guards: Phillip DePolo (1923-26) and Frank Kush (1945-47)

Center: John "Scare" Torquato (1925-26) shared with John "Jack" Roach (1924)

Backs: James "Whitey" Hagan (1920-1923); Edward "Bud" Bossick (1935-37); George Bokinsky (1936-37); Oscar Ripple (1929-32); Jack Freeman (1936)

Coach: Harold "Duke" Weigle

(The roster of starting lineups mentioned above is the roster Bill Gorgon showed to me in his barber shop more than twenty years ago.)

"Eddie" Chupek Tragedy

Souvenir Program

"Eddie" Chupek Night

EXHIBITION FOOTBALL GAMES

MONDAY, OCTOBER 25, 1948

POINT STADIUM
Johnstown, Pennsylvania
8:00 P.M.

Edward "Eddie" Chupek, age 16 and a stellar junior tackle on the Shade Twp. football team, was critically injured in the Shade-Windber game, September 11, 1948. He remained paralyzed from this injury until his death on March 15, 1990.

On Monday, October 25, 1948 a benefit exhibition football game for "Eddie" Chupek was held at Point Stadium in Johnstown. It was called "Eddie" Chupek Night. This exhibition football game consisted of five games between ten area high schools competing for ten minutes per game. The ten high schools included: Berlin, Boswell, Conemaugh, Conemaugh Twp., Johnstown, Meyersdale, Richland Twp., Shade Twp., Somerset, and Windber. According to the November 1, 1948 issue of the *Windber Era* This game was attended by over 7,500 fans and generated over 5,000 dollars.

The proceeds from Chupek Night were used to establish the Edward Chupek Trust Fund. The fund was used to pay nurses', doctors', and specialists' fees, hospital expenses, and other expenses necessary for the care of "Eddie."

Windber Stadium Award

The Windber Stadium Authority, who operates Windber Stadium, decided in 1950 to annually honor a football player who had played at Windber Stadium. The selection, by a committee from the Stadium Authority, was based on the player's athletic ability and the contribution they provided their team while playing a game or games at Windber Stadium. The award was presented for 15 years and then discontinued. The following Windber players were recipients of this award in the year indicated.

1950-Chester Tokarsky-Windber

1951

1952

1953-Bob Hudy & Ed Hordubay-Windber

1954

1955-Roy "Pete" Seese-Windber

1956-Charles "Chuck" Webb-Windber

1957-Tom Marron & Al "Hoko" Tavalsky-Windber

1958-Tom Marron & John Csordas-Windber

1959-John "Budder" Boruch-Windber

1960-

1961-Steve Kush-Windber

1962

1963

1964-Ron Vitucci & Bill Hunter-Windber

The years were no recipient is indicated are those years that a player from another school was selected. As of this printing I have not been able to locate these names.

Nunzio Marino Memorial Award

According to an article in the October 1, 1964 issue of the *Windber Era* the family of Nunzio Marino is making plans to establish the Nunzio Marino Memorial Award. The qualifications for this award includes; a senior athlete ranked in the upper 1/5 of their class scholastically, a two sport participant, and the individual must exhibit sportsmanship, leadership, and citzenship.

The three award winners:

1966-Michael D. Koshute

1970-James T. Lashinsky

1971-Timothy Berkey

As of this date the Nunzio Marino Memorial Award has been discontinued. There has not been a recepient since the year 1971.

Chrome Shovel Trophy

In 1955 the Windber Jaycees along with their counterparts in Johnstown and Altoona decided to award a traveling trophy to the team which had defeated the other two during the scholastic football season. This traveling trophy was to be emblematic of the three industrial towns; Altoona-Railroads, Johnstown-Steel Mills, and Windber-Coal Mining. The trophy was a Chrome #2 Shovel that could be displayed in a trophy case.

Any team defeating the other two in the same year for three consecutive seasons would keep the shovel. In 1963 Altoona defeated both Windber and Johnstown which they had accomplished the previous two seasons. The Chrome Shovel Trophy is now permanently held by Altoona. Between the years 1955 and 1963 Windber only once defeated Altoona (1960) and Johnstown (1957).

Lois Woods, Windber's Head Majorite, receives the "Silver Shovel" from Johnstown's Drum Major, as members of both Jaycees look on.

As I conclude this portion of the book, a photograph I found at Shaz's Barber Shop on Graham Ave., reminded me of the many fall Saturday mornings or afternoons I spent in my youth playing football at the various open lots around town. There was Meyer's field, the playground at 12th Street, Pomroy's Corner, the practice field beside the high school, Berwind Club House field, Methodist churchyard, Delaney Field, the field behind Mine 35 School, and some I have forgotten. All of these open areas were occupied by aspiring gridiron youngsters, willing to sacrifice a few bumps and bruises for the chance to score a touchdown and pretend to be a high school or college star of the day.

The teams were usually picked at random, however, on some occassions a team from one section of town would challenge one from another and play for bragging rights. Games were not supervised, nor was there much equipment used, except for a helmet or two. Most games were very spirited, it was not touch football or flag football. Tackle football was the game.

The photograph below would have been a very typical scene around Windber during the mid 1950"s when I was playing the game without a helmet. I sometimes think I played too many games without a helmet.

Front: (LR), Unknown, Steve Scaglione, Thomas "Tonto" Gillionardo, Anthony "Smuff" Pierre, Emery DiFlori, Don Bertino, Tom Scaglione, Joe "Hap" Hudack
Back: (LR), Cosmo Bertino, Steve "Skeeter" Gillionardo, Anthony "Mex" Dimuzio, George Spadone

This picture is dated 1938 and was taken on the practice field next to the old high school. This space is now occupied by the present day entrance to the high school auditorium.

Anthony "Mex" DiMuzio, third from the left in the backfield, went on to play for the high school team and in 1943 was selected as a second team offensive guard on the inagural *Johnstown Tribune Democrat* All Star Team. In 1944 he was selected as an All State offensive guard on the second team by the Associated Press (Over All Format) and went on to play college football at Drexel.

I hope you are looking forward to the 2008 Windber High School football season with enthusiasm. I can't wait. I love this game with a passion. I enjoy watching new gridiron heroes emerge, the elation of a win, the anguish of a loss, and the write ups following games. The most important thing, however, is that every new season continues to add to this history of Windber High School football The 2008 season will begin 95 years of scholastic competition and just as in the past, as in the future, games will be won or lost.

The story will continue, propelled by the players, coaches, and fans. I have truly enjoyed putting this document together and hope you can use it as a reference, not only to find that gridiron hero, but also to, rekindle memories of days gone by.

The next portion of this book contains reflections in drawings and caricatures, the Appendixes: Team Photographs and Records, and assorted records. They help bring my Reflection on Windber High School Football to a conclusion.

Go Ramblers

My wife, Carol, and my son, Charlie, both insisted that I include a picture of myself in uniform. I fullfilled their request by hiding these two pictures here.

Carl Mayer-1960

Carl Mayer-1961

21

Heckler's Reflection in Drawing and Caricature

During my research I contacted a number of teammates about some of the nicknames used and possibly how these nicknames originated. Terry Heckler, a 1960 graduate and quarterback for the 1959 Ramblers responded by sending me a story of how his nickname "Fern" originated. This story is found in Chapter 12 on page 93. With this story he sent a number of pictures taken at Camp Hamilton his senior year. He also included a collection of drawings and caricatures, with captions, which illustrate many of his memories during his participation in Windber High School football.

I contacted Terry and thanked him for sending the story. I also asked if I could use some of the pictures, drawings and caricatures. He responded saying: "I could use anything he had sent." I originally intended to use a few of the drawings and caricatures where applicable in pertinent chapters because of their theme. However, the more I looked at them, I could not believe how someone could capture such vivid memories by using a drawing or caricature.

When an article appeared in the April 30, 2006 edition of the *Tribune Democrat*, written by Randy Griffith, entitled **Windber native creates brand recognition**, I knew these drawings and caricatures had to be shared.

The article, by Griffith, dealt with how Terry Heckler made a name for himself in the advertising business. According to Griffith, Terry, is credited with helping name Starbucks and creating the Starbucks Coffee logo. A number of other named businesses, such as Cinnabon, Panera Bread, and New Balance Athletic Shoe, Inc. can also be added to the list. The article went on to give a short biography of Terry which included his athletic pursuits, education, art interest, and music ability.

I knew of his athletic ability because of being a teammate during his junior and senior years in high school. I can attest to his art ability having seen numerous caricatures, done in color, of teammates adorning the walls of the school cafeteria during the football banquet in 1960 and as to his music ability, I remember him playing the bass violin in a small band at high school sock hops.

Each drawing and caricature invoked countless memories, enjoy each one, they are priceless.

Camp Hamilton

Waiting for the bus to Camp Hamilton, always August 18th, early morning at the high school.

Shower Room with Cabins One and Two.

Jerseys and Pants drying on the hill, water spigot between Cabin One and the Shower Room.

Gump slamming cabin shutters on wake up call.

A Reflection on Windber High School Football

Showers at Camp Hamilton.

Atty would walk around on our stomachs when we did six inches. He had cleats on his shoes.

Big John
(Head Coach John Kawchak)

Big John throws Mouse Marron off the field for smiling funny.

Third day at Camp we decide to hit our hardest to raise the standard. Budder, Doc, and myself.

Len Rubal showed up at Camp to work out with us. He was playing at William and Mary. Had the biggest thighs I ever saw on a field.

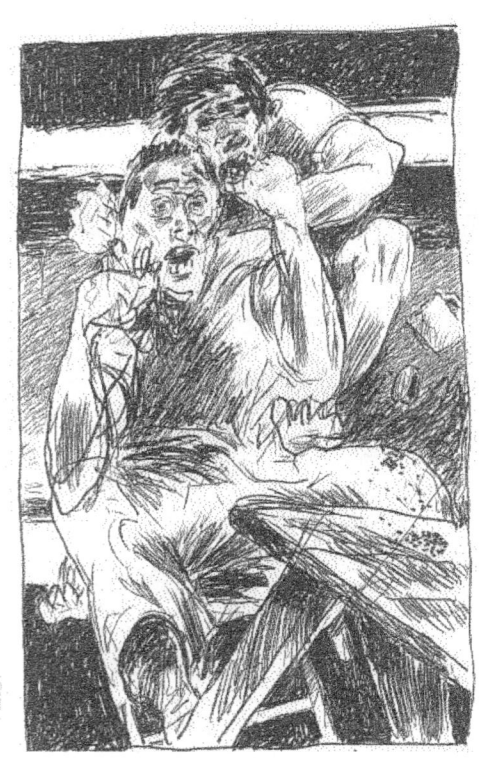

Rego Delimonte jumped Steve Kapash in Cabin 9. It was a bad fight over the end position. They both played, one on offense, one on defense. They ended up buddies.

Rego mixes his snuff with coffee grains.

A Reflection on Windber High School Football

People would come out early to be sure to watch Paul Piatek take his warm-up lap. Big John called it the "Boris Shuffle."

Hitting dummies on an August morning.

"Mouse" Marron and "Mooney" Csordas hit each so hard they smashed their helmets and they both were knocked out cold.

Dave "Dunnie" Dunmire power running during scrimmage.

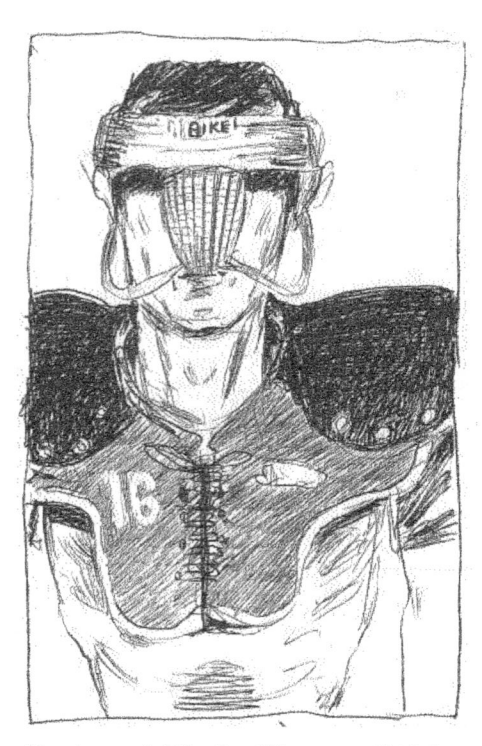

Freshman fall for the "Noseguard" trick.

Hosing down the field on a dry August day.

A Reflection on Windber High School Football

Teammates-1959

Tom "Doc" Sherwin - Fullback

Ed "Ridge runner" Hadix - Tackle

John "Budder" Borsch - End

Tom Bossi - Center

I was 2nd team defensive left half back my sophmore year and had to tackle "Budder" all night. Probably the best player in the state at age 14. Budder was a manboy.

Dave "Dunnie" Dunmire - Left halfback

Joe Gavalak - Right halfback

Paul "Woz" Wozniak - Guard

Joe Stopko
Joe with a hand dummy. Joe had the biggest head on the team. I had the smallest, I think.

Paul Piatek
Piatek and his orange black eye.

Bob Stawarz
Bob's face was twice its size and he looked like an old man. Bee stings!!!

Duane Senior
Duane's shoes were so big he tied the toes up. He got so used to them he always preferred over sized shoes.

Teammates-1958, 1957, 1956

Gene Heeter - 1958
Gene could wrap his hand around a ball touching his thumb and index finger.

Joe Kush - 1958

John Repko and Bob Minitti - 1958

Bob Minitti - 1958
All I had to do was beat Bob Minitti out for quarterback.

A Reflection on Windber High School Football

163

Tom "Bones" DePolo as Jerry Lee Lewis - 1958

Richard Marfizo - 1958

Don Dona - 1957

Aloysus "Hoko" Tavalsky - 1957

Chuck Shuster - Senior Center - 1957

Klemstine - Tackle - 1956

Chuck Webb wore number 41 the year before I wore it. Cabin captain my freshman year - 1956

A Reflection on Windber High School Football

Older Players

"Pete" Seese, Football star - 1954

George Winas, Quarterback -1954

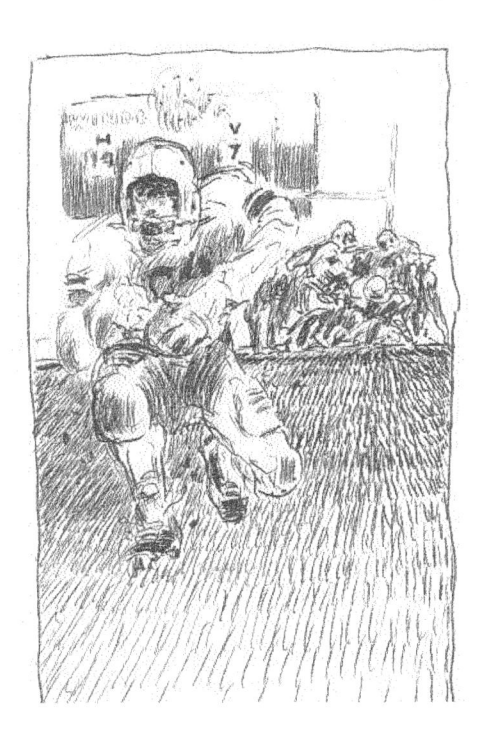

Chuck Shuster running T-X in Joe Johns game in junior high.-1954

The Opposition

Dean Stump, Johnstown Trojan center, in the hospital the same time as me when I broke my hand my sophmore year. I missed the Johnstown game.

Artie Patton (Cochran Jr. High) was the trickiest back we ever played against. Nobody could seem to hold on to him or get a clean shot.

Jim Curry, Altoona quarterback was 6' 6". In one jump he could move almost 4 yards in either direction. 1959 Altoona game.

A Reflection on Windber High School Football

Johnstown-Windber game 1959. Buchan was fullback for Johnstown, built like a fireplug. I was the only thing between him and a touchdown.

Johnstown's halfback, King, had the ball. No one knew except me and I made the tackle. Just another play. It could have gone for a touchdown. Johnstown game, 1959

Coaches and Others

Big John's standard camp uniform, white T-shirt, navy pants, brown hat, and a piece of rope for a belt.

Coach John Lochrie - Camp Hamilton - 1959

Coach Joe Flori

Alex Atty (trainer), lecture on blisters.

A Reflection on Windber High School Football

Gump had one eye. He told us he lost the other eye in the Johnstown game.

Gump grabbing his crotch. We were pieces of crap to him.

Bill Smutko, Junior High Coach, when I was a senior.

Mr. Mickle, the equipment man.

Dr. Rosenbaum

Coach Flori and his two man sled.

The McKeesport coaches, "Duke" Wiegle and "Ding" Schaeffer come into our locker room to see me and Tom Sherwin, to tell us they coached our dads. As if we didn't know. We beat their team.

Heckler

Windber Jr. High against Joe-Johns of Johnstown at Point Stadium. First game I played in 9th grade. I had a huge pimple on the end of nose that really hurt.

In 9th grade I had to ask Coach Flori to miss practice because of a violin lesson.

I was passing too good, so Mouse pounded my arm until I couldn't move it. Camp - 1958

I tackled Bob Minitti and we rolled into the weeds. He jumped up and kicked me in the face. I thought my nose blew off. It was just broke. Camp - 1958

On kickoff trials, I had a 40 yard running start. I hit Bucky Martell so hard he just snapped over. He thought I was all right after that.

Some of the big Chambersburg players in the hallway asked me if Bob Minitti really had two kids. I said "No, he had three."

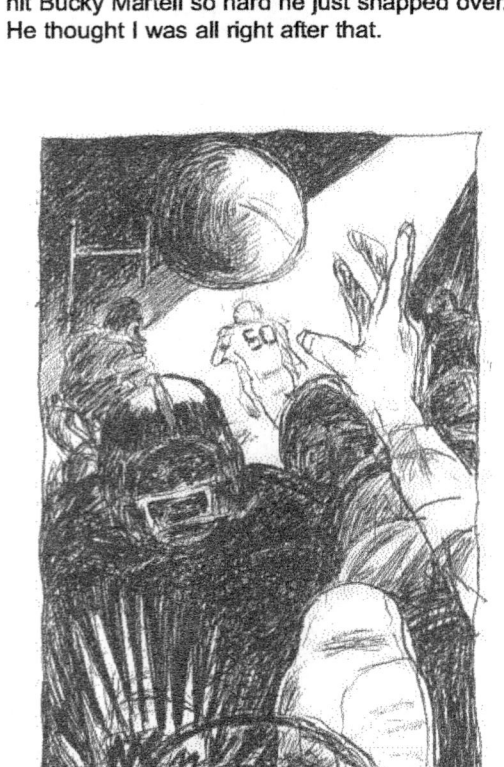

It was a jump pass to Budder. All my weight was on my left leg. A helmet shot through and blew my knee out. It's been a problem ever since.

Budder "iced" it back and I picked up an extra 30 yards against Indiana High School. - 1959

Juinior High School

We decide to "go out" for football around the St. Mary's sinkhole.

First Junior High practice. We had to run the grass down. Callen's Field, right behind the center of town.

The old junior high practice pants were blue with a big white stripe up the back. I remember earlier high school teams wearing them.

Practice at Sunset Field

Sunset Field below water tank on the hill.

Mouse and Bones make their entrance, first day of football practice.

Waiting for the coaches at Sunset Field over the hill, next to the Polish Cemetery. 1959

A Reflection on Windber High School Football

Heeter making fun of how Bones shifts at Sunset Field.

Polish Cemetery Field - (Southern California grass)
We had to walk past this to get to Sunset Field, the walk back wasn't much fun either.

Action Shots

Bones DePolo running interference for Mouse Marron at Camp Hamilton scrimmage.

The Homer City field was so high in the middle, we could hardly see the other team's bench across the field.

The lights blew up halfway through the Boswell scrimmage. They wanted us out of there.

Jack Creek was the best tackler on the team. He would fly at a group twice his size at full speed. Johnstown game at Point Stadium, 1958.

A Reflection on Windber High School Football

When Westinghouse came out, they didn't do any warm-up. They just yelled and jumped around in one big bunch. We never saw anything like that. It got Piatek pissed.

Just by the way he'd take the handoff I could tell "Doc" was going to break away. Tom Sherwin, fullback, later started at SMU.

Joe "Churchmouse" Pachella's first play, in a B-Game, went for a touchdown down the sideline at Altoona. 1958

Palumbo grabs the face mask and knees him in the face.-1956

The Old High School and More

The practice field beside the high school.

Curtains in the old high school auditorium.

Our practice field across from the stadium. The new highway took this field out our senior year.

Pep Rally in the old auditorium before the Johnstown game. We'd get a day off school if we beat them.

A Reflection on Windber High School Football

Running up 23rd Street after football practice.

Our letter jackets were a new design with circle of white on the shoulders. Bucky Martell.

Mouse Marron in back of Gump's truck. Summer work for football players.

Cheerleaders

Shirley Cotz

Sally Blackburn

Tootie Honadle

Windber Stadium

Game helmets ready in the Windber Stadium locker room.

We had heavy wool cloaks to wear on the sidelines.

Coach Flori came in the locker room at half time and immediately threw his hat on the floor, yelling son-of-a bitch. We were in trouble.

I threw the winning touchdown pass too high. Johnstown beat us by 6 points. 1959 game at Windber Stadium.

Starting backfield for the 1959 Windber Football Ramblers. Quarterback is Terry Heckler, the author of the drawings and caricatures, Right halfback, Joe Gavalak, Fullback, Tom "Doc" Sherwin, Left halfback, Dave "Dunnie" Dunmire. Picture taken by a *Tribune Democrat* photographer during pre-season training camp in August of 1959 at Camp Hamilton.

Team Photographs and Records

An introduction is needed for the use of the following Appendixes. The following pages contain both a pictorial, were possible, and written record of the 94 Windber High School Football Teams to date. **The year indicates the football year not the year of graduation.** The format used was that of including a team picture with players, coaches, and managers identified, season schedules with resulting scores of opponents played, any championships won or special accomplishments for that particular year. Unfortunately, there are five years, were no pictures of teams could be found, one team picture which could possibly be the wrong year, and 15 years were identification of team members, could not be located.

Included with a team picture and record are the starting offensive and defensive line-ups for that year, if found. After looking at the identification of players by position, I realized that a number of readers may not be familiar with the abrevations used by football junkies, and an explanation of these abrevations might be in order. Offensive and defensive formations in football are very varied and different names are used to identify a particular player. In order for coaches and players to simplify things, abrevations are used to identify a particular position. For example: RT, indicates that a player participated on the team as a Right Tackle, usually an offensive term or LB, which indicates this player was a Linebacker, a defensive term.

With these abrevations for position, players and coaches can diagram offensive and defensive formations, therefore, simplifying the learning of designated plays. Some abrevations are self explanaory while others need translation for better understanding. The following abrevations have been used throughout the 94 years of W.H.S. football. They are not unique to Windber football. These are football terms which fans, players, and coaches are familiar with. Individuals not familiar with the terminology will find this translation page very helpful as you continue your look at the history of Windber High School Football. I have also included some diagrams of various offensive and defensive formations with identification of positions by using the abrevations listed.

Offensive Positions

TE	Tight End
LT	Left tackle
LG	Left Guard
C	Center
RG	Right Guard
RT	Right Tackle
WB	Wing Back
QB	Quarterback
FB	Fullback
RB	Running Back
HB	Halfback
SE	Split End
WR	Wide Reciver
TB	Tailback
SB	Slotback
L	Lineman
OL	Offensive Lineman
E	End
IT	Inside Tackle
OT	Outside Tackle

Defensive Positions

DL	Defensive Lineman
LB	Linebacker
C	Corner
S	Safety
DT	Defensive Tackle
NG	Nose Guard
SS	Strong Safety
FS	Free Safety
MG	Middle Guard
DB	Defensive Back
DE	Defensive End
DG	Defensive Guard
OLB	Outside Linebacker
MLB	Middle Linebacker
CB	Corner Back
NT	Nose Tackle

Offensive Alignments

T-Formation

```
LE LT-LG-C-RG-LT-LE
        QB
   HB   FB   HB
```

Slot Formation

```
SE    LT-LG-C-RG-RT-TE
   SB        QB
          FB      RH
```

Wing I Formation

```
LE-T-G-C-G-T-RE
  QB           WB
  FB
  TB
```

Single Wing

```
TE-LT-LG-C-RG-RT
         FB        SB
     QB      RB
```

Unbalanced Line (right)

```
LE-LG-C-RG-IT-OT-RE
WB      QB
     FB    RB
```

Defensive Alignments

7 Diamond

```
DE-DT-DG-MG-DG-DT-DE
        MLB
DB                DB
        S
```

5-3-3

```
   DE-DT-NG-DT-DE
  OLB    MLB    OLB
  DB              DB
         S
```

6-2-3

```
DE-DT-DG-DG-DT-DE
     LB       LB
DB       S       DB
```

Windber High School Football-1914

No Photograph Avaliable

1914   **Head Coach: W.W. Lantz or Elmer Daily**   **Record:**   **Wins 1**   **Losses 3**   **Ties 1**

Offensive Sarting Line-up

LE	Jimmy Hyde or Mike Metz
LT	Homer Hoestine
LG	George Hasson or Al Berkey
C	Frank James
RG	Dave Bantley or John Hritz
RT	Leroy Williams or Angelo Marinelli
RE	Sheridan Hughes
QB	Bill McKendrick or L. Buck
LH	Ed Hughes
RH	Bill Severn
FB	Dave Parfitt

Season Schedule

W.H.S.		Opponent
0	Berwind	6
7	Colonials (Johnstown)	6
6	Colonials (Johnstown)	19
0	Hooversville	0
0	Cresson	6

Windber High School Football-1915

No Photograph Avaliable

1915   Head Coach: Dave Siebert   Record: Wins: 2   Losses: 1

Offensive Starting Line-up

Lineman	Harve Geisel
Lineman	John Clark
Lineman	Dave Bantley
Lineman	Wilfred Nevling
Lineman	Lee Mongel
Lineman	Jim Hyde
Lineman	Griff Truax
Lineman	Bill Holt
Lineman	Blue Kyle
Lineman	Alf Kough
Backfield	Bill McKendrick
Backfield	Dick Sipple
Backfield	Homer Hoenstein
Backfield	Bill Severn
Backfield	Ed Hughes

Season Schedule

W.H.S.		Opponent
58	South Fork	0
25	Latrobe	21
0	Johnstown	13

Windber High School Football-1916

No Photograph Avaliable

1916   Head Coach: Dave Siebert   Record: Wins: 3   Losses: 1

Offensive Starting Line-up

LE	Ellery Higgins or Bill Hold
LT	Wilfred Nevling
LG	Ben Adams or Andy Timko
C	Tony Buscaglia
RG	Dave Latz
RT	John Clark
RE	Blue Kyle
QB	Ed Mills or Clair Mills
LH	Carl Hoenstine
RH	Don Matherson
FB	Ed Hughes

Season Schedule

W.H.S.		Opponent
27	South Fork	0
12	South Fork	0
?	Scottsdale	?
6	Johnstown	12

The score for the Scottsdale game can not be found. It is reported that Windber won the game.

Windber High School Football-1917

Standing; (LR): Arnold Long, Ebbie Kyle, Coach Elmer Daily, Bernard Duncan, George Moore, Nick Nassard.
Line; (LR): Edgar Kyle, Carl Hoenstine, Ben Adams, Tony Buscaglia, Victor Zack, Wilford Nevling, Allen Mattherson.
Backs; (LR): Don Mattherson, George Brent (Identified as the colored man in the photograph found on page 20 in Chapter Three.), David Latz, Ed. Mills.

1917   **Head Coach: Elmer Daily**   **Record:**   **Wins 2**   **Losses 3**

Offensive Starting Line-up

LE	Allen Mattherson
LT	Wilfred Nevling
LG	Victor Zack or Arnold Long
C	Tony Buscaglia or Nick Nassard
RG	Ben Adams
RT	Carl Hoenstine or Bernard Duncan
RE	Edgar Kyle or George Moore
QB	Ed Mills
LH	Dave Latz (Captain)
RH	Don Mattherson
FB	George Brent

Season Schedule

W.H.S.		Opponent
8	Somerset	13
0	Altoona	16
13	Somerset	6
6	Altoona	0
0	Johnstown	40

Windber High School Football-1918

No Photograph Avaliable

1918   **Head Coach: Jim Hyde**   **Record:**   **Wins 2**   **Losses 0**

Offensive Starting Line-up

Lineman	Vic Zack
Lineman	Ben Adams
Lineman	Lou Middleman
Lineman	Nick Nazard
Lineman	Ladsy Polansky
Lineman	Mike Petronick
Lineman	Cliff Claycomb
Backfield	Don Matherson
Backfield	Allen Gochnour
Backfield	Pinky Polansky
Backfield	Dave Latz (Captain)

Season Schedule

W.H.S.		Opponent
12	Altoona	0
?	Somerset	?

No score found for the Somerset game, although reports indicate the game was won by Windber. The remaining games for this season were cancelled due to a flu epidemic.

Windber High School Football-1919

No Photograph Avaliable

1919   **Head Coach: Jim Hyde**   **Record:**   **Wins 0**   **Losses 4**   **Ties 1**

Offensive Starting Line-up

LE	John Piper
LT	Gus Hoffer
LG	Joel Smouse
C	Joe Aldstadt
RG	Mel Crum
RT	Charles Vallery
RE	All Matherson
QB	Clyde Kough
LH	Pinky Polansky
RH	Ladsy Polansky
FB	Clair Vickroy

Season Schedule

W.H.S.		Opponent
6	Windber Juniors	6
0	Altoona	7
7	Altoona	19
0	Somerset	19
6	Indiana Normal School	20

Windber High School Football-1920

Row 1: Piper, Cletus Crum, Gus Topper, Joe Aldstadt, Clair Vickroy, Joel Smouse, Charles Vallery, Roy Mills.
Row 2: Bob Koehler, P. Polansky, Thomas, Watts, Peterson, Solomon Solomon, Charles Hoestine, Jim Hagan.
Row 3: Jim Hyde-Head Coach, Don Thompson, Mike Hickey, C. Ripple, Jim Delehunt, Art Kelly, Clyde Kough, Augustine Ferline, C.C. Crawford-Superintendent of Schools.

1920   Head Coach: Jim Hyde   Record: Wins 5   Losses 2   Ties 2

Offensive Starting Line-up

LE	Roy Mills or Charles Vallery
LT	Joel Smouse
LG	Solomon Solomon
C	Joe Aldstadt
RG	Art Kelly or Gus Topper
RT	Cletus Crum
RE	Mike HIckey or Don Thompson
QB	Charles Hoenstine
LH	Clyde Kough
RH	Pinky Polansky or Jim Hagan
FB	Clair Vickroy or Bob Koehler

Season Schedule

W.H.S.		Opponent
14	Conemaugh	0
14	Altoona	13
0	Huntingdon	64
0	Windber Juniors	7
20	Johnstown Usher Club	0
20	Aflas	0
10	Bellefonte Academy	0
0	Windber Juniors	0

Windber High School Football-1921 ?

No Identification of Players Found

1921 **Head Coach: Jim Hyde** **Record:** **Wins 3** **Losses 3** **Ties 2**

Offensive Starting Line-up

LE	Pete White
LT	Cort Thompson or ? Hoffman
LG	Walt Piper
C	Fred Sell
RG	Bob Peterson or John Kinney
RT	Augustine Ferline
RE	Eugene Murphy or Mike Hickey
QB	John White
LH	Jim Hagan
RH	Jim Delehunt
FB	Charles Hoenstine

Season Schedule

W.H.S.		Opponent
0	Johnstown	27
32	Derry	0
21	St. Francis College	0
6	Clearfield	12
0	Altoona	0
20	South Fork Jrs.	0
0	Turtle Creek	0
0	Greensburg*	94

(*Not a regular season game)

Windber High School Football-1922

Row 1: L to R. Barton, Morgan, John Sharkey, T. Runco, Unknown, J. Smutko.
Row 2: L. to R. Parnell, John Lloyd, Unknown, Sngle, Fred Sell, Unknown, Unknown, Pete White.
Row 3: L. to R. A. Whalley, Unknown, Eugene Murphy, Unknown, Jim Hagan, Jim Delehunt, Unknown, Unknown, Coach Jim Hyde.

1922   Head Coach: Jim Hyde   Record: Wins 6   Losses 5   Ties 1

Season Schedule

Offensive Starting Line-up

LE	Lou Frulinger
LT	Bob Peterson or Phil DePolo
LG	Archur Kelly or J. Smutko
C	Fred Sell
RG	Gerald Snyder or Rod Wirick
RT	Augustine Ferline or Mel Crum
RE	John Lloyd or Pete White
QB	Jim Delehunt
LH	Jim Hagan
RH	Eugene Murphy
FB	Allen Gochnour

W.H.S.		Opponent
54	South Fork	0
60	Cresson	0
6	Johnstown	12
6	Hollidaysburg	6
33	Somerset	0
13	Altoona	6
0	Huntingdon	18
0	Lock Haven	34
0	Conemaugh	12
66	Everett	0
13	Derry	0
6	Latrobe	7

Windber High School Football-1923

No Identification of Players Found

First Undefeated Team

1923   Head Coach: H. L. Koehler   Record: Wins 9   Losses 0   Ties 1

Season Schedule

Offensive Starting Line-up

		W.H.S.	Opponent	
LE	Pete White			
LT	Philip DePolo	20	South Fork	0
LG	Wenard Kough	25	Clearfield	0
C	Fred Sell	32	Johnstown	0
RG	Raymond Wilson	32	Meyersdale	0
RT	Rodney Wilson	13	Lock Haven	0
RE	Louis Fruhlinger	34	Beaverdale	0
QB	Jim Hagan	24	Altoona	0
LH	Eugene Murphy	13	Huntingdon	3
RH	James Delehunt	13	Hollidaysburg	0
FB	Desiderius Polansky	0	Conemaugh	0

Other Players not listed as starters

John Lloyd-End, Gerald Snyder-Line, Carl Biss-Line, Thomas Boyd-Line, John Sharkey-Backfield, Richard Mickle-Manager.

Substitutes and Assistant Managers

James Camille, Ernest Carlis, Emanuel Gochnour, Dean Louder, Theodore Morgan, William Nevling, Solomon Solomon, Robert Norris, Blair Owens, Michael Picolo, Earnest Statler, John Smutko, Russell Yost, Russell Seese and Albert Plummer-Asst. Managers.

Windber High School Football-1924

No Identification of Players Found

1924   Head Coach: H. L. Koehler   Record: Wins 5   Losses 4   Ties 1

Offensive Starting Line-up

LE	Wenard Kough
LT	Ray Wilson
LG	John Wirick or Tom Boyd
C	John Roach
RG	Phil DePolo
RT	Gerald Snyder
RE	Pete White
QB	Jim Camille
LH	John Kinney
RH	Jim Delehunt
FB	Eugene Murphy

Season Schedule

W.H.S.	Opponent	
40	Beaverdale	0
0	Greensburg	60
0	Indiana Normal School	41
0	Lock Haven	15
7	Hollidaysburg	0
7	Altoona	3
0	Westinghouse Tech.	0
0	Norwin	13
19	Clearfield	0
7	Johnstown	0

Windber High School Football-1925

No Identification of Players Found

1925   Head Coach: Tom Zerbe   Record: Wins 4   Losses 3   Ties 2

Offensive Starting Line-up

LE	George Wilkinson
LT	Jim Zack
LG	Joe Congerski or John Roach
C	John Torquato
RG	Phil DePolo
RT	Ernest Carliss
RE	John Lloyd
QB	Jim Camille
LH	John Skarkey
RH	John Kinney
FB	Clifford Ripple

Season Schedule

W.H.S.	Opponent	
42	Beaverdale	7
0	Windber Ex-High	18
0	Tyrone	13
0	Somerset	0
0	Lock Haven	20
0	Hollidaysburg	0
9	Juniata	6
7	Altoona	0
7	Johnstown	6

Windber High School Football-1926

No Identification of Players Found

1926 **Head Coach: J. Nelson Hoffman** **Record:** **Wins 8** **Losses 1** **Ties 2**

Season Schedule

	Offensive Starting Line-up	W.H.S.		Opponent
LE	Howard Nevling			
LT	Jim Zack	42	Beaverdale	0
LG	Ernest Carliss	0	Indiana Normal School	0
C	John Torquato	6	Hollidaysburg	0
RG	Phil DePolo	19	Somerset	0
RT	Joe Congersky	26	Tyrone	0
RE	George Wilkinson	0	Lock Haven	0
QB	Jim Camille	70	Altoona	0
LH	Lou Colborn	28	Altoona Apprentice	0
RH	Nick Rillo	16	Bedford	7
FB	Harold "Duke" Weigle	40	Adams Twp.	3
		0	Johnstown	14

Windber High School Football-1927

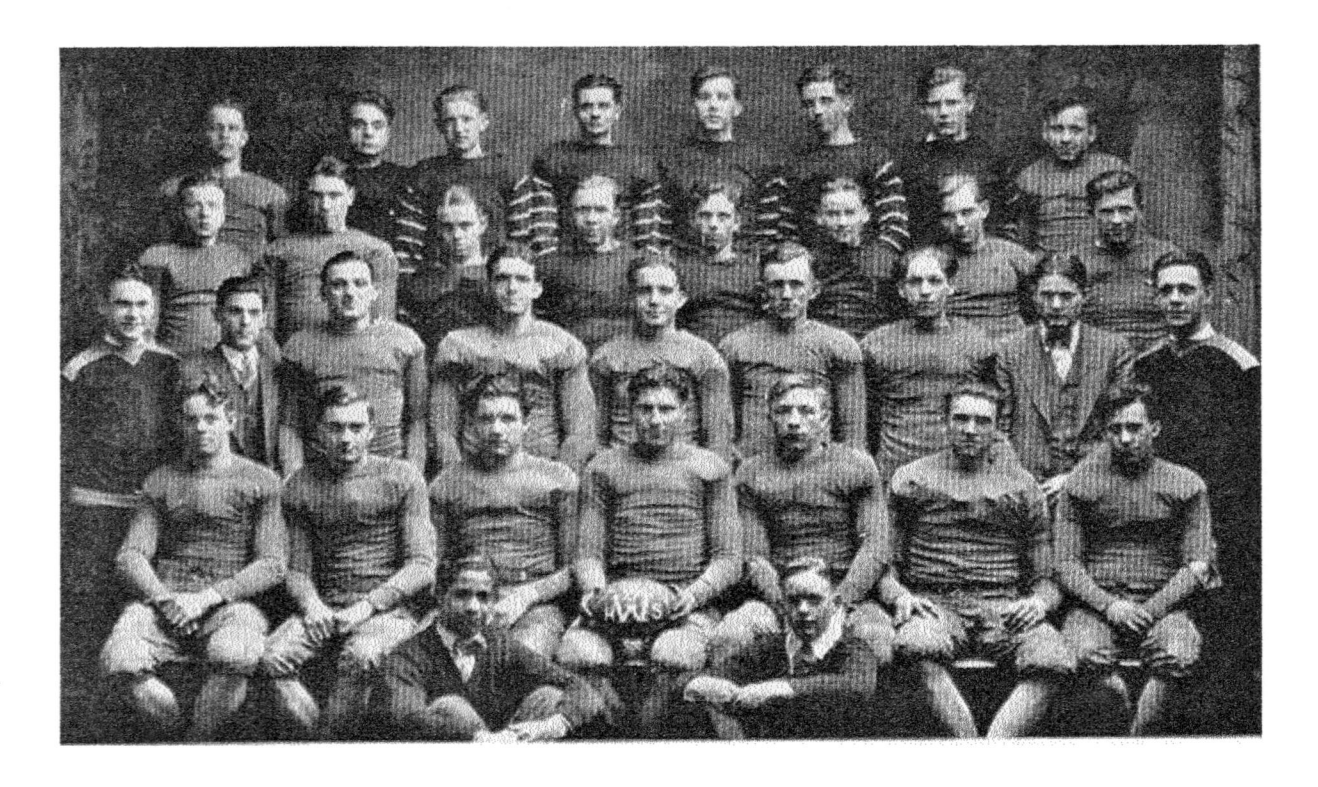

No Identification of Players Found

1927   Head Coach: Earl A. Unger   Record: Wins 3   Losses 5   Ties 1

Offensive Starting Line-up

LE	Gerald McFeeley
LT	Ralph Weigle
LG	Charles Gordon
C	Bob Honadle
RG	Jack Ferline
RT	Niles Dalberg or Adam Kohler
RE	Ted Helman or Nile Ripple
QB	Harold "Duke" Weigle
LH	Frances Murphy
RH	Joe Gates
FB	Nick Rillo

Season Schedule

W.H.S.	Opponent	
0	Beaverdale	0
0	Altoona Apprentice	19
15	Hollidaysburg	0
0	Somerset	14
7	Lock Haven	19
7	Altoona	9
20	Bedford	0
32	Adams Twp.	6
0	Johnstown	2

Windber High School Football-1928

No Identification of Players Found

1928   Head Coach: Earl A. Unger   Record: Wins 8   Losses 2

Offensive Starting Line-up

LE	Ted Keenan
LT	Ralph Weigle
LG	Joe Keenan
C	Bob Honadle
RG	Jack Ferline
RT	Niles Dalberg or Charles Gordon
RE	Gerald McFeeley
QB	Joe Gates
LH	John Marron or Nile Ripple
RH	Ken Faust
FB	Nick Rillo

Season Schedule

W.H.S.		Opponent
26	Beaverdale	0
0	Hurst	32
0	Portage	13
20	Altoona	6
39	Hollidaysburg	13
52	Somerset	7
18	Meyersdale	0
40	Bedford	0
30	Lilly	0
12	Johnstown	0

Windber High School Football-1929

No Identification of Players Found

1929   **Head Coach: Earl A. Unger**   **Record:**   Wins 4   Losses 4   Ties 1

Offensive Starting Line-up

LE	Leo Edwards
LT	Russell Anthony
LG	Joe Murphy
C	Bob Honadle
RG	Bill McCuch
RT	Niles Dalberg
RE	Earl Langley
QB	Joe Gates
LH	John Marron
RH	Oscar Ripple
FB	Jim Fagan

Season Schedule

W.H.S.		Opponent
78	Adams Twp.	0
53	Cresson	7
20	Portage	0
19	Bellefonte	25
9	Somerset	13
6	Altoona	47
39	Meyersdale	0
6	Bedford	7
0	Johnstown	0

Appendix I — A Reflection on Windber High School Football — 201

Windber High School Football-1930

Row 1: Coach-T.T. Allen, David Boyd, Russell Anthony, Niles Dalberg, John Marron (Captain), Joe Gates, William McCuch, Frank DeArmey, D.L. Quinsey,-Faculty Manager.
Row 2: Joe Murphy, Earl Langley, John Durbin, Don Worley, James Fagan, John Murphy, Alfred Burtnett.
Row 3: Edward Fife, Manager, Oscar Ripple, Nick Cicciarelli, John DeArmey, William Mayer, Jack Fagan, C. Bunton, Marlin Baumgardner, Elbert Weaver, Harold Smith, John Harding,-Manager.
Row 4: Kermit Olson, Edward Marron, Zolta Solma.

1930 **Head Coach: Tubby Allen** **Record:** **Wins 8** **Losses 2** **Ties 1**

Offensive Starting Line-up

LE	Leo Edwards or Dave Boyd
LT	Russell Anthony
LG	Joe Murphy
C	Don Worley
RG	Bill McCuch
RT	Niles Dalberg
RE	Earl Langley or Nick Cicciarelli
QB	Joe Gates
LH	John Marron
RH	Oscar Ripple or Harold Smith
FB	Jim Fagan or Frank DeArmy

Season Schedule

W.H.S.		Opponent
82	Carrolltown	0
27	Meyersdale	0
73	Bellefonte	0
7	Portage	0
33	Somerset	9
0	Hollidaysburg	6
6	LaSalle Inst.	7
37	Williamsburg	0
16	Ligonier	0
0	Johnstown	0
7	Johnstown	0

Windber High School Football-1931

Row 1: M. Baumgardner, H. Honadle, A. Roscetti, B. Sciotti, Z. Solma, A. Bartnett, J. Dell, ?. Spinelli, J. DeArmey, J. Cavacini, N. Petro, K. Parnell.
Row 2: C. Bunton, J. Fagan, E. Weaver, D. Worley, J. Murphy-Captain, O. Ripple, E. Langley, B. McCuch, J. Durbin W. Mayer, C. Mayer, H. Gimber.
Row 3: Tubby Allen-Head Coach, J. Wagner, B. Meyers, T. Marron, L. Fancourt, W. Wlson, J. Ziants, A. Prosseor, R. McFeely, G. George, ?. Senior, T. Harding-Manager.

1931   Head Coach: Tubby Allen   Record: Wins 5   Losses 4

Offensive Starting Line-up

LE	Earl Langley
LT	John Durbin
LG	Jack Fagan
C	Don Worley or Alf. Bartnett
RG	Carl Bunton
RT	William Mayer
RE	Marlin Baumgardner or Jim Cavacini
QB	Bill McCuch
LH	John Murphy (Capt.)
RH	Oscar Ripple
FB	Ken Parnell

Season Schedule

W.H.S.	Opponent	
13	Johnstown Catholic	6
6	Bedford	13
19	Bellefonte	14
0	Portage	6
19	Somerset	13
45	Hollidaysburg	0
0	LaSalle Institute	6
26	Meyersdale	0
0	Johnstown	6

Windber High School Football-1932

Row 1: T. Allen-Head Coach, N. Petro, W. Meyers, K. Parnell, E. Weaver, O. Ripple, (Mable Stringer-Mascot) J. Fagan, H. Honadle, J. Durbin, B. Ciotti, M. Beam-Faculty Manager.
Row 2: H. Weigle-Asst.Coach, R. McFeeley, G.Rollo, J.Dell, J.Cavacini, C Mayer, J. Wagner, J. Carliss, M. Beam.
Row 3: A. Garlathy, A. Roscetti, J. DeArmey, W. Farkas, C. Bartholomew, L. Fancourt, A. DePolo, T. Marron.
Row 4: G. Gordon, J. Bell, W. Lamb, W. Wilson, F. Saken, W. Kinney, V. Couperthwaithe, M. Mock F. Sherlock.
Row 5: M. Heckler, T. Harding, D. Faguani, R. Faguani, J. Daley, B. Gohn, Edward Fife-Manager, Bernard Murray-Manager, Dog: Pierre, (Name found in a scrap book photograph belonging to Earl Ripple, 1939 Quarterback).

1932   Head Coach: Tubby Allen   Record   Wins 8   Losses 2

Season Schedule

	Offensive Starting Line-up	W.H.S.		Opponent
LE	Bruno Ciotti			
LT	John Durbin	21	Shade	0
LG	Elbert Weaver	7	Johnstown Catholic	0
C	Bill Myers or Harold Honadle	21	Bedford	0
RG	Jack Fagan	19	Bellefonte	0
RT	Charles Mayer	6	Portage	12
RE	Jim Cavacini	13	Somerset	6
QB	Oscar Ripple	20	Westmont	6
LH	Nick Petro	25	Hollidaysburg	0
RH	George Rollo	14	Ferndale	7
FB	Ken Parnell or Armond Roscetti	10	Johnstown	19

Windber High School Football-1933
First State Champion Team

Row 1: T.T. Allen-Head Coach, R. Morgan-Mgr., H. Weigle-Asst. Coach, M. Mock, J. DeArmey, J. Cavacini, J. Wagner,(Captain), M. Stringer (Mascot), T. Marron, G. Gordon, L. Fancourt, B. Murray-Mgr.., M. Beam-Faculty Mgr., Robert Lorenzen-Principal.
Row 2: W. Lamb, C. Bartholomew, T. Harding, J. Carliss, A. Garlathy, W. Farkas, J. Bell.
Row 3: B. Allison, A. Sendek, W. Wilson, V. Couperthwaite, M. Heckler, J. Daily, F. Sakon, W. Beckley, F. Purcelli, W. DePolo, W. Gahagen.
Row 4: E. Larson, E. Yocca, C. Gilroy, A. LaMonaca, R. Parnell, A. Dzierski, W. Kinney, G. Katchmerick, W. Manotti, J. Sherlock, J. Freeman, T. Senella.
Row 5: E. George, M. Durbin, W. Cook, J. Bednar, R. Sherlock, E. Fagnani, J. DiGuilio, C. Wilson-Mgr., C. Pierre, J. Mastrolembo-Mgr., P. Ciotti, F. Hoffer., A. Abbatte-Mgr., A. DePolo, J. Mansour, T. Moraca.

1933 **Head Coach: Tubby Allen** **Record:** **Wins 9** **Losses 2**

Offensive Starting Line-up

LE	Andy Sendek or Tom Harding
LT	Arthur Garlathy
LG	Wilson Lamb
C	Melvin Mock
RG	George Gordon or Charles Bartholomew
RT	John DeArmey or John Daily
RE	Bill Farkas
QB	Jim Wagner
LH	Tom Marron
RH	Jim Cavacini
FB	John Carliss

Season Schedule

W.H.S.	Opponent	
27	Shade Twp.	6
18	Ferndale	0
27	Bedford	6
7	Portage	0
28	Somerset	18
13	Westmont	6
7	DuBois	12
6	Jersey Shore	13
27	Hollidaysburg	0
7	Johnstown	0
7	John Harris	6

Windber High School Football-1934

No Identification of Players Found

1934   Head Coach: Harold (Duke) Weigle   Record: Wins 7   Losses 0   Ties 5

Offensive Starting Line-up

LE	Andy Sendeck
LT	Arthur Garlathy
LG	Wilson Lamb
C	Bernard Allison
RG	Charles Bartholomew
RT	John Daily
RE	Tom Harding
QB	Bill Manotti
LH	Bill Farkas
RH	Jack Bell
FB	John Carliss

Season Schedule

W.H.S.		Opponent
18	Shade Twp.	0
0	Westmont	0
14	Johnstown Catholic	0
0	Ferndale	0
13	Altoona	13
12	Somerset	6
0	Portage	0
12	Dubois	6
47	Jesey Shore	0
40	Bedford	0
0	Pottsville	0
41	Altoona Catholic	0

Windber High School Football-1935

No Identification of Players Found

1935   Head Coach: Harold (Duke) Weigle   Record: Wins 11   Losses 0   Ties 1

Offensive Starting Line-up

LE	John Cavacini
LT	Bill Beckley
LG	Art Lamonica
C	Bernard Allison
RG	Ed Fagnani
RT	John Daily
RE	Jack Bell
QB	Bill Manotti
LH	Bill Farkas
RH	William DePolo
FB	Bud Bossick

Season Schedule

W.H.S.		Opponent
27	Punxsutawney	0
27	Pottsville	6
57	Westmont	0
59	Shade Twp.	0
28	Ferndale	0
27	Johnstown Catholic	0
54	Somerset	2
33	Portage	0
50	Curwensville	7
21	Ebensburg	0
46	Bedford	0
0	Johnstown	0

Windber High School Football-1936

Row 1: Sekela, Freeman, Bokinsky, Bossick, J. Sherlock, Beckley (Captain), Cicciarelli, La Monica, M. Durbin, Bodnar, Cavacini.
Row 2: Kinney, Weaver, DiGuilio, Wirick, Senella, Bartholomew, D. Sherlock, Surina, Miller, Hayes.
Row 3: Pierzchala, Rodgers, Barna, Maneval, H. Sherlock, F. Durbin, Antonishak, Redfoot, Fagan, Gorgon, Latz.
Row 4: Rusnock, Bell, Sakon, Allen Lubas, Palovich.
Row 5: Uhas, Heinrich, Badaczewski, Hagan, Yocca, Hamilton, Balogh, Izing, Saverino.

1936   Head Coach: Harold (Duke) Weigle   Record: Wins 13   Losses 0

Offensive Starting Line-up

LE	John Cavacini or Tom Senella
LT	Bill Beckley
LG	Art Lamonaca
C	Mike Durbin or Tony DiGuilio
RG	Nick Cicciarelli
RT	George Bodnar
RE	Jack Sherlock
QB	Jack Freeman
LH	Mike Sekela
RH	George Bokinsky
FB	Bud Bossick

Defensive Starting Line-up

LE	John Cavacini
LT	Art Lamonaca
LG	Nick Ciccarelli
MG	Mike Durbin
RG	George Bodnar
RT	Bill Beckley
RE	Jack Sherlock
LB	Mike Sekela
LB	George Bokinsky
HB	Bud Bossick
HB	Jack Freeman

Season Schedule

W.H.S.	Opponent		W.H.S.	Opponent	
60	Franklin	0	29	Bethlehem	0
48	Shade Twp.	0	20	Altoona	12
54	Fort Hill, Maryland	6	39	Curwensville	0
26	Conemaugh	12	57	Ebensburg	7
52	Punxsutawney	0	27	Emporium	14
32	Ferndale	13	39	Portage	0
52	Huntingdon	0			

Windber High School Football-1937
Second State Championship Team

Row 1: Pete Gorgone, Pete Pierzchala, Frank Durbin, George Wirick, George Bokinsky, Edward Bossick, Joe Rodgers, Paul Toth, William Hayes.
Row 2: Alvin Hagan, Victor Surina, Joe Tverdak, Hobart Sherlock, Frank Kinney, Joe Pierre, John Badaczewski, Steve Heinrick
Row 3: Arthut Daub-Asst. Coach, Earl Ripple, George Balog, Jack Morgan, John LaPlaca, Edward Sakon, Joe Bell, William Racine, John Tomaczewski, Nick Boblick, Ralph Weigle-Head Coach.
Row 4: Richard Mickle-Faculty Manager, Joe Flori, Edward Stanish, Andy Allen, Earl Berkey, David Latz, Robert Holsinger, James Verna, John Visnovsky, Charles Obbets, Steve Izing-Manager.
Row 5: Robert Sherlock, Elmer Barna, Robert Hamilton, Leo Torcato, Walter Dressick, Felix Guss, Mike Kundar.

1937   Head Coach: Ralph Weigle   Record: Wins: 11   Losses 1   Ties 1

Offensive Starting Line-up

LE	Bill Hayes or Frank Durbin
LT	Paul Toth
LG	Joe Rodgers or Steve Heinrich
C	Pete Pierzchala
RG	George Wirick
RT	John Badaczewski or Joe Tverdak
RE	Joe Pierre
QB	Edward "Bud" Bossick
LH	Vic Surina or Hobart Sherlock
RH	George Bokinsky
FB	Pete Gorgone

Season Schedule

W.H.S.		Opponent
9	Ferndale	0
0	Erie East	6
31	Shade Twp.	7
58	Fort Hill, Maryland	7
32	Conemaugh	0
20	Huntingdon	0
75	Bethlehem	12
54	DuBois	0
19	Curwensville	0
32	Johnstown Catholic	0
40	Portage	7
0	Johnstown	0
21	Steelton	0

Windber High School Football-1938

Row 1: William Hayes, Pete Gorgone, David Latz, Elmer Barna, Earl Ripple, Paul Toth, John Badaczewski, Steve Heinrich, Frank Durbin, Joe Pierre, Leo Turcato. **Row 2:** Robert Sherlock, Joe Flori, Andrew Allen, William Racine, Edward Stanish, Dominick Racine, Joe Polansky, Edward Sakon, John Alex, Felix Guss. **Row 3:** Manager-"Mace" Baranik, Walter Dressick, Bob Hamilton, George Balogh, Mike Kondas, Arnold Uhas, James Verna, Mike Jordan, Jack Morgan-Manager, Angelo Stevens. **Row 4:** Asst. Coach-Joe Gates, Head Coach-Don Fletcher.

1938   Head Coach: Don Fletcher   Record: Wins 7   Losses 4   Ties 1

Season Schedule

	Offensive Starting Line-up	W.H.S.		Opponent
LE	Leo Torquato	0	Ferndale	8
LT	Dave Latz	15	Portage	7
LG	Paul Toth	25	Johnstown Catholic	6
C	Elmer Barna	39	Shade Twp.	6
RG	Steve Heinrich	43	Conemaugh	6
RT	John Badaczewski	0	Erie East	34
RE	Joe Pierre	12	Scott High	18
QB	Pete Gorgone	19	DuBois	13
LH	Bill Hayes	8	Curwensville	7
RH	Earl Ripple	6	Pottsville	7
FB	Joe Polansky or Frank Durbin	13	Sharon	6
		6	Johnstown	6

Windber High School Football-1939

Seated: J. Coco, L. Torquato, J. Morgan, R. Yocca, E. Stanish, F. Guss, W. Cominsky, S. Kaplan, E. Ripple, M. Jordan, R. Sherlock, D. Racine, J. Polansky, M. Kondas, G. Bednar, E. Lehman, B Mitchell.
Standing: Head Coach-Joe Gates, Manager-A. Stevens, J. Hughes, A. Allen, S. Heinrich, J. Badaczewski, J. Bell, R. Hayes, C. Surina, G. Balogh, E. Shaffer, W. Dressick, J. Alex, L. Turcato, ? Weaver, Manager ? DiGuilo, Asst. Coach-Sam Donato.

1939   **Head Coach: Joe Gates**   **Record:**   Wins 10   Losses 1   Ties 1

Offensive Starting Line-up

LE	Leo Torquato
LT	John Badaczewski
LG	Steve Heinrich
C	Charles Surina
RG	Mike Jordan
RT	Andy Allen
RE	Dominick Racine
QB	Earl Ripple
LH	Bob Sherlock
RH	Joe Polansky or Ed Yocca
FB	Steve Kaplan

Season Schedule

W.H.S.	Opponent	
27	Conemaugh Twp.	13
0	Pottsville	12
13	Ferndale	13
7	Conemaugh	0
13	Portage	0
20	Scott High	7
20	DuBois	0
20	Patterson, New Jersey	6
25	Shade Twp.	0
20	Johnstown Catholic	13
40	Erie East	14
21	Rankin	6

Appendix I   A Reflection on Windber High School Football   211

Windber High School Football-1940

Row 1: (Left to Right) S. Kaplan, C. Surina, J. Hughes, J. Watts, W. Dressick, J. Verna, G. Bednar, M. Kondas.
Row 2: J. Lochrie, J. Morgan, R. Weaver, R. Hayes, P. Rodgers, W. Freeman, Joe Polansky.
Row 3: J. Katchmeric, A. Visnovsky, P. Kaplan, J. Cocco, W. Cominsky, G. Earhard.
Row 4: J. Battiste, M. Hegedus, J. Campitell, John Polansky, Ellis Lehman, J. Thomas, R. Yocca.

1940   **Head Coach: Joe Gates**   **Record:**   **Wins 4**   **Losses 6**   **Ties 2**

Offensive Starting Line-up

LE	Dominick Racine or Joe Katchmeric
LT	Ross Weaver
LG	Mike Jordan or George Earhard
C	Charles Surina or Ray Torquato
RG	Ed. Comminsky or Paul Rodgers
RT	Mike Kondas or Bob Hayes
RE	Ellis Lehman or Bill Freeman
QB	Steve Kaplan
LH	Walter Dressick or Walter Cominsky
RH	George Bednar or James Thomas
FB	Joe Polansky or John Polansky

Season Schedule

W.H.S.	Opponent	
6	Alumni (Whalley A.C.)	0
13	Erie East	19
6	Ferndale	0
6	Conemaugh	12
31	Portage	0
7	Rankin	13
6	DuBois	6
13	Larksville	6
0	Farrell	13
12	Johnstown Catholic	12
7	Shade Twp.	12
6	Donora	13

Windber High School Football-1941

Row 1-James Angelo, Arthur Toth, Louis Damico, George Dena, Ray Yocca, Edward Hunter, Andy Boyko.
Row 2-Joe Polansky, Nunzio Marino, James Thomas, Walter Cominsky, Charles Popelich, George Earhard, Paul Antolosky, Andy Visnovsky, Roy Lochrie.
Row 3-Ray Torquato, John Polansky, Jack Lochrie, James Campitell, Robert Hayes, Ross Weaver, Paul Rodgers, Joe Katchmeric, Pete Kaplan, Bill Freeman.

1941   Head Coach: Joe Gates   Record: Wins 9   Losses 2

Offensive Starting Line-up

LE	Joe Katchmeric
LT	Bob Hayes
LG	Paul Rodgers
C	Ray Torquato
RG	George Earhard
RT	Ross Weaver
RE	Pete Kaplan
QB	Nunzio Marino
LH	Walter Cominsky
RH	Joe Polansky or Charles Popelich
FB	John Polansky

Season Schedule

W.H.S.		Opponent
33	Boswell	0
40	Portage	2
0	Johnstown	9
14	Lewistown	6
31	Rankin	0
6	Farrell	7
21	Johnstown Catholic	12
38	Conemaugh	0
39	Ferndale	12
19	Donora	0
39	Conemaugh Twp.	6

Windber High School Football-1942

Row 1: John Polansky, Joe Katchmeric, Jim Campitell, George Solomon, Ray Torquato, Paul Rodgers, Jack Lochrie, Pete Kaplan, Jim Thomas.
Row 2: Nunzio Marino, Roy Lochrie, Jack Layland, Andy Boyko, Arthur Toth, Joe Campitell, Carl Geisel, Paul Antolosky, Walter Cominsky.
Row 3: Head Coach-Joe Gates, John Gibson, Ed. Wojicki, Richard Marino, Lester Shull, John Holovka, John Wojicki, Anthony DiMuzio, Ed. Hunter, Charles Popelich, Assistant Coach-Ray Jones.

1942   **Head Coach: Joe Gates**   **Record:**   Wins 8   Losses 0

Offensive Starting Line-up

LE	Joe Katchmeric
LT	Jim Campitell
LG	Paul Rodgers
C	Ray Torquato
RG	Bob Solomon
RT	Jack Lochrie
RE	Pete Kaplan
QB	Nunzio Marino
LH	Walter Cominsky
RH	Jim Thomas
FB	John Polansky

Season Schedule

W.H.S.		Opponent
64	Shade Twp.	0
40	Pittsburgh Central Catholic	0
41	Conemaugh	6
34	Portage	6
20	Johnstown	13
13	Altoona	7
26	Conemaugh Twp.	14
33	Johnstown Catholic	0

Windber High School Football-1943

Row 1: Manager-Alf Cantrine, Walter Cominsky, John Wojcicki, Edward Wojcicki, Carl Geisel, Tony DeMuzio, Manager-Tony Pierre, Arthur Toth, Joe DelSignore, Joe Campitell, Gerald Shaffer, Nunzio Marino, Don Thomas, Manager-Tony Panetti.
Row 2: Dwight Zimmerman, Tom Guiney, Walter Wozinski, Rufus Morocco, Jim Lewis, Bob Mucciola, John Holovka, Don Heeter, John Raccine, Mike Rosella, John McElhaney.

1943   Head Coach: Ray Jones   Record: Wins 10   Losses 0

Offensive Starting Line-up

LE	Gerald Shaffer
LT	Joe Campitell
LG	Joe DelSignore
C	Arthur Toth
RG	Tony DiMuzio
RT	Carl Geisel
RE	Ed Wojcicki
QB	Walter Cominsky
LH	John Wojcicki
RH	Don Thomas
FB	Nunzio Marino

Season Schedule

W.H.S.	Opponent	
54	Shade Twp.	14
47	Rankin	6
21	Johnstown Catholic	6
13	Portage	0
18	Johnstown	0
27	Lewistown	7
21	Altoona	7
27	Conemaugh Twp.	0
19	Johnstown	0
27	Conemaugh	0

Windber High School Football-1944

Row 1: Mehalko, Clement, Prisby, Lewis, Mucciola, Bauer, Kush, Vespa, Guiney.
Row 2: Morey, Berkey, Renaldi, Kutch, Laslo, Racine, Slishansky, McElhaney.
Row 3: Panetti (Manager), Leonardis, Rosella, Puckey, Badaczewski, Yocca, DiMuzio, Heeter.

1944   Head Coach: Joe Shevock   Record: Wins 4   Losses 4   Ties 1

Starting Offensive Line-up

LE	Charles Puckey or Fred Bauer
LT	Jim Lewis
LG	Tony DiMuzio
C	Don Heeter
RG	John Yocca
RT	Bob Mucciola
RE	Rufus Moraca
QB	Stan Prisby
LH	Paul Kutch or Leo Renaldi
RH	Mike Rosella
FB	Leo Renaldi or Bill Laslo

Season Schedule

W.H.S.		Opponent
0	Shade Twp.	12
6	Conemaugh	6
42	Portage	0
0	Johnstown	20
13	Adams Twp.	7
0	Altoona	34
6	Somerset	19
13	Johnstown Catholic	0
25	Conemaugh Twp.	0

Windber High School Football-1945

Row 1: Francis Swickla, Nick Mehalco, Millard Rounsley, Frank Kush, Joe Slishansky, Robert Mucciola, Pete Yocca, Fred Vespa, Tom Grebis, Gilbert Lochrie.
Row 2: John Morway, Russell Berkey, John Mehalic, James Morey, John Grieco, John Racine, Edward Hughes, Eugene Hagan, Melvin Berkey.
Row 3: Robert Appleyard, Hobart Berkey, Paul Kutch, Paul Clement, Leo Renaldi, Rufus Moraco, Don Heeter, Steve Leonardis, John Yocca, John Zahodine.
Row 4: Manager-John Torquato, Asst. Coach-Herb Wagner, Asst. Coach-John Kawchak, Head Coach-Steve Terebus, Athletic Director-Richard Mickle.

1945   Head Coach: Steve Terebus   Record: Wins 7   Losses 2   Ties 1

Season Schedule

Offensive Starting Line-up

LE	Robert Berkey or Bob Appleyard
LT	Steve Leonardis
LG	Frank Kush
C	Don Heeter
RG	John Yocca
RT	Robert Mucciola or Joe Slishansky
RE	Bob Appleyard or Rufus Morocco
QB	Paul Kutch
LH	Hobert Berkey
RH	James Morey or Leo Renaldi
FB	Paul Clement

W.H.S.	Opponent	
33	Shade Twp.	6
38	Conemaugh	0
32	Portage	6
0	Johnstown	0
7	Adams Twp.	13
19	Johnstown Catholic	0
12	Altoona	20
20	Somerset	6
34	Lewistown	6
14	Conemaugh Twp.	0

Appendix I — A Reflection on Windber High School Football

Windber High School Football-1946

Row 1: John Yocca, Frank Kush, Paul Kutch, Nick Mehalco, Joe Slishansky, Paul Clement, Joe Genovese.
Row 2: John Mehalic, Eugene Hagan, Joe Spadone, Bob Appleyard, Leo Renaldi, Richard Puto, Norbert Teklinsky.
Row 3: Fred Vespa, Bill Moraca, Sam Romano, Eddie Pruchnic, Gilbert Lochrie, Dwight Ling, Paul Komar, Frank Makoczy.
Row 4: Tom Sharpe, James Hobba, Eddie Hughes, James Klemstine, Jim Curtis, Joe Renaldi, John Zahodne, Russell Berkey, Millard Rounsley.
Row 5: Joe Koshute-Manager, Nick Yocca-Manager, Wilbur Berkey, Jim Morey, John Racine, Tom Grebis, Ronald Younker, Melvin Berkey-Manager, Edward Yuhas-Manager.
Row 6: Asst. Coach-John Kawchak, Head Coach-Ray Jones, Asst. Coach-Herb Wagner.

1946   **Head Coach: Ray Jones**   **Record:**   Wins 6   Losses 3   Ties 1

Offensive Starting Line-up

LE	Bob Appleyard or Russell Berkey
LT	John Mehalic
LG	Frank Kush
C	Nick Mehalko
RG	John Racine or Eugene Hagan
RT	John Yocca
RE	Joe Slishansky
QB	Paul Kutch
LH	Leo Renaldi
RH	Jim Morey or Joe Renaldi
FB	Paul Clement

Season Schedule

W.H.S.		Opponent
33	Shade Twp.	6
6	Sharpsville	21
34	Cresson	6
6	Johnstown	7
0	Adams Twp.	0
21	Conemaugh	0
12	Altoona	20
41	Somerset	6
26	Lewistown	0
20	Conemaugh Twp.	0

Windber High School Football-1947

Row 1: Manager-Jacobs, Heichel, Wasil, Gorgon, Curtis, Rounsley, Berkey, Komar, Teklinsky, T. Kush, Spadone, Manager-Aldstadt.
Row 2: Coach-Kawchak, Coach-Terebus, Gilbert, Klemstine, Makoczy, Moraca, F. Kush, Romano, Hughes, Lochrie, Ling, Grebis, Coach-Wagner, Coach-Farrell.
Row 3: Manager-Baranik, Renaldi, Cominsky, Campitell, Sam, Couperthwaite, Hunter, Gulick, Newcomer, Pruchnic, Kondas, Ott, Hobba, Sharpe, Younker.

1947   Head Coach: Steve Terebus   Record: Wins 3   Losses 6   Ties 1

Offensive Starting Line-up

LE	Joe Spadone or Sam Romano
LT	Frank Kush
LG	Millard Rounsley
C	Paul Komar or Wilbur Berkey
RG	James Curtis or Bill Gorgon
RT	Bill Moraca
RE	Tony Campitell
QB	Joe Renaldi or Ed Hughes
LH	Tom Grebis or Dwight Ling
RH	Gilbert Lochrie or Tom Sharpe
FB	Ronald "Link" Younker

Season Schedule

W.H.S.		Opponent
7	Shade Twp.	0
33	Lilly	6
12	Blairsville	25
6	Johnstown	7
0	Adams Twp.	0
25	Conemaugh	14
6	Donora	27
7	Altoona	35
0	Sharpsville	20
0	Conemaugh Twp.	2

Windber High School Football-1948

Row 1: M. Rounsley, N. Teklinsky, J. Curtis, J. Renaldi, W. Berkey, E. Newcomer, E. Pruchnic, J. Spadone, T. Kush, T. Sharpe.
Row 2: E. Oldham, S. Wasil, J. Gulick, N. Gilbert, A. Cominsky, L. Sam, R. Younker, A. Muscatello, A. Campitell, P. Komar.
Row 3: Dwight Erhard, B. Washko, Duane Erhard, B. Hunter, B. Morway, J. Voytko, J. Allen, E. DeMarco, J. Sasko, M. Yougovich.
Row 4: M. Berkey, E. Fluder, H. DiLoretto, Asst. Coach-A. Atty, Asst. Coach-E. Farrell, Head Coach-J. Kawchak.

1948   Head Coach: John Kawchak   Record: Wins 7   Losses 4

Season Schedule

	Offensive Starting Line-up	W.H.S.		Opponent
LE	Joe Spadone	19	Shade Twp.	0
LT	Norbert Teklinsky	6	Turtle Creek	0
LG	Millard Rounsley	6	Aliquippa	50
C	Wilbur Berkey or Paul Komar	23	Johnstown	7
RG	James Curtis	0	Adams Twp.	6
RT	Elmer Newcomer	14	Conemaugh Twp.	7
RE	Tony Campitell or Ed Pruchnic	18	Conemaugh	7
QB	Ted Kush or Chester Tokarsky	19	Punxsutawney	0
LH	Tom Sharpe	12	Meadville	6
RH	Ronald "Link" Younker	19	Ambridge	39
FB	Joe Renaldi	6	Allentown	27

Windber High School Football-1949

Row 1: E. Uhas-Manager, A. Muscatello, S. Wasil, R. Younker, P. Komar, A. Mock, C. Minitti, R. Cook-Manager.
Row 2: R. Hudy, B. Washko, J. Gulick, L. Rubal, M. Kush, J. Kochera, A. Cominsky, L. Sam.
Row 3: J. Campitell, W. Marfizo, D. Kopcik, J. Gillespie, R. Hrebik, W. Oldham.
Row 4: W. Appleyard, E. DeMarco, E. Iacona, G. Russian, P. Freeman, P. DePolo, J. Hordubay.
Row 5: C. Tokarsky, J. Sasko, W. Morway, J. Voytko, W. Hunter, R. DeBiase, J. Allen.

1949   Head Coach: John Kawchak   Record: Wins 8   Losses 1   Ties 1

Season Schedule

	Offensive Starting Line-up	W.H.S.		Opponent
LE	Louis Sam			
LT	John Gulick	40	Shade Twp.	0
LG	Alfred Mock or Al Comisky	20	Altoona	7
C	Paul Komar	7	Aliquippa	6
RG	Steve Wasil or Bill Gorgon	25	Johnstown	7
RT	John Sasko	20	Adams Twp.	6
RE	Tony Campitell	12	Conemaugh Twp.	6
QB	Chester Tokarsky	0	Conemaugh	26
LH	Bernard Washko or Pat Freeman	27	Punxsutawney	7
RH	Bill Morway	34	Meadville	0
FB	Ron "Link" Younker	0	Johnstown Catholic	0

Windber High School Football-1950

Row 1: Managers: John Kutsick, Joe Novak, George Petro, Edwood Wargo.
Row 2: Pat Freeman, Bob DeBiase, Eugene Iacona, Chester Tokarsky, Emil DeMarco, John Halkovich, John Sasko, Bill Morway, Jim Voytko, John Allen, Phil DePolo, Bill Hunter, Bernard Washko.
Row 3: Jack Kochera, Dan Kopcik, Steve Hancharik, Bill Marfizo, Leonard Rubal, Bill Oldham, Jim Hordubay, Bill Appleyarrd, Dick Hudy, Carl Minitti, Bob Hrebik, Bill Martell, Asst. Coach-Alex Atty.
Row 4: Head Coach-John Kawchak, George McKelvie, Ray Bossi, John Naylor, Marlin Berkey, Mike Kush, Carl Tokarsky, Jim Holman, Paul Stiffler, John Hamzik, Ernest Maxwell, Asst. Coach-Steve Kaplan.

1950   Head Coach: John Kawchak   Record: Wins 7   Losses 1   Ties 1

Offensive Starting Line-up

LE	Bill Marfizo or John Allen
LT	John Halcovich
LG	Emil DeMarco
C	Bob DeBiase
RG	John Sasko
RT	James Voytko
RE	Bill Hunter
QB	Chester Tokarsky
LH	Pat Freeman or Phil DePolo
RH	Bill Morway or Len Rubal
FB	Bernard Washko

Season Schedule

W.H.S.		Opponent
21	Shade Twp.	0
7	Altoona	7
13	Beaver Falls	7
12	Johnstown	6
13	Conemaugh Twp.	12
65	Conemaugh	7
7	Punxsutawney	13
19	Ebensburg	6
20	Adams Twp.	7

Windber High School Football-1951

Row 1: G. McKelvie, D. Kopic, D. Hudy, B. Oldham, B. Marfizo, L. Rubal, B. Appleyard, J. Kochera, J. Hordubay, B. Martell.
Row 2: G. Mnich, T. Kanas, T. Fagan, B. Hudy, R. Bossi, C. Tokarsky, J. Naylor, J. Holman, J. Sombronski.
Row 3: G. Kephart, D. Miller, S. Lubrano, J. Hajnos, E. Hordubay, C. Baughman, F. Berkey, R. Facciani, G. Petro.
Row 4: B. Hill, G. Zindash, F. Greene, D. Hunt, R. Halcovich.

1951   Head Coach: John Kawchak   Record: Wins 2   Losses 7

Offensive Starting Line-up

LE	Sam Holman
LT	Bill Oldham
LG	Bill Martell
C	Bill Marfizo or George McKelvie
RG	Dick Hudy
RT	Bill Appleyard
RE	Steve Hancharik
QB	Jack Kochera
LH	Len Rubal
RH	Bob Hudy
FB	Terry Fagan

Season Schedule

W.H.S.		Opponents
12	Shade Twp.	7
7	Altoona	12
0	Beaver Falls	25
7	Johnstown Catholic	16
0	Johnstown	7
0	Conemaugh Twp.	39
13	Cresson	7
7	Punxsutawney	10
7	Adams Twp.	32

Windber High School Football-1952

Row 1: F. Greene, T. Fagan, J. Naylor, B. Martell, J. Holman, G. McKelvie, R. Bossi, C. Tokarsky, B. Hudy, T. Kanas.
Row 2: A. Hancharik, G. Gephart, B. Halcovich, E. Hordubay, C. Baughman, J. Sombronski, B. Keller, R. Facciani, G. Zindash.
Row 3: R. Statler-Manager, J. Hajnos, J. Kush, J. Hordubay, N. Becky, A. Toth, E. Miller, G. Winas, J. Novak-Manager.
Row 4: Asst. Coach-A. Atty, B. Honadle, B. Stopko, E. Nelson, B. Bundy, B. Foltz, R. Dutzman, M. Spinazzola, D. Hunt, Head Coach-J. Kawchak.

1952   Head Coach: John Kawchak   Record: Wins 7   Losses 2   Ties 1

Season Schedule

Offensive Starting Line-up		W.H.S.		Opponents
LE	John Holman	24	Shade Twp.	26
LT	Ed. Hordubay or John Naylor	31	Altoona	6
LG	Bill Martell	13	Pittsburgh North Catholic	13
C	George McKelvie	39	Johnstown Catholic	6
RG	Tom Kanas	6	Johnstown	26
RT	Carl Tokarsky	30	Conemaugh	26
RE	Fred Green	2	Adams Twp.	0
QB	Bob Halcovich or Andy Hancharick	47	Punxsutawney	6
LH	Bob Hudy or Eugene Miller	40	Somerset	0
RH	Ray Bossi	12	Richland	0
FB	Terry Fagan			

Windber High School Football-1953

Row 1: Zindash, Kanas, Kephart, E. Hordubay, Hunt, Fagan, Greene, Sombronski, Hudy, Baughman, Keller, Halcovich, Facciani, Hajnos.
Row 2: Miller, Hancharik, J. Hordubay, Bundy, Honadle, J. Kush, Winas, Spinazzola, Nelson, Toth, Foltz, Dutzman, Becky.
Row 3: R. Brutts, Salko, Kondas, Bertsel, Spadone, Smutko, Lewark, Gahagan, Zeigler, Seese, DePolo, J. Brutts, Hritz, Finnegan, DeMarco.
Row 4: S. Kush, Clark, Sendek, Wargo-Managers, Head Coach-J. Kawchak, Asst. Coach-J. Lochrie, Asst. Coach-A. Atty.

1953   Head Coach: John Kawchak   Record: Wins 9   Losses 1

Offensive Starting Line-up

LE	Chuck Baughman
LT	Edward Hordubay
LG	G. Zindash or J. Sombronsky
C	Bill Keller
RG	Tom Kanas or Bob Halcovich
RT	Joe Hordubay or Dudley Hunt
RE	Fred Green
QB	Ralph Facciani
LH	Andy Hancharik or Eugene Miller
RH	Bob Hudy
FB	Terry Fagan

Season Schedule

W.H.S.		Opponents
28	Shade Twp.	12
35	Altoona	6
48	Johnstown Catholic	0
12	Johnstown	6
60	Portage	13
41	Conemaugh Twp.	0
0	Adams Twp.	6
26	Punxsutawney	19
46	Somerset	13
46	Richland	0

Windber High School Football-1954

Row 1: A. Toth, M. Spinazzola, G. Winas, W. Bundy, W. Honadle, E. Miller, A. Hancharik, J. Hordubay, J. Kush, R. Dutzman E. Nelson, N. Beckey.
Row 2: C. Custer, G. Gahagan, G. Kondas, S. Beretsel, R. Seese, Richie DePolo, C. Finnegan, R. Zeigler, M. Salko, H. Klimek, C. Webb, T. DeMarco, A. Palumbo.
Row 3: G. Zack, J. Lewark, W. Hritz, J. Brutts, G. Pauley, E. Lashinsky, W. Smutko, H. Polasko, Robert DePolo, R. Polgar, C. DiGiulio, G. Warshel.
Row 4: Student Trainer-W. Foltz, F. Klemstine, L. Sherwin, E. Borischak, E. Sherlock, T. Panetti, G. D'Arcangelo, Student Manager-J. Danko.

1954   Head Coach: John Kawchak   Record: Wins 9   Losses 1

Season Schedule

	Offensive Starting Line-up	W.H.S.		Opponents
LE	Charles Finnegan			
LT	Joe Hordubay	33	Shade	0
LG	Gwynn "Gatch" Gahagen or Nick Becky	27	Altoona	21
C	Joe Kush	21	Northern Cambria	0
RG	Bob Dutzman	14	Johnstown	7
RT	George Kondas	49	Portage	13
RE	Bill Honadle or Bill Bundy	7	Conemaugh Twp.	21
QB	George Winas or Bob Ziegler	34	Adams Twp.	7
LH	Andy Hancharik	40	Punxsutawney	6
RH	Eugene Miller	7	Johnstown Catholic	2
FB	Roy "Pete" Seese or Richie DePolo	15	Pittsburgh North Catholic	14

Windber High School Football-1955

Row 1: C. Custer, Joe Brutts, R. Zeigler, Richie DePolo, R. Seese, C. Finnegan, Robert Brutts, S. Beretsel, G. Gahagen, W. Hritz.
Row 2: W. Smutko, J. Lewark, G. Zack, N. Zindash, E. Lashinsky, A. Palumbo, G. Warshel, Robert DePolo, H. Klimek, M. Salko, G. Kondas.
Row 3: G. Patrick, J. Borovicka, G. Pauley, H. Polasko, C. Webb, C. DiGiulio, S. Kurcis, F. Klemstine, A. Pekala, A. Gaunt.
Row 4: J. Kosturko, W. Walters, D. Dona, A. Talvalsky, J. Kotch, M. Hynick, R. Zvolerin.

1955   Head Coach: John Kawchak   Record: Wins 6   Losses 4

Season Schedule

	Offensive Starting Line-up	W.H.S.		Opponents
LE	Charles Finnegan			
LT	John Lewark	33	Shade	7
LG	Gwynn "Gatch" Gahagen	7	Altoona	25
C	Steve Beretsel	0	Har-Brack	8
RG	Joe Brutts	7	Johnstown	13
RT	George Kondas or Harold Klimek	19	Bradford	0
RE	Clarence Custer or Chuck Webb	6	Conemaugh Twp.	7
QB	Bob Ziegler	53	Adams Twp.	18
LH	Art Palumbo or Henry Polasko	33	Punxsutawney	7
RH	Richie DePolo	61	Johnstown Catholic	6
FB	Roy "Pete" Seese	49	Pittsburgh North Catholic	6

Windber High School Football-1956

Row 1: R. Vespa-Manager, F. Klemstine, S. Kurcis, N. Zindash, G. Pauley, E. Lashinsky, A. Palumbo, C. Webb, H. Polasko, J. Zack, C. DiGiulio, R. DePolo, H. Klimek, G. Sabo-Manager.
Row 2: J. Kosturko, A. Tavalsky, W. Walters, T. Klena, R. Zvolerin, G. Patrick, J. Borovicka, M. Hynick, J. Kotch, B. Seese, A. Pekela, D. Holt, J. Weaver, D. Dona.
Row 3: Asst. Coach-R. Younker, Trainer-A. Atty, J. Rakoczy, J. Kush, J. Bokinsky, G. Stone, T. Congersky, C. Shuster, C. DePolo, T. DePolo, G. Heeter, S. Kapash, R. Minitti, T. Marron, R. Dalimonte, G. Maruschock, J. Repko, J. Csordas, Head Coach-J. Kawchak.

1956   Head Coach: John Kawchak   Record: Wins 6   Losses 3

Offensive Starting Line-up

LE	Jerry Zack
LT	Carmen DiGiulio
LG	Ed Lashinsky
C	Gary Pauley
RG	Nick Zindash or Bob Zvolerin
RT	Harold "Carbide" Klimek
RE	Chuck Webb
QB	Don Dona
LH	Art Palumbo
RH	Henry Polasko or Bob DePolo
FB	Steve Kurcis

Season Schedule

W.H.S.		Opponents
21	Shade	0
0	Altoona	14
13	Har-Brack	0
0	Johnstown	13
47	Bradford	13
12	Conemaugh Twp.	7
39	Adams-Summerhill	0
0	Pittsburgh North Catholic	31
7	McKeesport	0

Windber High School Football-1957

Row 1: J. Weaver, R. Zvolerin, D. Dona, M. Hynick, G. Patrick, T. Klena, J. Kosturko, D. Holt, A. Tavalsky.
Row 2: A. Pekala, G. Heeter, R. Minitti, C. Shuster, T. Marron, J. Kush, C. DePolo, R. Dalimonte, W. Seese.
Row 3: J. Bokinsky, T. DePolo, J. Repko, T. Congersky, S. Kapash, G. Stone, J. Csordas, J. Boruch.
Row 4: T. Sherwin, J. Stopko, W. Benko, G. Roman, T. Heckler, J. Gavalak, R. Marfizo, A. Friday.
Row 5: R. Novak-Manager, W. Walters-Manager, D. Clement-Manager, P. Sherlock, J. Creek, T. Bossi, E. Hadix, P. Wozniak, D. Martell.
Row 6: Asst. Coach-R. Younker, Asst. Coach-J. Lochrie, Trainer-A. Atty, Head Coach-J. Kawchak.

1957   Head Coach: John Kawchak   Record: Wins 5   Losses 3

Season Schedule

Offensive Starting Line-up		W.H.S.		Opponents
LE	Al Tavalsky	38	Monessen	37
LT	Tom Klena or Steve Kapash	7	Altoona	19
LG	John Csordas	33	Har-Brack	6
C	Chuck Shuster or Mike Hynick	21	Johnstown	13
RG	Bob Zvolerin	13	Chambersburg	20
RT	Joe Kosturko	39	Bedford	7
RE	John Boruch	6	Indiana	14
QB	Bob Minitti	41	McKeesport	21
LH	Tom Marron			
RH	George Patrick			
FB	Don Dona			

Games with Adams Twp. and Conemaugh Twp. were cancelled.(Flu Outbreak)

Windber High School Football-1958

Row 1: G. Heeter, J. Repko, J. Kush, T. Congersky, J. Csordas, R. Minitti, C. Shuster.
Row 2: E. Hadix, T. Sherwin, J. Boruch, S. Kapash, R. Dalimonte, T. Marron, T. DePolo.
Row 3: P. Minitti, D. Martell, P. Wozniak, P. Sherlock, J. Gavalak, T. Bossi, J. Stopko.
Row 4: J. Kawchak-Head Coach, J. Danko, R. Oyler, R. Marfizio, J. Hromack, M. Seese, E. Salko, J. Creek, T. Heckler, Trainer-A. Atty.
Row 5: J. Lochrie-Asst. Coach, B. Langley, R. Fetchko, C. Koach, F. Koshinskie, D. Dunmire, J. Dailey, E. Balser, Asst. Coach-J. Flori.
Row 6: S. Studniary, R. Stawarz, J. Hancharik, B. Hostetler, J. Koshinskie, N. Crider, P. Piatek.
Row 7: R. Sendek-Manager, L. Sabo-Manager, J. Pachella, J. Berkey.

1958   Head Coach: John Kawchak   Record: Wins 6   Losses 3   Ties 1

Offensive Starting Line-up

LE	Steve Kapash
LT	Joe Kush
LG	John Csordas
C	Charles Shuster
RG	John Repko
RT	Tom Congersky
RE	John Boruch
QB	Bob Minitti
LH	Tom Marron
RH	Gene Heeter
FB	Tom Sherwin

Season Schedule

W.H.S.	Opponent	Opponents
40	Monessen	14
6	Altoona	20
40	Har-Brack	6
13	Johnstown	36
14	Chambersburg	12
32	Conemaugh Twp.	20
44	Blairsville	7
7	Pittsburgh North Catholic	7
25	Indiana	0
0	McKeesport	20

Windber High School Football-1959

Row 1: J. Stopko, P. Wozniak, J. Creek, J. Gavalak, J. Boruch, T. Sherwin, P. Sherlock, T. Bossi, E. Hadix, T. Heckler.
Row 2: S. Kush, P. Piatek, D. Martell, D. Dunmire, F. Koshinskie, A. Langley, R. Oyler, J. Hancharik, P. Minitti, T. Fetsko.
Row 3: R. Stawarz, P. Roscetti, W. Sharpe, L. Mayer, C. Koach, R. Seese, R. Fetchko, E. Salko, E. Buday, C. Mayer.
Row 4: T. King, J. Toth, W. Smith, G. Tobias, J. Koshinskie, J. Pachella, J. Danko, B. Blair, J. Dutzman.
Row 5: A. Pipon, J. DiGiacomo, J. McCuch, C. Farbo, J. Fagan, T. Chuhta, H. Pomroy, R. Rubal, R. Ence, J. Zepka.
Row 6: R. Obett-Manager, S. Zahurak-Manager, R. Wozny-Manager, J. Molnar-Manager.

1959   Head Coach: John Kawchak   Record: Wins 5   Losses 2   Ties 1

Offensive Starting Line-up

LE	Jack Creek
LT	Ed Hadix
LG	Robert Oyler
C	Tom Bossi
RG	Paul Wozniak
RT	Pat Sherlock
RE	John Boruch
QB	Terry Heckler
RH	Joe Gavalak
LH	Dave Dunmire
FB	Tom Sherwin

Season Schedule

W.H.S.		Opponents
31	Westinghouse	6
12	Altoona	27
21	Indiana	0
13	Johnstown	20
32	Chambersburg	7
39	Conemaugh Twp.	7
12	Pittsburgh North Catholic	12
20	McKeesport	7

Windber High School Football-1960

Row 1: W. Sharpe, B. Blair, R. Ence, J. Pachella, J. Danko, J. Zepka, G. Tobias, J. McCuch, J. Cassanese, T. Chuhta, J. Sekela, D. Renfroe, T. Fetsko, E. Buday.
Row 2: S. Kush, R. Seese, D. Dunmire, P. Roscetti, A. Langley, R. Stawarz, F. Koshinskie, R. Oyler, P. Piatek, R. Fetchko, J. Hancharick.
Row 3: M. Sherlock, J. Bartholomew, W. Smith, H. Pomroy, C. Farbo, M. Alexander, E. Salko, J. Fagan, R. Rubal, J. DiGiacomo, F. Gaio. **Absent:** C. Mayer.

1960   Head Coach: John Kawchak   Record: Wins 5   Losses 4

Offensive Starting Line-up

LE	Richard Fetchko or Edward Salko
LT	John Danko
LG	Robert Oyler
C	Frank Koshinskie
RG	Albert Langley or Robert Stawarz
RT	Paul Piatek
RE	Pete Roscetti
QB	Joseph Hancharick
LH	Dave Dunmire
RH	Pat Minitti
FB	Robert "Mick" Seese

Season Schedule

W.H.S.		Opponents
28	Washington	12
7	Altoona	6
27	Indiana	19
0	Johnstown	26
18	Chambersburg	35
41	Conemaugh Twp.	14
7	Pittsburgh North Catholic	34
20	Shade	6
19	McKeesport	55

Windber High School Football-1961

Row 1: J. Flori-Asst. Coach, D. Oldham, R. Ence, J. Makuch, J. Lucas, S. Kush, G. Tobias, W. Smith, D. Dona, J. DiGiacomo, Head Coach-J. Lochrie.
Row 2: P. Freeman-Asst. Coach, J. Zepka, T. High, J. Bartholomew, J. Fagan, R. Robertson, B. Hadix, M. Alexander, F. Gaio, C. Mayer, Trainer-W. Smutko.
Row 3: J. Cassanese, W. Zemcik, J. Lynch, T. Chuhta, T. Rosa, J. Piatek, R. Rubal, B. Blair, A. Liska.
Row 4: M. Pekala, N. LaPlaca, G. Smith, C. Farbo, E. Buday, J. Facciani, R. Hobba, R. Seese.
Row 5: Manager-R. Wozny, Manager-D. Zahurak.

1961   Head Coach: John Lochrie   Record: Wins 2   Losses 7

Offensive Starting Line-up

LE	Carl Mayer
LT	James Bartholomew
LG	Steve Kush
C	Ernest Buday
RG	Charles Farbo
RT	James Fagan
RE	Tom Rosa
QB	Tom Chuhta
LH	George Tobias
RH	Ron Rubal
FB	Joe Zepka

Season Schedule

W.H.S.		Opponents
6	Washington	34
25	Altoona	32
20	Indiana	12
0	Johnstown	40
31	Conemaugh Twp.	12
12	Chambersburg	14
6	Pittsburgh North Catholic	41
7	Fort Hill, Maryland	18
20	Bishop McDevitt	27

Windber High School Football-1962

Row 1: D. Reese, C. Creek, R. Lapinsky, T. Tobias, G. Smith, S. Wozny, A. Koposko, D. Berkey, T. Watyka, V. Palumbo.
Row 2: J. Venzon, R. Wargo, J. Cassanese, J. Piatek, R. Ripple, A. Liska, R. Hobba, J. Facciani, W. Zemcik.
Row 3: J. Lynch, T. Rosa, N. LaPlaca, T. High, M. Alexander, S. Hancharik, R. Roberson, R. Vitucci, M. Liska, J. Bartholomew. **Absent:** D. Oldham, B. Hadix.

1962   Head Coach: John Lochrie   Record   Wins 3   Losses 5   Ties 2

Offensive Starting Line-up

LE	Dale Oldham
LT	James Bartholomew
LG	Nick LaPlaca or Ron Vitucci
C	Joe Cassanese or Gary Smith
RG	Bernard Hadix or Tom High
RT	Mike Alexander or Allen Liska
RE	Tom Rosa or James Lynch
QB	Jerry Facciani
LH	Bill Zemcik
RH	John Piatek
FB	Dale Dona

Season Schedule

W.H.S.		Opponents
6	Redstone	6
12	Altoona	43
20	Indiana	6
0	Johnstown	25
6	Johnstown Catholic	32
13	Conemaugh Twp.	6
7	Laura Lamar	7
18	Chambersburg	14
0	Fort Hill, Maryland	20
8	Bishop McDevitt	20

Windber High School Football-1963

Row 1: Manager-M. Papinchak, A. Ochoa, C. Hissong, H. Landy, B. Hunter, M. Koshute, G. Mickey, M. Spisok, S. Pallo, Manager-R. Hromak.
Row 2: Head Coach-R. Younker, R. Kohler, S. Wozny, W. Zemcik, R. Hobba, J. Venzon, M. Liska, S. Hancharik, R. Roberson, T. Holsopple, R. Ripple, R. Vitucci, J. Facciani, Asst. Coach-J. Camut.
Row 3: Manager-G. Gogo, B. Haynes, B. Mash, C. Creek, T. Tobias, R. Wargo, S. Novak, G. Smith, M. Piatek, A. Koposko, V. Palumbo, T. Cannoni, R. Jubik, Manager-J. Molesky, Asst. Coach-D. Keenan.
Row 4: D. Mack, A. Spadone, S. Skowron, D. Alexander, D. Kinkella, J. Decewicz, S. Potochar, B. Alexander, T. Watyka, J. Delorie, J. DiGuilio.

1963   Head Coach: Ronald Younker   Record: Wins 2   Losses 8

Season Schedule

	Offensive Starting Line-up	W.H.S.		Opponents
LE	Carl Creek			
LT	Mike Liska or Dave Kinkella	12	Ferndale	14
LG	Steve Wozny or Ron Vitucci	0	Altoona	30
C	Gary Smith	20	Indiana	6
RG	Richard Wargo	0	Johnstown	28
RT	Steve Hancharik	6	Bishop McCort	33
RE	Steve Novak	0	Conemaugh Twp.	14
QB	Jerry Facciani	0	Chambersburg	20
HB	Tom Tobias or Bob Hobba	7	Pittsburgh North Catholic	35
HB	Bill Zemcik or Virgil Palumbo	0	Fort Hill, Maryland	41
FB	Anthony Koposko	28	Bishop Guilfoyle	14

Windber High School Football-1964

Row 1: V. Palumbo, M. Papinchak, C. Creek, J. DiGuilio, M. Liska, J. Venzon, T. Holsopple, M. Piatek, J. Delorie.
Row 2: Asst. Coach-J. Camut, A. Ochoa, J. Cannoni, B. Hunter, B. Alexander, S. Potochar, M. Koshute, D. Alexander, G. Mickey, J. Decewicz, Head Coach-R. Younker.
Row 3: Asst. Coach-P. DePolo, J. Elias, P. DeMarco, A. DeBiase, J. Zankey, H. Barnes, G. Kohler, P. Korhut, M. Blair, G. Grove, Asst. Coach-D. Keenan.
Row 4: C. Hissong, R. Shark, F. Atty, J. Kitcho, C. DiLoreto, S. Pallo, T. Mash, L. Hunter, A. Spadone.

1964   **Head Coach: Ronald Younker**   **Record:**   **Wins 7**   **Losses 3**

Season Schedule

	Offensive Starting Line-up	W.H.S.		Opponents
LE	Carl Creek			
LT	Mike Liska	20	Ferndale	6
LG	Stan Skowron or Mike Piatak	39	Bishop Guilfoyle	6
C	Greg Mickey	40	Indiana	13
RG	Tom Holsopple	7	Johnstown	14
RT	Joe Delorie	33	Bishop McCort	13
RE	Ron Vitucci	39	Conemaugh Twp.	6
QB	Steve Pallo or John Venzon	13	Chambersburg	34
HB	Bill Hunter	55	Corry	26
HB	Joe Decewicz	49	Fort Hill, Maryland	0
FB	Virgil Palumbo	13	Altoona	33

Windber High School Football-1965

Row 1: Stanley Potochar, R. Manippo, J. Patas, J. Zemcik, B. Portante, R. Shark, J. Elias, P. DeMarco, R. Mash, Manager-D. Wargo, Manager-M. Zarnesky.
Row 2: T. Mash, S. Pallo, C. Hissong, H. Landi, M. Koshute, J. Cannoni, R. Meek, J. Decewicz, Steve Potochar, B. Hunter, S. Skowron, A. Spadone, G. Mickey, A. Ochoa, Line Coach-J. Camut.
Row 3: Head Coach-R. Younker, F. LaPlaca, R. Weaver, R. Chuta, J. Swaynos, J. Kitcho, P. Korhut, T. Cover, G. Grove, L. Hunter, S. Vargo, P. Lochrie, D. D'Arcangelo, J. Young, Backfield Coach-P. DePolo.
Row 4: Trainer-W. Smutko, J. Koot, L. Durst, J. Zankey, Tim Voytko, L. Elias, G. Kohler, T. Berkey, K. Newcomer, L. Wissinger, R. Walko, M. Blair, H. Barnes, Tom Voytko, A. DeBiase, Line Coach-D. Keenan.

1965   Head Coach: Ronald Younker   Record: Wins 6   Losses 4

Season Schedule

	Offensive Starting Line-up	W.H.S.		Opponents
LE	Mike Koshute			
LT	August Spadone or Joe Cannoni	7	Punxsutawney	12
LG	Phil DeMarco	7	Bishop Guilfoyle	6
C	Greg Mickey	14	Indiana	7
RG	Stan Skowron	7	Johnstown	18
RT	Alfred Ochoa	14	Bishop McCort	7
RE	Steve Potochar	35	Conemaugh Twp.	20
QB	Steve Pallo	20	Westmont	2
HB	Bill Hunter	20	Cambria Heights	21
HB	Joe Decewicz	27	Fort Hill, Maryland	13
FB	Tom Mash	7	Altoona	54

Windber High School Football-1966

Row 1: R. Manippo-Manager, T. Papinchak, L. Koposko, T. Rizzo, R. Younker, B. Portante, Jim Zemcik, R. Zemcik, G. Skowron, J.Miller-Manager.
Row 2: C. Petrilla-Manager, D. Holtzman-Manager, R. Shark, P. DeMarco, J. Kitcho, G. Kohler, H. Barnes, M. Blair, F. LaPlaca, P. Korhut, G. Grove, D. Wargo-Manager.
Row 3: Asst. Coach-P. DePolo, Trainer-W. Smutko, G. Gerula, J. Baranik, A. LaMonaca, J. Elias, L. Hunter, D. D'Arcangelo, R. Mash, P. Lochrie, Asst. Coach C. Finnegan, Head Coach-R. Younker.
Row 4: R. Chuhta, L. Elias, T. Cover, T. Berkey, K. Newcomer, B. Walko, L. Wissinger, D. Barnes, J. Swaynos.

1966   Head Coach: Ronald Younker   Record: Wins 4   Losses 6

Offensive Starting Line-up

LE	Tom Berkey
LT	Mark Blair
LG	Phil DeMarco
C	Gary Grove
RG	Richard Shark
RT	Tom Cover or Ken Newcomer
RE	Larry Wissinger
QB	Ron Chuta
HB	Larry Hunter
HB	George Kohler or Bob Portante
FB	Tim Voytko

Season Schedule

W.H.S.		Opponents
6	Punxsutawney	12
20	Bishop Guilfoyle	19
14	Indiana	6
0	Johnstown	21
14	Bishop McCort	34
19	Conemaugh Twp.	0
13	Westmont	14
7	Cambria Heights	25
0	Lewistown	32
7	Altoona	52

Windber awarded forfeit win over Johnstown, player ineligible.

Windber High School Football-1967

Row 1: R. Chuhta, A. LaMonaca, L. Elias, M. Morgan, Tim Voytko, J. Swaynos, G. Baranik.
Row 2: T. Rizzo, J. Hodowanes, R. Mash, B. Portante, D. D'Arcangelo, R. Younker, P. Lochrie, J. Zemcik.
Row 3: D. Wargo-Manager, D. Barnes, Tom Voytko, T. Berkey, K. Newcomer, B. Walko, L. Wissinger, T. Cover, J. Miller-Manager.

Row 1: T. Blair, J. Cochran, F. Swiokla, T. Papinchak, S. Oyler, P. Stiffler, R. Pekala, P. Sambor.
Row 2: J. Zemcik, N. Costantino, R. Zemcik, S. Korhut, L. Marx, P. Mishko, J. Lashinsky, G. Skowron, A. Turk.
Row 3: B. Gasper-Manager, M. Soika, T. Elias, G. Gerula, L. Koposko, D. Hajnos, D. Shaffer, R. Ochoa, C. Petrilla.
Row 4: H. Swincinski, M. Potochar, N. DePolo, N. Mulcahy, S. Beechan, R. Radowski, E. Pruchnic, R. Koshinskie.

1967   Head Coach: Harold Price   Record: Wins 5   Losses 4   Ties 1

Season Schedule

Offensive Starting Line-up		W.H.S.		Opponents
LE	Bill Walko			
LT	Tom Cover	34	Homer City	13
LG	Pat Lochrie	10	Northern Cambria	6
C	Don Barnes	14	Indiana	21
RG	Jack Zemcik	7	Punxsutawney	7
RT	Larry Wissinger	19	Bishop McCort	14
RE	Tom Berkey	37	Conemaugh Twp.	0
QB	Ron Chuhta	0	Westmont	7
HB	Bob Portante	14	Cambria Heights	7
WB	Gary Baranik or Ron Mash	7	Lewistown	13
FB	Tim Voytko	0	Johnstown	13

Windber High School Football-1968

Row 1: P. Sambor, J. Durst, T. Papinchak, F. Swiokla, D. Hoffman, G. Thomas, J. DeBiase, S. Oyler, D. Weaver, R. Wojcicki, M. Petrilla.
Row 2: R. Ochoa, M. Soika, T. Elias, W. Walerysiak, G. Skowron, A. Turk, D. Hajnos, J. Zemcik, J. Cerwinsky, D. Shaffer, P. Stiffler.
Row 3: Manager-M. Gibson, Manager-D. Sepety, T. Rizzo, G. Gerula, G. Pruchnic, L. Marx, N. Costantino, J. Lashinsky, S. Korhut, P. Mishko, R. Zemcik, R. Younker, Manager-C. Petrilla, Manager-D. Wise.
Row 4: A. LaMonaca, R. Zepka, L. Newcomer, N. Mulcahy, M. Potochar, D. Barnes, S. Beechan, T. Slatcoff, R. Badowski, E. Battiste, L. Koposko.

1968   Head Coach: Harold Price   Record: Wins 2   Losses 7   Ties 1

Season Schedule

Offensive Starting Line-up

Pos	Player	W.H.S.	Opponents	
LE	Leo Koposko	7	Bishop Guilfoyle	19
LT	Norbert Mulcahy	20	Northern Cambria	20
LG	George Gerula	0	Indiana	13
C	Sam Beechan	6	Punxsutawney	39
RT	Greg Skowron	0	Somerset	6
RE	Gene Pruchnik	0	Conemaugh Twp.	20
QB	Jim Lashinsky	7	Westmont	6
HB	Nick Costantino	13	Cambria Heights	0
WB	Ron Zemcik	13	Forest Hills	14
FB	Tony Rizzo	6	Johnstown	40

Windber High School Football-1969

Row 1: M. Gibson-Manager, D. Sepety-Manager, M. Petrilla, J. Chliek, D. Furguiele, R. Ochoa, S. Oyler, G. Heinrich, D. Swincinski, R. Wojcicki, P. Sambor, M. Grieco, G. Lehman, D. Bencie, Manager-D. Wise, Manager-D. Berkey.
Row 2: R. Papinchak, R. Domonkos, D. Kebisek, D. Weaver, J. Badowski, S. Elias, D. Hoffman, D. Dembinsky R. DeBiase, G. Thomas, T. Wojcicki, B. Newcomer, J. Furmanchik, J. Chizmar.
Row 3: Head Coach-H. Price, Asst. Coach-E. Price, Manager-M. Portante, A. Turk, D. Ling, F. Swiokla, P. Stiffler, M. Thomas, P. Mishko, T. Herczegh, B. Ciotti, J. Lashinsky, J. Durst, J. Zemcik, D. Hoffer, M. Soika, Manager-S. Yuhas, Backfield Coach-R. Conway, Line Coach-M. Spinazzola.
Row 4: E. Hunt, M. Nagy, E. Battiste, S. Beechan, R. Badowski, L. Newcomer, N. Mulcahy, T. Slatcoff, R. Zepka, S. Korhut, D. Donato, W. Walerysiak.

1969   Head Coach: Harold Price   Record: Wins 9   Losses 1

Offensive Starting Line-up

LE	Steve Korhut
LT	Bob Badowski
LG	Jim Zemcik
C	Sam Beechan
RG	Steve Oyler
RT	Paul Stiffler
RE	Pete Misko
QB	Jim Lashinsky
HB	Richard Ochoa or Albert Turk
HB	Frank Swiokla
FB	Mike Soika

Season Schedule

W.H.S.		Opponents
12	Bishop Guilfoyle	8
22	Northern Cambria	0
7	Richland	19
12	Punxsutawney	7
26	Somerset	6
27	Conemaugh Twp.	21
20	Westmont	0
28	Cambria Heights	0
6	Forest Hills	0
6	Central Cambria	0

Windber High School Football-1970

Row 1: K. Sadveri, D. Bencie, M. Petrilla, D. Hoffman, R. Domonkas, D. Stiffler, V. Ochoa, G. Hajnos, M. Koshute.
Row 2: Manager-D. Sepety, G. Heinrich, G. Thomas, B. Stopko, J. Durst, B. Hoffer, D. Rizzo, M. Thompson, B. Newcomer, Manager-W. Noel.
Row 3: Asst. Coach-R. Conway, P. Crognale, W. Walerysiak, B. Garland, T. Slatcoff, S. Robatin, J. Barwatt, M. Badowski, J. Yasko, D. Ling, Manager-D. Berkey.

Row 1: Manager-M. Portante, D. Furgiele, J. Grieco, J. Dill, J. Chizmar, J. Furmanchik, D. Kebisek, J. Chliek, J. LaMonaca, Manager-D. Wise.
Row 2: S. Elias, D. Dembinsky, R. DeBiase, J. Grisin, M. Cannoni, B. Miller, J. Badowski, D. Weaver.
Row 3: Head Coach-Harold Price, T. Herczegh, B. Ciotti, E. Battiste, R. Zepka, L. Newcomer, M. Nagy, D. McCuch, T. Keim, Manager-S. Yuhas.

1970   Head Coach: Harold Price   Record: Wins 9   Losses 1

Pos	Player		W.H.S.	Season Schedule	Opponents
LE	Walt Walerysiak	**Offensive**			
LG	Dan Dembinsky	**Starting**	20	Bishop Guifoyle	14
C	Richard Zepka	**Line-up**	19	Northern Cambria	8
RG	Larry Newcomer		0	Richland	20
IT	Ed Battiste		27	Punxsutawney	16
OT	Mike Nagy		28	Somerset	9
RE	Greg Thomas		20	Conemaugh Twp.	8
QB	Tony Slatcoff		13	Westmont	12
HB	Jim Durst		20	Cambria Heights	0
HB	Matt Pertrilla		16	Forest Hills	6
FB	Dean Hoffman		6	Central Cambria	0

Windber High School Football-1971

Row 1: J. Pallo, K. Sadvari, J. Damico, S. Maystorovich, G. Soika, M. Weyant, D. Bencie, D. Kebisek, G. Hajnos, J. LaMonaca, A. Lapinsky, J. Furmanchik.
Row 2: Head Coach-H. Price, R. DeMarco, P. Crognale, B. Newcomer, G. Heinrich, T. Herczegh, B. DeBiase, J. Greico, R. Domonkos, J. Chliek, D. Rizzo, J. Chizmar, D. Stiffler, V. Ochoa, M. Koshute, J. Dill, Asst. Coach-M. Spinazzola.
Row 3: E. Price-Asst. Coach, M. Elias, B. Hoy, M. Cannoni, B. Hoffer, D. Ling, B. Ciotti, B. Garland, S. Robatin, J. Barwatt, A. Mulcahy, T. Keirn, J. Yasko, B. Miller, J. Grisin, M. Petrllia, M. Badowski, Asst. Coach-R. Conway.
Row 4: Manager-J. France, Manager-D. Berkey, J. Slatcoff, M. Bencie, G. DeBiase, M. Cocco, J. Hudack., D. Berkey, D. Pruchnik, B. Newcomer, J. Lapinsky, M. Thompson, S. Elias, R. Mucciola, Manager-W. Noel, Manager-D. Barzensky.

1971   Head Coach: Harold Price   Record: Wins 6   Losses 3   Ties 1

Offensive Starting Line-up

LE	Bill Garland
LT	John Grieco
LG	Robert DeBiase
C	Brad Ciotti
RG	John Chliek
RT	Terry Herczegh
RE	Bill Hoffer
QB	Dave Rizzo
HB	Greg Heinrich
HB	Donald Ling
FB	Dave Bencie

Season Schedule

W.H.S.		Opponents
7	Bishop Guilfoyle	6
26	Northern Cambria	20
13	Richland	18
18	Punxsatawney	14
6	Somerset	0
7	Conemaugh Twp.	18
7	Westmont	0
8	Cambria Heights	13
7	Forest Hills	0
6	Central Cambria	6

Windber High School Football-1972

Row 1: G. Soika, A. Lapinsky, J. Slatcoff, M. Badowski, J. Barwatt B. Garland, J. Yasko, M. Koshute, B. Feathers, C. Badowski.
Row 2: D. Rizzo, K. Berkey, D. Oatman, B. Clark, R. Livingston, F. Alt, R. Snyder, R. DeMarco, D. Stiffler, B. Moore, V. Ochoa, D. Mash, D. Domonkos, J. Ercole, V. Koshute, M. Weyant.

Row 1: J. LaMonaca, M. Cannoni, S, Robatin, J. Grisin, J. Dill.
Row 2: L. Moschgat, J. Lapinsky, M. Furda, D. Pruchnic, J. Creek, J. Pallo, R. Mucciola, M. LaMonaca.
Row 3: R. Patterson, J. Hudack, T. Battiste, D. Wright, D. Matta, M. Elias, M. Petrilla, F. Wozny.

1972   **Head Coach: Joe Flori**   **Record:**   **Wins 10**   **Losses 1**

Offensive Starting Line-up

LE	Bill Garland
LT	Steve Robatin or Mark Elias
LG	Jim Dill
C	Robert Mucciola
RG	Mike Cannoni or Jim LaMonaca
RT	Joe Grisin
RE	Joe Barwatt
QB	Dave Rizzo
HB	Dale Stiffler
HB	Victor Ochoa
FB	Joe Yasko

Season Schedule

W.H.S.	Opponent	Opponents
20	Bishop Guilfoyle	0
Win	Northern Cambria-Forfeit	0
20	Huntingdon	14
34	Richland	7
38	Punxsutawney	0
6	Somerset	0
0	Conemaugh Twp.	28
35	Westmont	14
39	Cambria Heights	6
19	Forest Hills	0
40	Central Cambria	6

Windber High School Football-1973

First Undefeated Team Since 1943

Row 1: V. Ferrante, D. Oatman, R. Cocco, S. Bencie, M. Furda, D. Koshute, N. Angelo, J. Campitelli, R. Chizmar, M. Shaffer, R. Frame.
Row 2: Manager-J. France, Manager-M. Cocco, L. Moschgat, R. Snyder, R. Livingston, D. Petrilla, D. Domonkos, C. Badowski, K. Brumbaugh, M. Weyant, J. Creek, V. Koshute, Manager-B. Barzensky, Manager-D. DiPaola.
Row 3: M. LaMonica, D. Mash, M. Elias, F. Alt, J. Slatcoff, G. Soika, S. Campitell, R. Patterson, A. Lapinsky, D. Pruchnic, T. Slatcoff.
Row 4: Asst. Coach-T. Voytko, Head Coach-J. Flori, J. Hudack, R. DeMarco, B. Clark, K. Berkey, T. Battiste, D. Wright, R. Moore, M. Petrilla, M. Sam, F. Wozny, R. Mucciola, C. Bowers, Asst. Coach-P. Pollino, Asst. Coach-J. Hancharick.

1973   Head Coach: Joe Flori   Record: Wins 10   Losses 0

First Undefeated Team Since 1943

	Offensive Starting Line-up
LE	Alex Lapinsky or George Soika
LT	Frank Wozny or Mark Elias
LG	Mark LaMonica
C	Robert Mucciola
RG	Dave Wright or Mike Furda
RT	James Hudack or Larry Moschgat
RE	Jeff Slatcoff
QB	Kevin Berkey
HB	Mike Weyant or Dave Oatman
HB	Ralph DeMarco
FB	Robert Moore or Mike Weyant

Season Schedule

W.H.S.		Opponents
19	Bishop Guilfoyle	0
40	Northern Cambria	0
33	Richland	6
27	Punxsutawney	12
19	Somerset	0
8	Conemaugh Twp.	0
40	Westmont	14
21	Bishop McCort	7
28	Forest Hills	0
33	Central Cambria	14

Windber High School Football-1974

Row 1: E. Petrilla, R. Palumbo, W. Koshute, V. Ferrante, R. Frame, J. Spencer, D. Oatman, J. Stossel, P. Katch.
Row 2: M. Furda, J. Creek, J. Campitelli, T. Harclerode, D. Koshute, K. Brumbaugh, V. Koshute, S. Bencie, R. Livingston, D. Petrilla, Manager-R. Shaffer.
Row 3: Head Coach-J. Flori, Asst. Coach-T. Voytko, Manager-J. Geiger, M. LaMonaca, G. Domonkos, V. Partsch, T. Slatcoff, J. Gentile, N. Angelo, R. Snyder, D. Domonkos, L. Moschgat, C. Badowski, Asst. Coaches: J. Hancharick and P. Pollino.
Row 4: R. Patterson, F. Alt, M. Sam, T. Battiste, D. Wright, R. Moore, F. Wozny, D. Mash, T. Keirn.

1974   Head Coach: Joe Flori   Record: Wins 8   Losses 2

Offensive Starting Line-up

LE	Frank Alt
LT	Frank Wozny or Larry Moschgat
LG	Mark LaMonaca
C	Jim Creek or Tony Battiste
RG	Richard Patterson
RT	Dave Wright or Mark Sam
RE	Mike Furda
QB	Dave Domonkos
HB	Bob Snyder
HB	Dave Oatman
FB	Robert Moore or Dennis Mash

Season Schedule

W.H.S.		Opponents
12	Johnstown Vo-Tech.	0
25	Northern Cambria	6
28	Richland	6
3	Punxsutawney	7
26	Somerset	6
20	Conemaugh Twp.	12
39	Westmont	28
34	Bishop McCort	6
7	Forest Hills	8
26	Central Cambria	6

Windber High School Football-1975

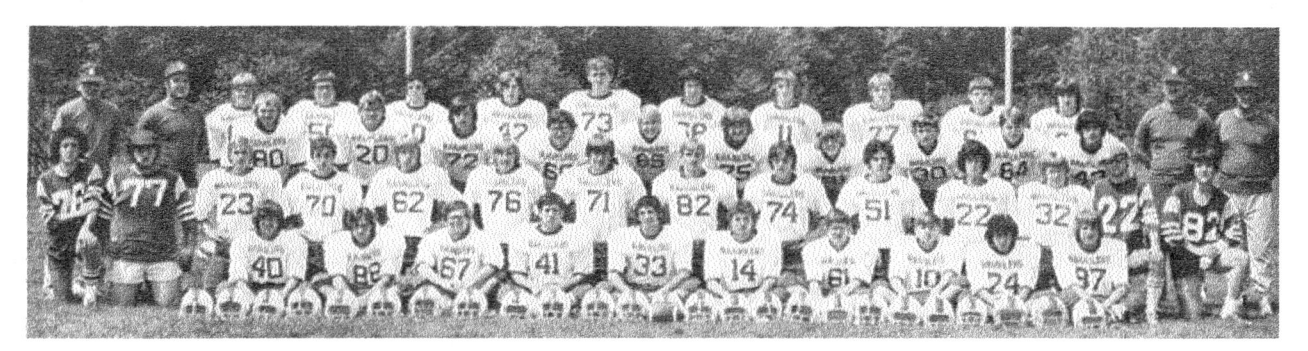

Row 1: Tony Ferrante, Gary Heinrich, Jim Stossel, Tony Costantino, Jim Finella, Ray Palumbo, Randy Frame, Dale Tomlinson, Mike Muscatello, Glenn Statler.
Row 2: Jim Byrne, Bryan McCuch, Ed Naugle, Bill Koshute, Bob Jacobs, Bob Phillips, David Wozny, Ken Martin, Ken Klonicke, Jim Gentile, Brett Shaffer, Paul Katch, Randy Livingston, Matt DiNinno.
Row 3: David Petrilla, Steve Bencie, Roy Oyler, Dan Koshute, Greg Domonkos, Chris Walerysiak, Jeff Spencer, Jim Campitelli, Ryan Frame, Vince Ferrante.
Row 4: Head Coach-Joe Flori, Asst. Coach-Tim Voytko, Keith Brumbaugh, Tom Slatcoff, Tom Harclerode, John Gentile, Bill Elko, Chuck Ozimok, Keith Danel, Tom Keirn, Victor Partsch, Nick Angelo, Asst. Coach-Joe Hancharick, Asst. Coach-Pat Pollino.

1975   **Head Coach: Joe Flori**   **Record:**   **Wins 5**   **Losses 5**

Offensive Starting Line-up

LE	Dave Petrilla
LT	Bill Elko or Chris Walerysiak
LG	Dan Koshute
C	Tom Slatcoff or Victor Partsch
RG	James Stossel or Randy Frame
RT	Tom Keirn
RE	Keith Brumbaugh
QB	Keith Danel or Ray Palumbo
HB	Nick Angelo or Vince Ferrante
HB	James Campitelli
FB	Steve Bencie

Season Schedule

W.H.S.		Opponents
27	Johnstown Vo-Tech.	7
7	Shady Side Academy	28
13	Richland	12
14	Bedford	42
12	Somerset	13
27	Conemaugh Twp.	0
13	Westmont	42
22	Bishop McCort	43
31	Forest Hills	14
13	North Star	12

Windber High School Football-1976

Row 1: Manager-Andy Mattis, Mike Muscatello, Mike Adore, Matt Pruchnik, Bill Tallyen, Jim Spinos. **Row 2:** Mark Berkey, Dale Tomlinson, Ray Palumbo, Dave Wozny, Jeff Oldham, Gary Berkey. **Row 3:** Matt DiNinno, Head Coach-Joe Flori, Jim Gentile, John Costa, Chris Walerysiak, Bob Jacobs, Rodger Shepko. **Row 4:** Bill Koshute, Greg Domonkos, Brian Petrilla, John Gentile, Bill Elko.

Row 1: M. Gyurik, J. Petrilla, P. Finella, P. Katch, T. Gill.
Row 2: M. Newcomer, K. Martin, T. Costantino, T. Ferrante, J. Stossel, W. Horner, C. Muscatello.
Row 3: R. Frame, J. Marko, R. Oyler, J. Holden, B. Patrick, E. Naugle, Asst. Coach-T. Voytko.
Row 4: D. Alt, T. Badowski, T. Keim, M. Paskovich, T. Harclerode, Asst. Coach-P. Pollino.

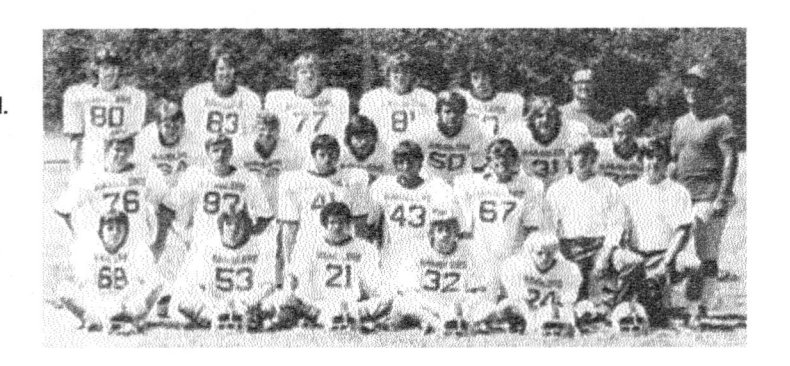

1976   Head Coach: Joe Flori   Record: Wins 7   Losses 2   Ties 1

Offensive Starting Line-up

LE	Greg Domonkos
LT	Roy Oyler or Chris Walerysiak
LG	Bill Elko
C	Dave Wozny
RG	James Stossel
RT	Tom Keirn
RE	Ken Martin or John Costa
QB	Ray Palumbo
HB	Paul Katch or Ed Naugle
HB	John Gentile or Tony Ferrante
FB	Blase Patrick or Tony Costantino

Season Schedule

W.H.S.		Opponents
17	Johnstown Vo-Tech.	6
27	Bishop Carroll	14
15	Richland	6
19	Bedford	16
9	Somerset	6
7	Conemaugh Twp.	6
12	Westmont	12
6	Bishop McCort	21
0	Forest Hills	12
35	North Star	6

Windber High School Football-1977

Row 1: Head Coach-J. Flori, D. Hutchison, J. Loffredo, G. Petrilla, P. Finella. **Row 2:** Asst. Coach-J. Hancharick, C. Muscatello, A. Constantino, D. Tomlinson, J. Petrilla, S. Constantino. **Row 3:** M. DiNinno, M. Weaver, J. Costa, R. Jacobs, J. Holden, R. Frame. **Row 4:** R. Shepko, B. Petrilla, J. Stopko, T. Badowski, D. Alt.

Row 1: J. Finella, T. Ferrante, M. Adore, T. Gill, A. Mattis, Asst. Coach-T. Voytko. **Row 2:** J. Spinos, M. Tewksbury, B. Tallyen, M. Pruchnic, M. Berkey, Asst. Coach-P. Pollino. **Row 3:** C. Walerysiak, J. Gentile, G. Berkey, K. Martin, W. Horner. **Row 4:** B. Elko, P. Gerula, B. Walko, M. Pascovich, D. Wozny.

1977   Head Coach: Joe Flori   **Record: Wins 7   Losses 3**

Offensive Starting Line-up

LE	John Costa
LT	Chris Walerysiak
LG	Bill Elko
C	Dave Wozny
RG	Bob Jacobs
RT	Ryan Frame
RE	Ken Martin
QB	Dale Tomlinson
HB	Jim Finella or Rodger Shepko
HB	Tony Ferrante
FB	Tony Constantino

Season Schedule

W.H.S.		Opponents
27	Johnstown Vo-Tech.	7
41	Bishop Carroll	13
15	Richland	19
21	Bedford	20
0	Somerset	27
42	Conemaugh Twp.	14
28	Westmont	13
7	Bishop McCort	14
20	Forest Hills	13
48	North Star	0

Windber High School Football-1978

Row 1: Head Coach-J. Flori, Tom Gill, Todd Hoffman, K. Martell, Pierre Finella, Gary Petrilla, John Swaynos, Robert Hegedus, Brian Crognale, Steve Costa, Matt Ferrante, Asst. Coach-Tim Voytko.
Row 2: Asst. Coach-Robert-Rullo, Robert Zabrucky, Steve Costantino, Matt Pruchnik, Bill Tallyen, M. Miele, Rich Rosa, Mike Adore, Mike Crum, Asst. Coach-Pat Pollino.
Row 3: Emil Petrilla, B. Siska, Gary Berkey, Mike Tewkesbury, Joe Loffredo, Wayne Webb, Rodger Shepko, Jim Spinos, Jeff Thomas, John Boyer, B. Szadvari.
Row 4: Wade Homer, Jeff Petrilla, Mark Weaver, Jeff Stopko, Pete Gerula, Robert Walko, Tom Badowski, Brian Petrilla, John Holden, Mike Pascovich, Dave Weaver.

1978   Head Coach: Joe Flori   Record: Wins 5   Losses 5

Offensive Starting Line-up

LE	Jim Spinos
LT	Brian Petrilla
LG	Gary Berkey
C	Jeff Petrilla
RG	Jeff Stopko
RT	Mike Adore or John Holden
RE	Tom Badowski
QB	Bill Tallyen
HB	Pierre Finella
HB	Rodger Shepko
FB	Matt Pruchnik

Season Schedule

W.H.S.		Opponents
35	Johnstown Vo-Tech.	12
14	Bishop Carroll	12
27	Richland	28
19	Bedford	13
6	Somerset	19
19	Conemaugh Twp.	28
30	Westmont	8
6	Bishop McCort	7
7	Forest Hills	24
46	North Star	24

Windber High School Football-1979

Row 1: Head Coach-Joe Flori, Wayne Webb, Bob Zabrucky, Joe Loffredo, Steve Costa, Gary Petrilla, Jeff Thomas, Kelly Rish.
Row 2: Mike Crum, Steve Costantino, Mark Weaver, Bob Walko, Jeff Stopko, Mike Tewksbury, John Boyer, Emil Petrilla, Asst. Coach-Robert Rullo.
Row 3: Paul Gentile, Matt Ferrante, John Wargo, Mike Csordas, Todd Hoffman, Bob Hegadus, John Swaynos, Doug Faith, Brian Crognale.
Row 4: Asst. Coach-Tim Voytko, Dave Weaver, John Sanow, Mark Paulochik, Tim Ishman, Tim Yesh, George Pipon, Jim Miller, Tony Williams, Rich Rosa.

1979   **Head Coach: Joe Flori**   **Record:**   **Wins 5**   **Losses 5**

Offensive Starting Line-up

LE	Pete Gerula or Kelly Risch
LT	Joe Loffredo
LG	Mike Tewksbury
C	Jeff Thomas
RG	Jeff Stopko
RT	Mark Weaver
RE	Bob Walko
QB	Bob Zabrucky
HB	Wayne Webb
HB	Gary Petrilla or Steve Costa
FB	Steve Costantino

Season Schedule

W.H.S.		Opponents
40	Johnstown Vo-Tech.	14
6	Bishop Carroll	13
25	Richland	6
0	Bedford	34
6	Somerset	20
20	Conemaugh Twp.	7
27	Westmont	13
0	Duquesne	34
19	Forest Hills	16
15	North Star	20

Windber High School Football-1980

Row 1: Jerry Simmers, Leroy Miller, Bob Cerwinsky, Joe Sutor, Kevin Koshute, Keith Koshute, Don Snoeberger, Pete Bartolomucci, James Harr, Paul Gentile.
Row 2: Vince George, Keith Charney, Harry Gosnell, Danny Webb, Darren Miller, Bob Hegedus, Tony Williams, John Boyer, Todd Hoffman, Tom Kohler, Dave Weaver.
Row 3: Head Coach-Joe Flori, Asst. Coach-Mike Furda, Mike Crum, Jim Miller, Ed. Marcinko, Emil Petrilla, Robert Vargo, Rob Dudinack, Rick Dudinack, Rich Rosa, Greg Jacobs, Doug Ledney, Asst. Coach-Robert Rullo.
Row 4: John Sanow, John Niovich, Rich Oldham, Kevin Charney, John Wargo, George Pipon, Doug Faith, Mike Sotosky, Tim Yesh, Dan Koot, Asst. Coach-Tim Voytko.

1980   Head Coach: Joe Flori   Record: Wins 0   Losses 10

Season Schedule

	Offensive Starting Line-up	**W.H.S.**		**Opponents**
LE	Tom Kohler or Doug Faith			
LT	Ed Marcinko	7	Johnstown Vo-Tech.	27
LG	Mike Crum	7	Bishop Carroll	28
C	Danny Koot	0	Richland	30
RG	Bob Hegedus	21	Bedford	38
RT	Rob Dudinak or Rick Dudinak	6	Somerset	34
RE	Dave Weaver	0	Conemaugh Twp.	6
QB	Todd Hoffman	14	Westmont	40
HB	Harry Gosnell	6	Central Cambria	34
HB	Paul Gentile or John Wargo	0	Forest Hills	38
FB	John Boyer or Dan Webb	20	North Star	42

Windber High School Football-1981

Row 1: Manager-Jim Mattis, Bob Burkett, Keith Will, Mark Kurcis, Keith Koshute, Brian Crognale, Pete Bartolomucci, Kevin Faith, Jeff Haman, Charley Block.
Row 2: Manager-Jerry Simmers, Jon Marhefka, Harry Gosnell, Danny Webb, Jim Harr, Brian Boyer, Don Snoeberger, Bob Hegedus, Bill Gearhart, Randy Jurich, Dave Gentile, Manager-Rick Manges.
Row 3: Kevin Koshute, Joe Teklinsky, Paul Gentile, Bob Vargo, Mike Sotosky, Darrell Datko, Greg Jacobs, Mike Spinnazola, Doug Ledney, Scott Newcomer.
Row 4: Jason Durst, Joe Shenego, George Pipon, Tony Williams, Ed. Marcinko, Emil Petrilla, Doug Faith, Kevin Griffin, John Wozny, Rick Dudinack, John Wargo, Marty Patterson, Kevin Charney, John Sanow, Rich Oldham, Keith Charney, John Niovich, Danny Koot.

1981   Head Coach: Bill Smutko   Record: Wins 4   Losses 6

Offensive Starting Line-up
LE	Doug Faith
LT	Greg Jacobs
LG	Pete Bartolomucci
C	Danny Koot
RG	Bob Hegedus
RT	Ed Marcinko or John Niovich
RE	George Pipon
QB	John Sanow
HB	Harry Gosnell
HB	Paul Gentile or John Wargo
FB	Dan Webb

Season Schedule
W.H.S.		Opponents
27	Johnstown Vo-Tech.	14
23	Bishop Carroll	0
7	Richland	6
12	Bedford	13
7	Somerset	26
14	Conemaugh Twp.	21
6	Westmont	24
14	Central Cambria	30
6	Forest Hills	40
8	North Star	6

Defensive Starting Line-up
LE	Doug Faith
T	Greg Jacobs
G	Pete Bartolomucci or Brian Crognale
G	John Niovich
T	Ed Marcinko
RE	Rick Dudinack
LB	Don Snoeberger
LB	Bob Hegedus
HB	Paul Gentile
HB	John Wargo
HB	George Pipon

Windber High School Football-1982

Row 1: Dave Gentile, Doug Ledney, Dan Koot, Rick Dudinack.
Row 2: Steve Strayer, Bob Cerwinsky, Ted Thomas, Mark Kurcis, Keith Will, Bob Burkett, Chris Fisher, Charlie Block.
Row 3: Brian Boyer, Kevin Koshute, Danny Webb, Mike Maluchnik, Don Snoeberger, Harry Gosnell, Keith Koshute, Dave Burkett, John Horner.
Row 4: Joe Tessari, Bill Gearhart, Mike Spinazzola, Joe Teklinsky, Greg Jacobs, Jeff Haman, Scott Newcomer.
Row 5: Ed Marcinko, John Niovich, Keith Charney, Kevin Charney, Rich Oldham, Marty Patterson.

1982   Head Coach: Bill Smutko   Record: Wins 3   Losses 7

Offensive Starting Line-up
LE	Rich Oldham
LT	Greg Jacobs
LG	Mike Spinazzola
C	Danny Koot
RG	Rick Dudinack
RT	Ed Marcinko
RE	Keith Charney or Doug Ledney
QB	Kevin Charney
HB	Harry Gosnell
HB	Keith Koshute
FB	Dan Webb

Season Schedule
W.H.S.		Opponents
21	Johnstown Vo-Tech.	8
14	Johnstown	21
16	Richland	14
6	Bedford	26
0	Somerset	19
15	Conemaugh Twp.	12
0	Westmont	48
0	Central Cambria	14
0	Forest Hills	23
16	North Star	26

Defensive Starting Line-up
T	Charles Block
G	Joe Tessari
G	Joe Teklinsky
LE	Marty Patterson
LB	Don Snoebeger
LB	John Niovich
HB	Bill Gearhart
HB	Jeff Haman
HB	Kevin Koshute
HB	Keith Will
S	Bob Burkett

Windber High School Football-1983

Row 1: Chris Coat, Brian Buchkovich, Dave Toma, Curt Manges, Eric Whetzel, David Sotosky, Ken Lute.
Row 2: Asst. Coach-Ralph DeMarco, Chris Blough, Steve Strayer, Keith Will, Bob Burkett, Louie Pierce, Jim Spinos, Bill Wargo, Tony Campitell, Asst. Coach-Phil DeMarco, Brian Felski.
Row 3: Manager-David Campitell, Manager-Joe Sepp, Mike Seger, Brian Boyer, Joe Teklinsky, Matt Maruschok, Scott Newcomer, Joe Tessari, Ted Thomas, Mike Maluchnik, Bill Gearhart, Ed Damico.
Row 4: Asst. Coach-Ray Conway, Asst. Coach-Mike Spinazzola, Dave Burkett, Mark Kurcis, John Horner, Kevin Griffin, Marty Patterson, Dave Gentile, Jeff Haman, Steve Chizmar, Head Coach-Ed Price.

1983   Head Coach: Ed Price   Record: Wins 1   Losses 9

Offensive Starting Line-up

LE	Marty Patterson or Mike Maluchnik
LT	Kevin Griffin
LG	Brian Boyer
C	Joe Tessari
RG	Scott Newcomer
RT	Ted Thomas or Matt Maruschok
RE	Dave Gentile
QB	Jeff Haman
HB	Keith Will
HB	Steve Strayer or Bill Gearhart
FB	Joe Teklinsky

Season Schedule

W.H.S.		Opponents
0	Johnstown Vo-Tech.	6
0	Conemaugh Valley	7
0	Richland	15
6	Bedford	53
6	Somerset	10
0	Conemaugh Twp.	28
6	Westmont	14
6	Central Cambria	24
0	Forest Hills	12
33	North Star	6

Windber High School Football-1984

Row 1: Manager-David Campitell, Erik Whetzel, Steve Strayer, Ken Lute, Steve Chizmar, Brian Costa, Josh. Puricelli, Ted Thomas, Manager-Ed Nelson.
Row 2: Don Koshute, Dave Toma, Louie Pierce, Jim Spinos, Eugene Phillips, Curt Manges.
Row 3: Bob Wagner, Todd Thomas, Larry Betcher, Richard Feldbauer, Larry Becker, Mike Betcher, Arron Shawley.
Row 4: Asst. Coach-Carl Mayer, Matt Maruschok, Gene Mattis, Benno DeLuca, Joe Ondesko, Tom Williams, Joe Tessari, Asst. Coach-Mike Spinazzola.
Row 5: Head Coach-Ed Price, Tony Campitell, Dave Sotosky, John Horner, Paul Romanchok, Chris Coat, Jason Durst-Trainer. **Missing:** Chris Blough, Dave Burkett, Nick Enoch, Asst. Coach-Ray. Conway.

1984   Head Coach: Ed Price   Record: Wins 1   Losses 10

Offensive Starting Line-up
LE	Joe Onderko
LT	Larry Betcher
LG	Ted Thomas or Chris Blough
C	Joe Tessari
RG	Gene Mattis or Matt Maruschok
RT	Tom Williams
RE	Curt Manges
QB	John Horner
HB	Steve Strayer or Eugene Phillips
HB	Benno Deluca
FB	Tony Campitell

Season Schedule

W.H.S.		Opponents
6	Meyersdale	14
0	Conemaugh Valley	40
14	Richland	32
6	Bedford	32
0	Somerset	27
12	Conemaugh Twp.	50
26	Westmont	56
6	Central Cambria	48
0	Forest Hills	35
3	North Star	0
8	Johnstown Vo-Tech.	14

Defensive Starting Line-up
LE	Gene Mattis
LT	Ted Thomas
LG	Joe Tessari
RG	Tom Williams
RT	Larry Betcher
RE	Dave Burkett
LB	Tony Campitell or Chris Blough
LB	Benno DeLuca
HB	Curt Manges
HB	Dave Toma or Don Koshute
S	Steve Strayer or Erik Whetzel

Windber High School Football-1985

Row 1: G. Gaye, A. Shawley, J. Heinrich, L. Hoffman, J. Russo, S. Wright, D. Toma, M. Betcher, R. Kaniuk, R. Keyser, M. Maurizio, R. Wagner.
Row 2: M. Grohal, L. Becker, M. Dzurko, E. Shaffer, J. Hicks, L. Koharchik, J. Hancharik, T. Piscitella, D. Webb, R. Kukenberger, S. Amann.
Row 3: Mgr.-C. Gaye, D. Koshute, J. Boyer, B. Costa, J. Jarvis, M. Allison, K. Lute, S. Chizmar, C. Manges, J. Lewark, G. Burke.
Row 4: J. Spinos, V. Palumbo, J. Fuschino, J. Decker, S. Penrod, E. Whetzel, T. Petrilla, F. Blair, G. Burke, N. Enoch, Mgr.-J. Sepp.
Row 5: L. Betcher, B. Gearhart, R. Feldbauer, T. Campitell, S. Paczek, P. Romanchok, D. Sotosky, S. Lute, C. Coat, J. Drzewiecki, L. Pierce.

1985   Head Coach: Phil DeMarco   Record: Wins 4   Losses 7

Offensive Starting Line-up

SE	Brian Costa
LT	Mike Betcher or Jay Hicks
LG	Ken Lute
C	Jim Spinos
RG	Lou Pierce
RT	Larry Betcher
TE	Tony Campitell
FL	Curt Manges
QB	Paul Romanchock
HB	Don Koshute
HB	Larry Becker

Season Schedule

W.H.S.		Opponents
7	Meyersdale	22
19	Berlin	16
6	Richland	20
12	Bedford	37
20	Somerset	28
6	Conemaugh Twp.	20
13	Westmont	18
20	Central Cambria	14
0	Forest Hills	30
14	North Star	0
26	Johnstown Vo-Tech.	7

Defensive Starting Line-up

LE	Larry Betcher
LT	Mike Betcher
RT	Lou Pierce
RE	Steve Chizmar
LB	Brian Costa
LB	Tony Campitell
LB	Ken Lute
C	Erik Whetzel
C	Dave Toma
SS	Don Koshute
FS	Curt Manges

Windber High School Football-1986

Row 1: P. Hoffer, C. Yonish, B. Wagner, B. Hostetler, M. Walerysiak, S. Pruchnic, J. Heinrich, D. Ondesko.
Row 2: Mgr.-Joe Hicks, J. Oyler, A Madoskey, R. Cameron, Gary Burke, R. Elliot, M. Corle, Mgr.-M. Campitell.
Row 3: B. Meyers, D. Kreinbrook, J. Lewark, P. Buza, T. Piscitella, D. Koshute, J. DePolo, J. Hancharick, Jay Hicks, M. Betcher.
Row 4: M. Dzurko, J. Fuschino, J. Russo, D. Webb, J. Foster, S. Wright, S. Penrod, D. Adamczyk, V. Palumbo, Greg Burke, M. Facciani.
Row 5: B. Costa, J. Jarvis, B. Horner, B. Gearhart, P. Romanchock, S. Lute, B. Gephart, J. Drzewiecki, F. Blair, M. Grohal.

1986   Head Coach: Phil DeMarco   Record: Wins 9   Losses 1   Ties 1

Offensive Starting Line-up
SE   Brian Costa
LT   John Drzewiecki
LG   Mike Betcher
C   Joe Hancharick
RG   Frank Blair
RT   Jay Hicks or
     Matt Grohal
TE   Brian Gearhart
FL   Joe Russo or
     Bob Wagner
QB   Paul Romanchock
HB   Don Koshute
HB   Virg Palumbo

Season Schedule

W.H.S.		Opponents
20	Meyersdale	14
30	Berlin	14
14	Richland	7
35	North Star	0
34	Everett	12
49	Conemaugh Twp.	22
28	Westmont	28
42	Northern Maryland	0
46	Chestnut Ridge	22
42	Williamsburg	13

Defensive Starting Line-up
LB   Greg Burke
LT   John Drzewiecki
LG   Frank Blair
RG   Scott Wright
RT   Jay Hicks
LB   Don Koshute
LB   Mike Betcher
LB   Virg Palumbo
HB   Brian Gearhart
S   Paul Romanchock or
     Brian Horner
HB   Brian Costa or
     Bob Wagner

District 5 Championship Windber 34   Bedford 36

Windber High School Football-1987

Row 1: J. Heinrich, P. Hoffer, C. Palumbo, E. Gosnell, A. Kostick, A. Pierce, J. Wargo, K. Damico, J. Prince.
Row 2: Greg Burke, V. Palumbo, S. Wright, J. Suto, E. Romanchock, Gary Burke, D. Webb, A. Madosky, T. Negrey.
Row 3: B. Toomey, R. Cameron, J. Fuschino, J. Hicks, D. Adamczyk, S. Pruchnic, M. Hess, M. Dzurko, R. Elliot, M. Corle.
Row 4: B. Hostetler, J. Oyler, N. Fraska, M. Facciani, J. Russo, D. Ondesko, K. Halaburda, M. Walerysiak, B. Burkett.
Row 5: J. Hancharick, J. Foster, M. Grohal, B. Gearhart, B. Horner, B. Gephart, S. Lute, J. Drzewiecki, F. Blair, J. Lewark.
Row 6: S. Penrod, T. Piscitella, D. Kreinbrook, M. Penrose, J. Jarvis, P. Buza, M. Gray, J. DePolo, J. Panetti.

1987   Head Coach: Phil DeMarco   Record: Wins 6   Losses 4

Offensive Starting Line-up
WR	Gary Burke
LT	John Drzewiecki
LG	Jim Jarvis
C	Joe Hancharick
RG	Frank Blair
RT	Matt Grohal
TE	Brian Gearhart or S. Penrod
WR	Joe Russo or John Fuschino
QB	Brian Horner
RB	Virg Palumbo
RB	Greg Burke

Season Schedule

W.H.S.		Opponents
20	Meyersdale	0
12	Berlin	28
26	Richland	6
27	North Star	0
26	Everett	0
54	Conemaugh Twp.	0
6	Westmont	13
17	Weirton Madonna, WVa.	20
7	Chestnut Ridge	20
31	Williamsbburg	18

Defensive Starting Line-up
DL	Frank Blair
DL	John Drzewiecki
DL	Matt Grohal
DL	Jay Hicks
LB	Doug Webb
LB	Scott Wright
LB	Virg Palumbo
DB	Gary Burke
DB	Mike Dzurko
DB	Greg Burke
DB	John Fuschino or Joe Russo

Windber High School Football-1988

Row 1: Mgr.-Mike Corle, E. Gosnell, K. Damico, M. Kozar, A. Kostick, J. Wargo, C. Palumbo, Mgr.-Jim Prince.
Row 2: Asst. Coach-S. Pallo, K.Ott, A. Pierce, P. Hoffer, B. Hostetler, M. Walerysiak, B. Kaniuk, T. Dzurko, R. Tallion.
Row 3: D. Thacher, J. Oyler, R. Quinn, N. Fraska, D. Wagner, K. Halaburda, D. Ondesko, B. Burkett, J. Rhodes.
Row 4: Head Coach-P. DeMarco, C. Risch, J. Suto, R. Cameron, R. Elliot, J. Panetti, M. Moore, E. Romanchock, B. Toomey, D. Adamczyk, M. Facciani, Asst. Coach-Jeff Slatcoff.
Row 5: Asst. Coach-R. DeMarco, J. DePolo, S. Pruchnic, D. Kreinbrook, J. Foster, B. Horner, B. Gephart, M. Gray, P. Buza, M. Penrose, Asst. Coach-N. Williams.

1988   Head Coach: Phil DeMarco   Record: Wins: 2   Losses 8

Offensive Starting Line-up
WR	Jason DePolo
WR	Rick Elliot or Dave Ondesko
OL	Jim Foster
OL	Bo Toomey
OL	David Kreinbrook
OL	Sean Pruchnic
OL	Bill Gephart or Kevin Halaburda
TE	Jason Oyler
QB	Brian Horner
RB	Mike Facciani
RB	Ed Gosnell or Chris Palumbo

Season Schedule
W.H.S.	Opponents	
6	Blairsville	7
30	Saltsburg	0
14	Richland	17
14	Conemaugh Twp.	25
6	Shade	8
7	North Star	26
6	Berlin	16
14	Meyersdale	0
19	Chestnut Ridge	20
14	Portage	21

Defensive Starting Line-up
DL	Jamie Wargo
DL	David Thacker or Jim Foster
LB	John Panetti
LB	Jason Oyler or Bo Toomey
LB	Matt Penrose
DB	Barry Hostetler or Ed Gosnell
DB	Rick Elliott or Matt Walerysiak
DB	Brian Horner or David Ondesko

Windber High School Football-1989

Row 1: C. McMullin, C. Marsh, J. Wargo, J. Hicks, R. Tallion, E. Gosnell, C. Palumbo, D. Senior.
Row 2: Asst. Coach-S. Pallo, P. Mulcahy, D. Prince, J. Oyler, K. Damico, B. Kaniuk, A. Kostick, A. Pierce, S. Nihoff, C. Gaye, R. Pruchnic, Asst. Coach-Jeff Slatcoff.
Row 3: Head Coach-P. DeMarco, M. Kosar, D. Barnes, K. Ott, N. Fraska, G. Walko, E. Penrod, J. McDonald, B. Drzewiecki, E. Badowski, D. Thacker, T. Dzurko, Asst. Coach-R. DeMarco.
Row 4: B. Quinn, J. Suto, J. Panetti, T. Toomey, M. Moore, E. Romanchock, M. Gray, M. Penrose, J. Rhodes, D. Wagner, C. Risch, K. Halaburda.

1989   Head Coach: Phil DeMarco   Record: Win 8   Losses 2   Ties 1

Offensive Starting Line-up
- WR Matt Penrose or Kevin Damico
- LT Joe Suto or Jamie Rhodes
- LG Bo Toomey
- C   Jamie Wargo
- RG Art Pierce or Matt Gray
- RT Kevin Halaburda
- TE Eric Romanchock
- QB John Panetti
- RB Ed Gosnell
- FB Bryan Kaniuk or Tim Dzurko
- RB Chris Palumbo

Season Schedule

W.H.S.		Opponents
19	Ferndale	6
14	Berlin	6
26	Richland	6
14	North Star	0
21	Marion Center	14
51	Conemaugh Twp.	0
0	Shade	10
7	Meyersdale	7
19	Chestnut Ridge	20
21	Portage	0

District 5 "A" Championship
Windber 23   Meyersdale 19

Defensive Starting Line-up
- DL Kevin Halaburda
- DL David Thacker
- DL Jamie Wargo
- LB John Panetti
- MLB Matt Penrose
- LB Bo Toomey
- C   Kevin Damico or Ryan Pruchnic
- SS Matt Kozar
- FS Nick Fraska or Bryan Kaniuk
- C   Ed Gosnell or Alex Kostick

Windber High School Football-1990

Row 1: N. Matera, C. Marsh, R. Tallion, E. Potts, T. Rasko, S. Rummel, T. Vatavuk, J. Hicks, D. Senior.
Row 2: Asst. Coach-S. Pallo, J. Oyler, J. Ott, T. Dzurko, D. Prince, D. Barnes, R. Hancharick, R. Pruchnic, S. Nihoff, M. Kozar, S. Birtle, Asst. Coach-J. Slatcoff.
Row 3: Head Coach-P. DeMarco, K. Ott, J. Figard, R. Jacobs, P. Gray, G. Walko, C. Risch, B. Badowski, E. Heinrich, C. Gaye, J. Madosky, D. Thacker, Asst. Coach-R. DeMarco.
Row 4: D. Marx, R. Rummel, S. Lybarger, E. Penrod, J. Czinka, M. Moore, D. Wagner, J. McDonald, B. Quinn.

1990   Head Coach: Phil DeMarco   Record: Wins 3   Losses 7

Offensive Starting Line-up

TE	Bob Badowski
LT	Bob Quinn
LG	Chad Risch
C	Eric Penrod
RG	Kevin Ott
RT	Jamie Rhodes
WB	Matt Kozar
QB	Mike Moore
FB	Tim Dzurko
RB	Cory Marsh
RB	Joe Hicks

Season Schedule

W.H.S		Opponents
0	Homer Center	21
14	Berlin	8
7	Richland	20
7	North Star	16
12	Marion Center	13
13	Conemaugh Twp.	28
13	Shade	10
18	Meyersdale	26
15	Chestnut Ridge	22
19	Portage	8

Defensive Starting Line-up

DL	Bob Quinn
DL	Jamie Rhodes
DL	Cory Gaye
DL	Dan Marx
LB	Kevin Ott
LB	Tim Dzurko
LB	Chad Risch
C	Ryan Pruchnic
C	Matt Kozar
S	Mike Moore
S	Ron Tallion

Windber High School Football-1991

Row 1: M. Sendek, B. George, D. Senior, S. Rummel, T. Rasko, T. Vatavuk, J. Hicks, C. Marsh, C. Titus, Manager-J. Gartland.
Row 2: Asst. Coach-S. Pallo, E. Potts, V. Brunetto, J. Oyler, J. Grillo, J. Shuster, J. Jablon, R. Pruchnic, S. Nihoff, T. Bonitz, J. Madoskey, Asst. Coach-J. Slatcoff.
Row 3: Head Coach-P. DeMarco, J. Ott, R. Hancharick, S. Mock, D. Prince, B. Badowski, C. Gaye, D. Barnes, B. Russo, B. Custer, S. Birtle, Asst. Coach-R. DeMarco.
Row 4: J. Quinn, M. Louchart, P. Gray, J. Figard, J. McDonald, J. Czinka, E. Penrod, S. Lybarger, G. Walko, E. Heinrich, R. Jacobs, M. Adamczyk.

1991   Head Coach: Phil DeMarco   Record: Wins 5   Losses 4   Ties 1

Offensive Starting Line-up

TE	Bob Badowski
LT	John McDonald
LG	Derek Barnes
C	Eric Penrod
RG	Dan Prince or Pat Gray
RT	Cory Gaye
WR	Jarod Oyler or Ryan Pruchnic
QB	Scott Lybarger
HB	Duane Senior
FB	Jason Ott or Joe Hicks
HB	Cory Marsh
Punter-Scott Lybarger	

Season Schedule

W.H.S	Opponents	
34	Bishop Carroll	7
14	Berlin	20
7	Richland	21
7	North Star	6
6	United	7
7	Conemaugh Twp.	7
28	Shade	7
27	Meyersdale	22
26	Chestnut Ridge	35
8	Portage	0

Defensive Starting Line-up

DT	John McDonald
DT	Eric Penrod
NG	Pat Gray
LB	Bob Badowski
LB	Scott Birtle
LB	Jarod Oyler
LB	Jason Ott
C	Duane Senior
C	Joe Hicks
SS	Shawn Nihoff
FS	Ryan Pruchnic
Kicker-John McDonald	

Windber High School Football-1992

Row 1: R. Ott, N. Vatavuk, T. Dolan, B. Minor, L. Blough, B. Gerula, J. Franko, M. Sendek, J. Banjak, D. Wargo, M. Russo.
Row 2: Asst. Coach-B. Gennett, C. Titus, T. Richards, N. Kiss, E. Potts, D. Hechler, S. Birtle, S. Rummel, H. Barnes, B. Mock, J. Gartland, Asst. Coach-J. Slatcoff.
Row 3: Head Coach-P. DeMarco, T. Vatavuk, D. Gephart, N. Gray, J. Jablon, P. Gray, O. Fermariello, J. Shuster, T. Bonitz, T. Rasko, E. Korhut, Asst. Coach-R. DeMarco.
Row 4: M. Louchart, J. Grillo, R. Hancharick, J. Ott, M. Miranda, B. Custer, J. Gutteridge, J. Madoskey, J. Figard, B. Russo.
Row 5: M. Thomas, S. Mock, E. Heinrich, C. Hanik, J. Czinka, A. Korhut, S. Lybarger, M. Adamczyk, J. Quinn.

1992   Head Coach: Philip DeMarco   Record: Wins 8   Losses 2

Offensive Starting Line-up
TE	Scott Birtle
LT	Ernie Heinrich
LG	Pat Gray
C	Rob Hancharick
RG	Scott Rummel
RT	Joe Quinn
SE	Todd Rasko
QB	Scott Lybarger
HB	Tim Vatavuk
FB	Jason Ott
HB	Joe Madoskey

Season Schedule
W.H.S		Opponents
20	Bishop Carroll	0
28	Berlin	13
21	Richland	0
28	North Star	0
15	United	22
21	Conemaugh Twp.	6
28	Shade	6
21	Meyersdale	7
21	Chestnut Ridge	22
28	Portage	6

Defensive Starting Line-up
DT	Erinie Heinrich
DT	Rob Hancharick
MG	Pat Gray
DE	Jason Ott
DE	Joe Madoskey
LB	Scott Birtle
LB	Barry Russo
LB	Jeff Shuster
DB	Jake Grillo
DB	Mike Louchart
DB	Todd Rasko

Appalachian Conference Section III Champions
Somerset County Champions

Windber High School Football-1993

Row 1: D. Kohler, D. Wargo, N. Vatavuk, G. Turner, J. Banjak, T. Dolan, M. Russo, J. Beabes, R. Ott, D. Chippie.
Row 2: M. Sendek, B. Stiffler, J. Franko, R. Natta, T. DiPaola, L. Blough, N. Kiss, J. Claar, B. Gerula, E. Korhut, R. George, B. Minor.
Row 3: Head Coach-P. DeMarco, M. DeBiase, B. Mock, H. Barnes, J. Shuster, J. Grillo, M. Louchart, N. Davis, M. Pekala, D. Rininger, B. Russo, J. Jablon, T. Bonitz, Asst. Coach-C. Gunby, Asst. Coach-B. Gennett.
Row 4: Asst. Coach-R. DeMarco, J. Figard, N. Gray, S. Mock, J. Quinn, T. Hanik, A. Korhut, C. Hanik, M. Adamczyk, D. Dzurko, M. Thomas, D. Gephart, C. Romani, Asst. Coach-J. Slatcoff.

1993   Head Coach: Phil DeMarco   Record: Wins 7   Losses 3   Ties 1

Offensive Starting Line-up

TE	Jason Jablon or Barry Russo
LT	Aaron Korhut or Lenny Blough
LG	Todd Bonitz or Justin Banjak
C	Mike Sendek
RG	Matt Adamczyk or Brian Mock
RT	Joe Quinn
WR	Chip Hanik or Tony DiPaola
QB	Mike Louchart
RB	Brad Minor
RB	Randy Ott
FB	Jake Grillo

Season Schedule

W.H.S		Opponents
28	Berlin	0
48	Shade	0
7	Conemaugh Twp.	12
48	North Star	6
20	Blacklick Valley	0
6	Conemaugh Valley	9
14	Meyersdale	6
40	Ferndale	7
22	Portage	12
14	Marion Center	14

Defensive Starting Line-up

DT	Joe Quinn
DT	Shannon Mock
DG	Mike Russo
DG	Brian Mock
DE	Chip Hanik
DE	Jason Jablon or Mike Thomas
LB	Barry Russo
LB	Jeff Shuster
C	Nate Gray
C	Brad Minor
SS	John Franko
FS	Jake Grillo

District 5 "A" Playoff
Windber 7   Conemaugh Twp. 14

Windber High School Football-1994

Row 1: B. Hunter, N. Vatavuk, R. Bantly, M. Grohal, D. Chippie, D. Kohler, R. Ott, J. Kozar.
Row 2: Head Coach-P. DeMarco, M. Russo, D. Alexander, B. Minor, D. Thomas, L. Blough, B. Mock, J. Banjak, S. Malisko, M. Unsnik, T. Dolan.
Row 3: Asst. Coach-R. DeMarco, R. Mash, R. George, B. Stiffler, E. Korhut, B. Gall, T. DiPaola, J. Claar, J. O'Hara, B. Gerula, J. Franko, Asst. Coach-J. Slatcoff, Asst. Coach-B. Gennett.
Row 4: M. DeBiase, N. Davis, J. Figard, M. Thomas, M. Pekela, C. Hanik, A. Korhut, N. Gray, D. Rininger, H. Barnes, R. Mateljan.

1994   Head Coach: Phil DeMarco   Record: Wins 9   Losses 2   Ties 1

Offensive Starting Line-up

TE	Tony DiPaola
LT	Aaron Korhut
LG	Justin Banjak
C	Mike Russo
RG	Brian Mock
RT	Len Blough
WR	Chip Hanik
QB	Nate Gray
RB	Eric Korhut or Brad Minor
RB	Randy Ott
FB	Neil Vatavuk

Season Schedule

W.H.S		Opponents
56	Berlin	7
40	Shade	0
20	Conemaugh Twp.	20
47	North Star	21
46	Blacklick Valley	12
27	Conemaugh Valley	13
20	Meyersdale	0
14	Ferndale	16
40	Portage	18

District 5 "A" Champions
PIAA Playoffs:

Windber 27	Northern Bedford	0
Windber 21	Conemaugh Twp.	7
Windber 0	Homer Center	17

Defensive Starting Line-up

DT	Harry Barnes
DT	Aaron Korhut
MG	Mike Russo
DE	Mike THomas
DE	Chip Hanjik
LB	Justin Banjak
LB	John Franko
C	Brad Minor
C	Eric Korhut
SS	Ben Gerula
SS	Todd Dolan

Windber High School Football-1995

Row 1: J. Marsh, R. Bantly, J. Kozar, D. Chippie, M. Gregory, D. Kohler, M. Grohal, J. Schirato, T. Harr.
Row 2: Manager-B. Vaught, D. Piatek, D. Alexander, R. Mash, B. Stiffler, R. George, S. Malisko, J. DiPaola, M. Verostick, Manager-R. Christner.
Row 3: Head Coach-P. DeMarco, Asst. Coach-S. Pallo, D. Thomas, D. Weyandt, J. Hite, J. O'Hara, R. Gall, D. Henger, J. Mock, Asst. Coach-J. Slatcoff, Asst. Coach-P. Katch.
Row 4: Asst. Coach-R. DeMarco, N. Davis, M. DeBiase, D. Rininger, R. Mateljan, D. Decewicz, M. Pekala, C. Ramoni, J. Figard, T. Panetti, Asst. Coach-G. Buchsen.

1995   Head Coach: Phil DeMarco   Record: Wins 7   Losses 4

Offensive Starting Line-up
WR	Tony DiPaola
WR	Bobby Gall or Bill Stiffler
LT	Mike Pekala
LG	Dominick Chippie
C	Scott Malisko
RG	Mike Grohal
RT	Dirk Rininger
QB	Nathaniel Davis
RB	Ryan George
RB	Ron Mash
FB	Jeff Figard
Kicker-Mike Grohal	

Season Schedule
W.H.S		Opponents
7	Portage	34
7	Ferndale	6
12	Meyersdale	21
20	Conemaugh Valley	12
28	Blacklick Valley	12
20	North Star	6
12	Conemaugh Twp.	13
20	Shade	8
7	Berlin	3

Defensive Starting Line-up
OLB	Mike DeBiase
OLB	Nathaniel Davis
MLB	Don Thomas
DL	Mike Pekala
DL	Dominick Chippie
DL	Dirk Rininger
DL	Jeff Figard
CB	Bill Stiffler
CB	Bobby Gall
S	Ryan George
S	Tony DiPaola
Punter-Ryan George	

PIAA Playoffs
Windber 14   Tussey Mountain 13
Windber 0   Northern Bedford 13

Windber High School Football-1996

Row 1: Josh Marsh, Tom Harr, Jon Kozar, Steve Sollenberger, Mike Grohal, Rich Bantly, Adam Divine.
Row 2: Asst. Coach-Jeff Slatcoff, Joe Cannoni, Jim O'Brien, Matt Verostick, Dave Henger, Doug Alexander, Ron Mash, Ryan Berkey, Jerry Schirato, Trainer-Ruth Kline, Asst. Coach-Gary Buchsen.
Row 3: Head Coach-Phil DeMarco, Greg Berezansky, Joe Young, Don Thomas, Jeff Mock, Jason Thomas, Scott Malisko, Chad Hasse, Brad Fedorko, Jeff Jablon, Asst. Coach-Ralph DeMarco.
Row 4: Bob Gall, Todd Moss, Jim O'Hara, Tom Panetti, Dave Decewicz, Rick Mateljan, Jason Hite, Damien Weyandt, Jeff Berkey, Joe Pallo.

1996   Head Coach: Phil DeMarco   Record: Wins 2   Losses 7

Offensive Starting Line-up
- WR Bobby Gall
- WR Jerry Schirato or Jim O'Hara
- LT Jason Hite or Rick Mateljan
- LG Doug Alexander
- C   Scott Malisko
- RG Mike Grohal
- RT Damien Weyandt
- TE Doug Henger
- QB Tom Panetti
- RB Ron Mash
- RB Jon Kozar
- FB Don Thomas
- Kicker-Mike Grohal

Season Schedule

W.H.S		Opponents
14	Portage	12
14	Ferndale	28
33	Meyersdale	34
25	Conemaugh Valley	35
20	Blacklick Valley	26
0	North Star	14
13	Conemaugh Twp.	7
6	Shade	26
14	Berlin	20

Defensive Starting Line-up
- OLB Don Thomas
- OLB Scott Malisko
- MLB Steve Sollenberger
- DL   Damien Weyandt
- DL   Joe Pallo
- DL   Doug Alexander
- DL   Jason Hite
- DL   Mike Grohal
- CB   Jerry Schirato
- CB   Ron Mash
- S   Jim O'Hara
- S   Bobby Gall
- Punter-Doug Henger

Windber High School Football-1997

Row 1: P. Dello, D. Kostick, J. Marsh, T. Harr, J. Telek, C. Lushko, M. Ferrante, D. Piatek.
Row 2: J. DeBiase, J. Doyka, A. Orlovsky, J. Helman, B. Moore, E. Toath, S. Klonicke, M. Alexander, J. Pitera.
Row 3: S. Sollenberger, J. O'Brien, J. Bahorik, A. Devine, J. Pallo, R. Patsy, J. Schirato, J. Cannoni, N. Rizzo.
Row 4: Head Coach-P. DeMarco, R. Berkey, B. Reid, L. Wozniak, M. Trachok, G. Wright, G. Berzansky, J. Jablon, J. Young, M. Verostick, Asst. Coach-G. Buchsen, Asst. Coach-R. DeMarco.
Row 5: C. Hasse, R. Dalla Valle, D. Blackburn, J. Thomas, T. Panetti, J. Berkey, J. Hite, T. Moss, D. Weyandt, J. Mock.

1997   Head Coach: Phil DeMarco   Record: Wins 6   Losses 4

Offensive Starting Line-up

WR	Jerry Schirato
WR	Jeff Berkey
LT	Jason Hiter
LG	Josh Marsh
C	Jason Thomas
RG	Chad Hasse
RT	Damien Weyandt
TE	Matt Verostick
QB	Tom Panetti
FB	Jeff Mock
TB	Joe Cannoni

Punter-Luke Wozniak or Joe Cannoni

Season Schedule

W.H.S	Opponent	Opp
0	Portage	21
12	Ferndale	0
7	Meyersdale	13
18	Conemaugh Valley	13
54	Blacklick Valley	0
32	North Star	0
19	Conemaugh Twp.	28
8	Shade	21
28	**Berlin***	**0**
34	Richland	8

Defensive Starting Line-up

OLB	Jeff Berkey
OLB	Tom Panetti
MLB	Steve Sollenberger
DT	Damien Weyandt
DT	Chad Hasse
NT	Joe Pallo
DE	Jeff Mock
DE	Josh Marsh or Matt Verostick
CB	Tom Harr
CB	Nick Rizzo
S	Jeff Jablon

Kicker-Jeff Jablon

District 5 "A" Champions   *49 Regular Season Games Winning Streak Begins

Windber High School Football-1998

Row 1: P. Dello, J. Telek, J. Spinelli, M. Ferrante, F. Tallyen, M. Cominsky, J. O'Roark, J. Whitaker, G. Pallo, D. Kostik, S. Kozar,
Row 2: Head Coach-P. DeMarco, J. Pitera, R. Kolson, S. Sollenberger, C. Wozniak, S. Garczynski, A. Orvlosky, R. Moore, J. Helman, J. Cannoni, M. Alexander, F. Solensky, Asst. Coach-R. DeMarco.
Row 3: Asst. Coach-G. Buchsen, P. Donato, R. Berkey, J. DeBiase, J. Jablon, J. Pallo, G. Berzansky, S. Jones, N. Rizzo, J. Slatcoff, J. Doyka, S. Horner, Asst. Coach-J. Slatcoff.
Row 4: A. Devine, W. Reed, R. Dalla Valle, D. Blackburn, J. Berkey, J. Thomas, B. Gindlesperger, T. Moss, M. Hayes, G. Wright, M. Weaver.

1998   Head Coach: Phil DeMarco   Record: Wins 11   Losses 1

Offensive Starting Line-up
TE	Luke Wozniak
LT	Todd Moss
LG	John Telek
C	Jason Thomas
RG	Ryan Berkey or Garret Wright
RT	Joe Pallo
WR	Dan Blackburn or Nick Rizzo
SE	Jeff Berkey
QB	Jeff Jablon
TB	Joe Cannoni
FB	Steve Sollenberger

Punter-Luke Wozniak

Season Schedule
W.H.S		Opponents
41	Blacklick Valley	0
48	Meyersdale	6
46	North Star	0
41	Conemaugh Valley	18
49	Berlin	12
32	Conemaugh Twp.	0
26	Ferndale	3
31	Shade	6
42	Portage	6

Defensive Starting Line-up
DE	Jeff Berkey
DT	Mike Alexander
NT	Joe Pallo
DT	Bob Moore
DE	Garret Wright
LB	Steve Sollenberger
LB	Jeremy Helman
CB	Joe Cannoni
CB	Nick Rizzo
S	Bill Reid
S	Jeff Jablon

Kicker-Luke Wozniak

Somerset County Champions
District 5 "A" Champions

PIAA Playoffs
Windber 7   Southern Huntingdon 6
Windber 28   Conemaugh Twp. 26
Windber 14   Bishop Carroll 34

Windber High School Football-1999

Row 1: E. Berkey, J. Weyandt, B. Ward, D. Kostick, J. Byer, N. Costantino. **Row 2:** Asst. Coach-S. Pallo, J. Simon, S. Krauss, S. Kozar, G. Pallo, M. Ferrante, P. Dello, B. Yonish, T. Wozniak, Asst. Coach-R. DeMarco, Asst, Coach-G. Buchsen. **Row 3:** Head Coach-P. DeMarco, J. O'Roark, M. Alexander, J. Helman, L. Wozniak, B. Moore, F. Tallyen, J. Pitera, F. Solensky, J. Spinelli, Asst. Coach-J. Slatcoff. **Row 4:** R. Kolson, J. Beckley, M. Phillips, M. Coulter, S. Horner, S. Garcyznski, M. Allison, P. Donato, K. Slezak, M. Cominsky. **Row 5:** G. Heinrich, S. Jones, M. Weaver, J. Slatcoff, B. Gindlesperger, M. Hayes, B. Reid, G. Wright, N. Rizzo, A. Orlovsky.

1999   Head Coach: Phil DeMarco   Record: Wins 10   Losses 1

Offensive Starting Line-up

TE	Luke Wozniak
LT	Josh Spinelli
LG	Garrett Wright
C	Matt Hayes
RG	Gabe Pallo
RT	Bob Moore
WR	Phil Dello or
	Robby Kolson
WR	Jeff Slatcoff
QB	Nick Rizzo
TB	Jeremy Helman
FB	Bill Reid or
	Frank Tallyen
Punter-Luke Wozniak	

Season Schedule

W.H.S	Opponents	
28	Blacklick Valley	6
42	Meyersdale	7
36	North Star	0
39	Conemaugh Valley	14
55	Berlin	6
39	Conemaugh Twp.	7
42	Ferndale	14
49	Shade	6
41	Portage	12

Defensive Starting Line-up

DE	Garrett Wright
DT	Mike Alexander
MG	Jim Pitera or
	Keith Slezak
DT	Bob Moore
DE	Brian Gindlesperger or
	Gabe Pallo or
	Frank Solensky
LB	Jeremy Helman or
	Matt Hayes
DB	Nick Rizzo
DB	Jeff Slatcoff
DB	Bill Reid
DB	Robby Kolson
Kicker-Luke Wozniak	

Somerset County Champions
Appalachian Conference: South Champions
PIAA-District 5 "A" Champions

PIAA Playoffs
Windber 30   Southern Huntingdon 12
Windber 20   Bellwood-Antis 36

Windber High School Football-2000

Row 1: J. Mock, A. Hostetler, J. Weyandt, K. Dale, E. Berkey, J. Huntsman, G. Pallo. **Row 2:** Asst. Coach-S. Pallo, J. Simon, S. Kozar, J O'Roark, J. Byer, R. Simmons, B. Ward, N. Costantino, M. Cominsky, Asst. Coach-J. Slatcoff. **Row 3:** Head Coach-P. DeMarco, J. Spinelli, R. Kolson, F. Tallyen, G. Heinrich, A. Cambell, T. Walls, J. Kolson, P. DeMarco, First Asst. Coach-R. De-Marco. **Row 4:** J. Beckley, M. Phillips, K. Slezak, M. Allison, B. Yonish, S. Garzynski, M. Coulter, T. Wozniak. **Row 5:** M. Weaver, J. Slatcoff, S. Slatcoff, A. Strittmatter, B. Gindlesperger, M. Hayes, M. Gindlesperger, J. Miller, J. Curlej.

2000   Head Coach: Phil DeMarco   Record: Wins 12   Losses 1

Offensive Starting Line-up
TE	Brian Gindlesperger
LT	Matt Coulter
LG	Josh Spinelli
C	Matt Hayes
RG	Gabe Pallo
RT	Mike Phillips
WR	Robbie Kolson
WR	Tom Wozniak
QB	Jeff Slatcoff
RB	Jake O'Roark or Matt Weaver
FB	Frank Tallyen or Keith Slezak

Punter-John Curlej

Season Schedule
W.H.S		Opponents
49	Berlin	0
41	Shade	0
48	Conemaugh Twp.	0
41	North Star	0
47	Blacklick Valley	0
14	Conemaugh Valley	7
33	Meyersdale	12
33	Ferndale	0
25	Portage	13

Defensive Starting Line-up
DE	Brian Gindlesperger
DT	Mike Phillips
MG	Josh Spinelli
DT	Keith Slezak
DE	Gabe Pallo
LB	Sean Kozar
LB	Frank Tallyen
LB	Matt Hayes
DB	Jeff Slatcoff
DB	Jake O'Roark
DB	Matt Weaver or Steve Slatcoff

Kicker-Adam Strittmatter

Somerset County Champions
West Pac Conference Champions
PIAA District 5 "A" Champions
PIAA District 5 and 6 "A" Regional Champions

PIAA Playoffs
Windber 54   Conemaugh Twp. 0
Windber 33   Bishop Guilfoyle 12
Windber 10   Bishop Carroll 7
Windber 6   Sharpsville 28

Windber High School Football-2001

Row 1: J. Stevens, J. Huntsman, A. Statler, S. Pitera, J. Weyandt, G. Guy, J. Smith, C. Shaffer, E. Verostick, J. Hobba, D. Helman. **Row 2:** Asst. Coach-S. Pallo, D. Schropp, B. Berkey, C. Erickson, D. Podrasky, R. Dale, W. Blackburn, A. Hostetler, J. Boyer, E. Berkey, J. Lehman, Asst. Coach-J. Slatcoff. **Row 3:** Head Coach-P. DeMarco, N. Costantino, J. Grisin, J. Simon, T. Harrigan, S. Litzinger, J. Byer, R. Simmons, J. Mock, R. McNeal, D. Carter, B. Ward. **Row 4:** M. Phillips, J. Thomas, J. Beckley, C. Perkosky, B. Yonish, G. Heinrich, M. Coulter, T. Wozniak, P. DeMarco, J. Kolson, Asst. Coach-R. DeMarco. **Row 5:** J. Gleto, C. Stanton, M. Allison, C. Trusch, M. Gindlesperger, S. Slatcoff, J. Curlej, K. Slezak, J. Miller, A. Cambell, T. Walls.

2001   Head Coach: Phil DeMarco   Record: Wins 11   Losses 1

Offensive Starting Line-up
TE	Brett Yonish
LT	Matt Coulter
LG	Josh Simon
C	Philip DeMarco
RG	Josh Weyandt or Bruce Ward
RT	Mike Phillips
WR	Tom Wozniak
WR	Jarrod Mock
QB	Steve Slatcoff
TB	John Kolson or Greg Guy
FB	Keith Slezak

Punter-John Curlej

Season Schedule

W.H.S	Opponents	
49	Berlin	0
47	Shade	0
28	Conemaugh Twp.	0
52	North Star	0
35	Blacklick Valley	0
19	Conemaugh Valley	6
35	Meyersdale	7
28	Ferndale	0
20	Portage	7

Defensive Starting Line-up
DE	Brett Yonish
DL	Keith Slezak
DL	Jason Miller
DL	Mike Phillips or Philip DeMarco
DE	Gary Heinrich or John Curlej
LB	Josh Simon
LB	Bruce Ward or John Kolson
CB	Mark Gindlesperger
CB	Jarrod Mock
SS	Tom Wozniak
FS	Steve Slatcoff

Kicker-John Curlej or Jarrod Mock

PIAA Playoffs
Windber 26   Homer Center 6
Windber 36   Junitia Valley 0
Windber 7   Bishop Carroll 35

Somerset County Champions
West Pac. Conference Champions
PIAA District 5 "A" Champions

Windber High School Football-2002

Row 1: J. Stevens, A. Hostetler, S. Pitera, A. Statler, A. Clement, J. Jones, S. Hostetler, D. Helman. **Row 2:** Asst. Coach-F. Blair, J. Huntsman, G. Guy, J. Boyer, C. Erickson, J. Smith, J. Lehman, J. Hobba, E. Verostick, D. Podrasky, Asst. Coach-R. DeMarco. **Row 3:** Asst. Coach-J. Slatcoff, B. Berkey, D. Kitcho, A. Dulak, J. Grisin, F. Rummel, J. Hicks, W. Blackburn, D. Clark, D. Schropp, Head Coach-P. DeMarco. **Row 4:** R. Barnes, M. Gleto, R. McNeel, A. Campbell, B. Seese, T. Harrigan, D. Carter, S. Pekala, J. Kolson, P. DeMarco. **Row 5:** J. Mock, J. Gleto, C. Perkosky, M. Gindlesperger, S. Slatcoff, J. Curlej, C. Trusch, C. Stanton, J. Miller, J. Thomas.

2002   Head Coach: Phil DeMarco   Record: Wins 11   Losses 1

Offensive Starting Line-up

TE	John Curlej
LT	Adam Campbell
LG	Jay Miller
C	Philip DeMarco
RG	Jeff Thomas
RT	John Gleto or
	Jordan Grisin
WR	Josh Hobba or
	Jay Stevens
WR	Jarrod Mock
QB	Steve Slatcoff
TB	John Kolson
FB	Adam Hostetler or
	Steve Pitera

Punter-John Curlej

Season Schedule

W.H.S		Opponents
33	Portage	14
27	Ferndale	0
34	Meyersdale	7
35	Conemaugh Valley	0
28	Blacklick Valley	6
42	North Star	8
7	Conemaugh Twp.	0
55	Shade	8
48	Berlin	12

Defensive Starting Line-up

DE	John Curlej
DL	Jay Miller
DL	Jordan Grisin or
	Brock Seese
DL	Philip DeMarco
DE	Chris Perkosky
LB	John Gleto
LB	Jeff Thomas
CB	Jarrod Mock
CB	Dan Clark or
	David Kitcho
SS	Jake Boyer
FS	Steve Slatcoff

Kicker-Jarrod Mock

Somerset County Champions
West Pac. Conference Champions
PIAA District 5 "A" Champions

PIAA Playoffs

Windber 6	Bellwood-Antis 0
Windber 20	Bishop Guilfoyle 0
Windber 12	Bishop Carroll 13

Windber High School Football-2003

Row 1: M. Ulatsky, D. McCann, J. Erickson, C. Sturtz, S. Pitera, A. Clement, A. Statler, S. Papinchak, A. Peterson, D.J. Helman, J. Stevens. **Row 2:** Asst. Coach-J. Slatcoff, D. Podrasky, D. Schropp, M. Dello, J. Smith, G. Guy, E. Verostick, J. Lehman, B. Dale, R. Crawford, Asst. Coach-F. Blair. **Row 3:** Head Coach-P. DeMarco, D. Kitcho, D. Clark, J. Hobba, A. Dulak, M. Wilson, J. Grisin, K. Simmons, C. Erickson, J. Boyer, K. Snell, B. Berkey, Asst. Coach-R. DeMarco. **Row 4:** M. Mucciola, G. Seese, F. Rummel, A. Newcomer, J. Petrunak, J. Thomas, R. Barnes, M. Claar, C.W. Beckley, J. Horner, C. Ovington. **Row 5:** M. Gleto, R. McNeel, B. Seese, J. Gleto, C. Perkosky, C. Trusch, C. Stanton, T. Harrigan, S. Pekala, B. Franchic.

2003   Head Coach: Phil DeMarco   Record: Wins 7   Losses 3

Offensive Starting Line-up

TE	Chris Trusch or John Lehman
LT	Brock Seese
LG	Chris Perkosky
C	Jeff Thomas
RG	John Gleto or Charlie Erickson
RT	Jordan Grisin
WR	Josh Hobba
WR	Jay Stevens or D.J. Helman
QB	Tim Harrigan or David Kitcho
FB	Steve Pitera
TB	Greg Guy or Dan Clark

Punter-Chris Trusch
Extra Points & Field Goals-Josh Hobba

Season Schedule

W.H.S		Opponents
21	Portage	16
32	Ferndale	0
7	**Meyersdale***	**9**
39	Conemaugh Valley	8
37	Blacklick Valley	6
16	North Star	7
35	Conemaugh Twp.	6
42	Shade	6
21	Berlin	32

PIAA District 5 "A" Champions

*49 Consecutive Regular Season Game Win Streak Ends 1997 to 2003

PIAA Playoffs
Windber 0   Northern Cambria 42

Defensive Starting Line-up

DE	Chris Perkosky
DT	Jordan Grisin or Brock Seese
DT	Brian Berkey or Clinton Stanton
DE	Josh Smith or Chris Trusch
LB	Jake Boyer
LB	Jeff Thomas
CB	Dan Clark
CB	David Kitcho
SS	Steve Pitera or Evan Verostick
FS	Greg Guy or Frank Rummel

Kicker-Chris Trusch

Appendix III   A Reflection on Windber High School Football   277

Windber High School Football-2004

Row 1: S. Papinchak, K. Korzi, M. Snyder, P. Ferrante, C. Sturtz, A. Peterson, M. Ulatsky. **Row 2:** Head Coach-P. DeMarco, A. Clement, J. Lehman, M. Andrascik, R. Crawford, J. Kotula, W. Sipko, J. Shuster, J. Erickson, Asst. Coach-R. DeMarco. **Row 3:** N. Berkey, C. Ovington, D. Gardner, J, Gathagan, D. Kitcho, J. Mash, J. Heinrich, M. Holden, M. Rancourt, Asst. Coach-F. Blair, **Row 4:** D. Clark, A. Dulak, K. Simmons, G. Seese, P. Walker, M. Wilson, J. Horner, B. Dale, M. Dello, K. Snell. **Row 5:** C.W. Beckley, M. Gleto, S. Pekala, J. Petrunack, B. Seese, F. Rummel, M. Mucciola, S. Hudak, A. Newcomer, J. Ward.

2004   Head Coach: Phil DeMarco   Record: Wins 6   Losses 4

Offensive Starting Line-up

TE	Josh Petrunak
T	Josh Horner
T	Grant Seese or Marcus Snyder
C	C. W. Beckley
G	Tony Clement
G	Brock Seese
SE	Frank Rummel or Brenan Franchic
RB	Dan Clark or Patrick Ferrante
FB	Aaron Peterson or Nick Berkey
QB	David Kitcho or Brad Dale

Punter-Matt Wilson or Kris Korzi

Season Schedule

W.H.S		Opponents
13	Blacklick Valley	20
48	North Star	6
21	Conemaugh Twp.	0
60	Shade	7
19	Berlin	20
39	Conemaugh Valley	14
35	Meyersdale	0
13	Ferndale	17
12	Portage	7

Defensive Starting Line-up

DE	Chris Ovington
DT	Brock Seese
MG	Matt Gleto
DT	Shayne Pekala
DE	Brenan Franchic
LB	Josh Kotula
LB	Jason Mash
CB	Dan Gardner
CB	Chuck Sturtz
S	Brad Dale or Matt Dello
S	Dan Clark or Frank Rummel

Kicker-Dan Gardner or Alan Newcomer

PIAA Playoffs
Windber 0   North Star 6

Windber High School Football-2005

Photograph taken by Cover Studio

Row 1: Mike Webb, Ricky Aufman, Vince Walls, Jim Greathouse, Jonathan Ferensic, Mike Smith, Garret Ursino, Domenic Mash, Matt Koot. **Row 2:** Josh Kotula, Kris Korzi, Brock Smith, Dominic Balash, Vinnie Paczek, Josh Mock, Joe Arcuri, Taylor Keiper, Marcus Snyder **Row 3:** Matt Rancourt, Matt Andrascik, Nick Berkey, Jason Mash, Paul Walker, Justin Gathagan, Jake Lehman, Bill Sipko, Mike Holden. **Row 4:** Brenan Franchic, Josh Horner, Kevin Simmons, Stephen Hudak, Head Coach-Phil DeMarco, Jason Ward, C.W. Beckley, Matt Wilson, Grant Seese.
Row 5: Asst. Coach-Matt Grohal, Chris Ovington, Aaron Peterson, Patrick Ferrante, Matt Ulatsky, Ray Crawford, Brad Dale, Matt Dello, Dan Gardner, Statistician-Dave Senior. **Row 6:** Volunteer-Philip DeMarco, Volunteer-Frank Tallyen, Trainer-Robert Christner, Asst. Coach-Jeff Slatcoff, Asst. Coach-Ralph DeMarco, Volunteer-Paul Katch, Statistician-Glenn Gaye, Jr., Statistician-Glenn Gaye, Sr.

2005   Head Coach: Phil DeMarco   Record: Wins 10   Losses 2

Offensive Starting Line-up
TE	Brenan Franchic
T	Matt Rancourt
T	Josh Horner
G	Stephen Hudak
G	Marcus Snyder
C	C.W. Beckley
SE	Matt Wilson
FB	Aaron Peterson
TB	Matt Andrascik
FL	Patrick Ferrante
QB	Brad Dale

Punter-Kris Korzi or Matt Wilson

Season Schedule

W.H.S		Opponents
14	Blacklick Valley	7
41	North Star	7
42	Conemaugh Twp.	14
57	Shade	0
46	Berlin	0
12	Conemaugh Valley	0
22	Meyersdale	7
38	Ferndale	0
21	Portage (Overtime)	22

PIAA District 5 "A" Champions

Defensive Starting Line-up
DE	Jake Lehman
DL	Josh Horner
DL	Chris Ovington
DL	Nick Berkey
DE	Brenan Franchic
LB	Josh Kotula
LB	Jason Mash
CB	Matt Wilson
CB	Dan Gardner
SS	Dominic Balash
FS	Mike Holden

Kicker-Dominic Balash

PIAA Playoffs

Windber 13	Meyersdale 6
Windber 42	Tussey Mountain 7
Windber 0	Duquesne 18

Appendix III — A Reflection on Windber High School Football — 279

Windber High School Football- 2006

Photograph taken by Life Touch, Hancock Studio

Row 1: R.J. Gathagan, Brock Smith, Joe Arcuri, Nick Seitz, Head Coach-Phil DeMarco, Taylor Keiper, Mike Clark, Mark Horner, Mike Domonkos, Trainer Bob Christner.

Row 2: Asst. Coach-Ralph DeMarco, Josh Kotula, Matt Andrascik, Marcus Snyder, Kris Korzi, Luke McDannell, Josh Shuster, Dominic Balash, Kevin Erickson, Patrick Ferrante, Nick Berkey, Volunteer-Paul Katch.

Row 3: Asst Coach-Jeff Slatcoff, Justin Gathagan, Bill Sipko, Mike Holden, Mike Webb, Domenic Mash, Robert Coughenour, Rick Aufman, Matt Koot, Dan Gardner, Vince Walls, Dr. Patrick Gray, Support Staff-Bob Smith.

Row 4: Volunteer-Philip Demarco, Statistician-Glenn Gaye, Sr., Statistician-Glenn Gaye, Jr., Jonathan Ferensic, Stephen Hudak, Vinnie Paczek, Robert Lupton, Jake Lehman, Matt Rancourt, Jarod Spinelli, Paul Walker, Jason Mash, Jason Ward, Statistician-Dave Senior, Asst. Coach Matt Grohal.

2006   Head Coach: Phil DeMarco   Record: Wins 9   Losses 2

Offensive Starting Line-up
TE	Jason Mash
T	Matt Rancourt
T	Jonathan Ferensic
G	Stephen Hudak
G	Marcus Snyder
C	Matt Koot
SE	Dan Gardner
FB	Jake Lehman
TB	Matt Andrascik
FL	Patrick Ferrante or Mike Webb
QB	Kris Korzi

Punter-Kris Korzi

Season Schedule
W.H.S		Opponents
20	Blacklick Valley	0
28	Shade	0
44	Conemaugh Valley	0
20	North Star	0
46	Berlin	0
14	Conemaugh Twp.	0
26	Portage	7
9	Meyersdale	21
41	Ferndale	0

Defensive Starting Line-up
DE	Jake Lehman
DL	Vinnie Paczek
DL	Jason Ward
DL	Nick Berkey
DE	Bill Sipko
LB	Josh Kotula
LB	Jason Mash
DB	Mike Webb
DB	Dan Gardner
DB	Dominic Balash
DB	Mike Holden

Kicker-Dominic Balash

PIAA Playoffs
Semi-final Round	Windber 8	North Star 0
District 5 Championship	Windber 14	Meyersdale 20 (Overtime)

Windber High School Football- 2007

Photograph taken by Life Touch, Hancock Studio

Row 1: L-R: Tyler Weaver, Kyle Smith, Ben Pavlick, Joe Arcuri, Taylor Keiper, Mike Clark, Mark Horner, Nick Seitz, Sam Weaver
Row 2: Coach-Ralph DeMarco, Statistician-Glenn Gaye, Jr., Trainer-Robert Christner, Rick Aufman, Cory Hancock, Kody Lupton, Kevin Erickson, Max Thomassy, Domenic Mash, Luke McDannell, Robert Keim, R.J. Gathagan, Coach-Philip DeMarco, Statistician-Glenn Gaye, Sr. **Row 3:** Volunteer Coach-Paul Katch, Mike Domonkos, Erick Strapple, Eric Solar, Jesse Ward, Head Coach-Phil DeMarco, Brandon Ulasky, Josh Hogue, Matt Koot, Vinnie Pazeck. **Row 4:** Coach-Matt Grohal, Paul Turcato, Dr. Patrick Gray, Vinnie Walls, Jarod Spinelli, Mike Kasuba, Seth Michaels, Levi Allison, Robert Lupton, Kegan Ashbrook, Jonathan Ferensic, Statistician-Dave Senior, Mike Webb, Volunteer Coach-Paul Buza.

2007   Head Coach: Phil DeMarco   Record: Wins 7   Losses 3

Offensive Starting Line-up

TE	Domenic Mash
T	Jarod Spinelli
T	Jonathan Ferensic
G	Rick Aufman
G	Vinnie Paczek
C	Matt Koot
SE	Mike Webb
FB	Vince Walls
TB	Kevin Erickson
FL	Mike Clark
QB	Taylor Keiper

Punter-Kevin Erickson

Season Schedule

W.H.S	Opponents	
35	Blacklick Valley	14
42	Shade	7
35	Conemaugh Valley	14
27	North Star	13
27	Berlin	0
13	Conemaugh Twp.	14
0	Portage	14
13	Meyersdale	7
49	Ferndale	0

Defensive Starting Line-up

DE	Domenic Mash
DL	Jarod Spinelli
DL	Vinnie Paczek
DL	Matt Koot
DE	Jonathan Ferensic
LB	Kevin Erickson
LB	Vince Walls
DB	Mike Webb
DB	Mike Clark
DB	Taylor Keiper
DB	R. J. Gathagan or Brandon Ulasky

Kicker-Kevin Erickson

PIAA Playoffs
Semi-final Round   Windber 0   North Star 29

Appendix IV — A Reflection on Windber High School Football — 281

Windber Rambler Opponents

A very interesting question was presented to me near the end of the 2005 season. Someone asked me how many different teams Windber High School had played? I had no idea at the time and decided to compile a list of schools. The list consisted of all schools played from the 1914 season, the first official year of high school football at Windber, thru the 2007 season. There have been a few schools change their name. I included their records together. A few schools also merged, however, I did not combine these records. There are also a number of high schools listed which no longer exist because of mergers. All teams listed are from the state of Pennsylvania unless otherwise noted. At the conclusion of the entire list, I show the teams Windber has played 20 or more times.

Opponent	Total Games	Wins	Losses-Wbr. Wins	Ties
Adams Twp.	16	4	10	2
Aflas	1	1	1	1
Aliquippa	2	1	1	
Allentown	1	1		
Altoona	41	21	17	3
Altoona Apprentice	2	1	1	
Altoona Catholic (Bishop Guilfoyle)	13	1	12	
Alumni (Whalley A.C.)	1		1	
Ambridge	1	1		
Beaver Falls	2	1	1	
Beaverdale	6		5	1
Bedford	22	11	11	
Bellefonte	4	1	3	
Bellefonte Academy	1		1	
Bellwood Antis	2	1	1	
Berlin	23	6	17	
Berwind	1	1		
Bethlehem	2		2	
Bishop Carroll	12	5	7	
Bishop McDevitt	2	2		
Blacklick Valley	15	2	13	
Blairsville	3	2	1	
Boswell	1		1	

Opponents	Total Games	Wins	Losses-Wbr. Wins	Ties
Bradford	2		2	
Cambria Heights	8	3	5	
Carrolltown	1		1	
Chambersburg	8	5	3	
Chestnut Ridge	7	6	1	
Clearfield	3	1	2	
Conemaugh	18	3	13	2
Conemaugh Twp.	71	21	48	2
Conemaugh Valley	17	4	13	
Corry	1		1	
Cresson	5	1	4	
Curwensville	4		4	
Derry	2		2	
Donora	3	2	1	
Dubois	6	1	4	1
Duquesne	2	2		
Ebensburg (Central Cambria)	15	5	9	1
Emporium	1		1	
Erie East	4	3	1	
Everett	3		3	
Farrell	2	2		
Ferndale	28	5	21	2
Forest Hills	18	10	8	
Fort Hill, Maryland	7	3	4	
Franklin	1		1	
Greensburg	2	2		
Har-Brack	4	1	3	
Holidaysburg	11	1	8	2
Homer City (Laura Lamar)	5	2	2	1
Hooversville	1			1

Appendix IV — A Reflection on Windber High School Football

Opponents	Total Games	Wins	Losses-Wbr. Wins	Ties
Huntingdon	6	2	4	
Hurst (Mt. Pleasant)	1	1		
Indiana	12	3	9	
Indiana Normal School (College) (IUP)	3	2		1
Jersey Shore	2	1	1	
John Harris	1		1	
Johnstown	51	28	16	7
Johnstown Catholic (Bishop McCort)	31	8	21	2
Johnstown Colonials	2	1	1	
Johnstown Usher Club	1		1	
Johnstown Vo-Tech.	12	3	9	
Juniata	1		1	
Junitia Valley	1		1	
Larksville	1		1	
LaSalle Institute, Maryland	2	2		
Latrobe	2	1	1	
Lewistown	6	2	4	
Ligonier	1		1	
Lilly	2		2	
Lock Haven	6	4	1	1
Marion Center	3	1	1	1
McKeesport	5	2	3	
Meadville	2		2	
Meyersdale	32	9	22	1
Monessen	2		2	
North Star	36	8	28	
Northern Bedford	2	1	1	
Northern Cambria	10	1	8	1
Northern Maryland, Maryland	1		1	

Opponents	Total Games	Wins	Losses-Wbr. Wins	Ties
Norwin	1	1		
Paterson, New Jersey	1		1	
Pittsburgh Central Catholic	1		1	
Pittsburgh North Catholic	9	4	2	3
Portage	40	8	31	1
Pottsville	4	2	1	1
Punxsutawney	20	6	13	1
Rankin	4	1	3	
Redstone	1			1
Richland	27	12	15	
Saltsburg	1		1	
Scott High	2	1	1	
Scottsdale	1		1	
Shade	45	7	38	
Shady Side Academy	1	1		
Sharon	1		1	
Sharpsville	3	3		
Somerset	38	16	21	1
South Fork	4		4	
South Fork Juniors	1		1	
Southern Huntingdon	2		2	
St. Francis College	1		1	
Steelton	1		1	
Turtle Creek	2		1	1
Tussey Mountain	2		2	
Tyrone	2	1	1	
United	2	2		
Washington	2	1	1	
Weirton Madonna, West Virginia	1	1		

Appendix IV — A Reflection on Windber High School Football

Opponents	Total Games	Wins	Losses-Wbr. Wins	Ties
Westinghouse	2		1	1
Westmont	27	10	14	3
Williamsburg	3		3	
Windber Ex-Hi	1	1		
Windber Juniors	3	1	2	

Teams which have played Windber at Least 20 or More Times

Opponent	Total Games	Wins	Losses-Wbr. Wins	Ties
Conemaugh Twp.	71	21	48	2
Johnstown	51	28	16	7
Shade	45	7	38	
Altoona	41	21	17	3
Portage	40	8	31	1
Somerset	38	16	21	1
North Star	36	8	28	
Meyersdale	32	9	22	1
Richland	27	12	15	
Westmont	27	10	14	3
Ferndale	28	5	21	2
Bedford	22	11	11	
Berlin	23	6	17	
Punxsutawney	20	6	13	1

Four Year Letter Winners
Windber High School Football
1914-2007

During the first thirty years of Windber High School Football, boys in the freshman, sophomore, junior, and senior classes, were eligible to play varsity football. The elite group of boys who earned four letters all played during this time frame. When a junior high school football program was initiated during the mid 1940's, freshman boys were no longer eligible to participate at the varsity level. This change in the football program eliminated the possibility of any boys becoming four year letter winners. The following eight boys demonstrated their football skills when they were freshman and must be considered among the most elite in the history of Windber High School Football.

Name	Position	Years Played
Jim Hagan	Running Back & Quarterback	1920-1923
James Delehunt	Running Back	1921-1924
Philip DePolo	Guard & Tackle	1923-1926
Niles Dalberg	Tackle	1927-1930
Joe Gates	Quarterback & Running Back	1927-1930
Oscar Ripple	Running Back & Quarterback	1929-1932
Joe Polansky	Fullback & Running Back	1938-1941
Walter Cominsky	Running Back & Quarterback	1940-1943

I must include an update, beginning in the fall of 2008, freshman will be eligible to participate at the varsity level. The freshman program will be discontinued because schools in the area have eliminated their freshman programs. We undoubtedly will see more boys added to this elite list.

Coaching Records
Windber High School
Football
1914-2007

Years	Seasons	Coach	Wins	Losses	Ties	Winning Percentage
1914	1	W. W. Lantz	1	3	1	.200
1915-1916	2	Dave Siebert	5	2	0	.714
1917	1	Elmer Daily	2	3	0	.400
1918-1922	5	Jim Hyde	16	14	6	.444
1923-1924	2	H. L. Koehler	14	4	2	.700
1925	1	Thomas Zerbe	4	3	2	.444
1926	1	J. Nelson Hoffman	8	1	2	.727
1927-1929	3	Earl Unger	15	11	2	.536
1930-1933	4	Thurman "Tubby' Allen	30	10	1	.732
1934-1936	3	Harold "Duke" Weigle	31	0	6	.837
1937	1	Ralph Weigle	11	1	1	.846
1938	1	Don Fletcher	7	4	1	.583
1939-1942	4	Joe Gates	31	9	3	.721
1943 & 1946	2	Ray Jones	16	3	1	.800
1944	1	Joe Shevock	4	4	1	.444
1945 & 1947	2	Steve Terebus	10	8	2	.500
1948-1960	13	John Kawchak	82	36	5	.666
1961-1962	2	John Lochrie	5	12	2	.263
1963-1966	4	Ronald "Link" Younker	19	21	0	.475
1967-1971	5	Harold Price	31	16	3	.620
1972-1980	9	Joe Flori	57	33	1	.626
1981-1982	2	William Smutko	7	13	0	.350
1983-1984	2	Edward Price	2	19	0	.095
1985-2007	23	Phil DeMarco	170	74	5	.683
		Total	578	304	47	**.618**

Windber High School Football Players Who went on to become Head Coaches At the High School Level

Player's Name	High School
Jim Hyde	Windber, Erie Central, Erie East, Erie Academy
Joe Gates	Windber, Greensburg, Wheeling Central Catholic, Nanty-Glo
Mike Durbin	Blairsville, Holidaysburg, Chenago Valley-Binghamton, NY
Arnold Bricker	Emporium
Harold "Duke" Weigle	Windber, Tamaqua, Phillipsburg-NJ, Johnstown, McKeesport
Ralph Weigle	Windber
Oscar Ripple	Shade
Bill Freeman	Wheeling Central Catholic-WV
Nunzio Marino	St. Bernard's Catholic-Bradford, PA
John "Jack" Lochrie	Windber
Ron "Link" Younker	Oil City, Chestnut Ridge, Windber
William Smutko	Windber
Robert Oyler	Central Cambria
Richard Shark	Richland
Emil DeMarco	Richland
Edward Pruchnic	Richland
Phil DeMarco	Windber
Stanley "Skip" Skowron	Westmont
Bud Bossick	Pottsville
Patrick Sherlock	Westmont
James Foster	Somerset
Arthur Palumbo	Shade-Central City
Virgil Palumbo	Quigley Catholic High School
Nick Campitelli (non-player)	Richland

Windber High School Football Alumni Who Participated at the College Level 1908-2007

Through out the 94 year history of Windber High School Football, there have been approximately 165 alumni who moved on to play college football. The following list gives the player's name, last year of high school football and college or university they attended. The accuracy of this list is primarily based on newspaper articles from the *Johnstown Tribune Democrat*, *Windber Era*, and *Hi-Times* and by no means should the reader infer that all these individuals played four years of college football and/or graduated from the college or university they attended.

This list I'm sure is not 100 percent accurate, although from research done, it does provide a very good record of those individual Windber High School players who continued their gridiron experience at the college level.

Name	Football Senior Year	College
William Farber	1908	Syracuse University
James Hyde	1915	Indiana Normal School
James Hagan	1923	University of Pittsburgh
Gerald Snyder	1924	University of Maryland
Jim Delehunt	1924	Duquesne
John Roach	1924	Susquehanna University
John Lloyd	1925	Juniata
Jim Zack	1926	University of Maryland
Ernest Carliss	1926	University of Maryland
Louis Colborn	1926	Dickinson
Jim Camille	1926	Juniata, Lebanon Valley
John Torquato	1926	St. Francis (Loretto)
Phil DePolo	1926	Lebanon Valley
Harold "Duke" Weigle	1927	Albright
Francis Murphy	1927	Class team-Notre Dame
Nick Rillo	1928	St. Francis (Loretto)
Ted Keenan	1928	University of Maryland
Ralph Weigle	1928	Albright
Bob Honadle	1929	University of Maryland
Joe Gates	1930	St. Francis (Loretto), Duquesne University
Oscar Ripple	1932	Concord W. Va. State Teachers College
Harold Honadle	1932	Albright
Bill Meyers	1932	Dickinson
James Cavacini	1933	University of Indiana
John DeArmy	1933	University of Maryland

Name	Football Senior Year	College
Charles Bartholomew	1934	Franklin & Marshall
Johnny Carliss	1934	West Virginia University
William Farkes	1935	University of Pittsburgh & Franklin & Marshall
Edward Fagnani	1935	Dickinson
Jack Bell	1935	Franklin & Marshall, Albright
Billy Manotti	1935	Franklin & Marshall, Albright
Bernard Allison	1935	Franklin and Marshall
Glenn Ream	1935	Lenoir Rhyne College
George Bodnar	1936	Franklin & Marshall, Dickinson
Mike Sekela	1936	University of Pittsburgh
John Cavacini	1936	Concord W. Va. State Teachers College
Mike Durbin	1936	Concord W. Va. State Teachers College
Bill Beckley	1936	Dickinson Prep.
Arnold Bricker	1936	Dickinson Prep.
Jack Freeman	1936	Notre Dame and William & Mary
Art Lamonaca	1936	University of Pittsburgh
Pete Gorgone	1937	Muhlenburg
Bud Bossick	1937	Muhlenburg
George Bokinsky	1937	Duke University
Pete Pierzchala	1937	Bucknell
George Wirick	1937	Muhlenburg
Frank Durbin	1938	Rutgers
Paul Toth	1938	Western Reserve
Joe Pierre	1938	University of Pittsburgh
Bill Hayes	1938	Leheigh
John Badaczewski	1939	Western Reserve
Steve Heinrich	1939	Western Reserve
Earl Ripple	1939	University of Pittsburgh
Albert Lamonaca	1939	University of Pittsburgh
Steve Kaplan	1940	Scranton University
Bill Freeman	1940	St. Vincent
Bob Hayes	1941	U.S. Military Academy (Army)
Jack Lochrie	1942	St. Vincent
Pete Kaplan	1942	California State Teachers College
Nunzio Marino	1943	Notre Dame, St. Bonaventure
Walter Cominsky	1943	Penn State
Jim Campitell	1943	Drexel
Anthony DiMuzio	1944	Drexel
John Yocca	1946	Michigan State
Paul Clement	1946	St. Vincent
Frank Kush	1947	Washington & Lee, Michigan State
Tom Grebis	1947	Drexel
James Curtis	1948	John Hopkins University
Ron "Link" Younker	1949	Penn State
John Gulick	1949	Indiana State Teachers College
Paul Komar	1949	Kutztown State Teachers College
Emilio DeMarco	1950	William & Mary
Pat Freeman	1950	William & Mary

Appendix IV — A Reflection on Windber High School Football

Name	Football Senior Year	College
Bill Marfizo	1951	William & Mary
Leonard Rubal	1951	William & Mary
George McKelvie	1952	Concord
John Naylor	1952	Clarion
Chuck Baughman	1953	Wayne State University
Edward Hordubay	1953	North Carolina State
William Keller	1953	Wayne State University
Robert Halcovich	1953	Kent State
Tom Kanas	1953	William & Mary
Ralph Facciani	1953	Columbian Prep., U. S. Naval Academy
Terry Fagan	1953	Wayne State University
Andrew Hancharik	1954	Arizona State University
Joe "Gunda" Kush	1954	Hillsdale College
Joe Hordubay	1954	University of Pennsylvania
Bob Dutzman	1954	Elon
Gwynn "Gatch" Gahagan	1955	West Virginia University
George Kondas	1955	West Virginia University
Roy "Pete" Seese	1955	North Carolina State
Bill Smutko	1955	Clarion
Chuck Webb	1956	Wyoming University
Steve Kurcis	1956	Clarion
Art Palumbo	1956	Concord W.Va. State Teachers College
Jerry Zack	1956	Juniata
Al "Hoko" Tavalsky	1957	Juniata
Bob Zvolern	1957	University of Pittsburgh, Univ. of Tennessee
George Patrick	1957	Juniata
Dave Holt	1957	Millersville
Don Dona	1957	Arizona Univ., Palo Verde, Panhandle A & M.
Bob Minitti	1958	Arizona State University
Tom Marron	1958	Michigan State, Arizona State University
Chuck Shuster	1958	Arizona State University
Gene Heeter	1958	West Virginia University
Tom Congersky	1958	Juniata
Joe Kush	1958	Arizona State University
John Repko	1958	Clarion
Jack Creek	1959	Slippery Rock
Tom Bossi	1959	Cornell
Pat Sherlock	1959	Slippery Rock
John "Budder" Boruch	1959	Cornell
Terry Heckler	1959	Carnegie Tech
Tom Sherwin	1959	Southern Methodist University
Joe Gavalak	1959	Indiana University of Pennsylvania, (IUP)
Joe Hancharick	1960	Clarion
Dave Dunmire	1960	University of Mississippi
Bob Oyler	1960	Southern Methodist University
Pete Rosscetti	1960	Parson Jr., Washburn, Panhandle A & M
Steve Kush	1961	West Virginia University

Name	Football Senior Year	College
Carl Mayer	1961	Indiana University of Pennsylvania, (IUP)
Jim Fagan	1961	West Virginia University
George Tobias	1961	Clarion
Nick LaPlaca	1962	Fairmont State, W.Va., University of Pacific
Tom Rosa	1962	Fairmont State, W.Va.
Jerry Facciani	1963	Lafayette
Bill Zemcik	1963	California University of Pennsylvania
Ron Vitucci	1964	Panhandle A & M
Joe Delorie	1964	Lafayette
Virgil Palumbo, Sr.	1964	Frederick College, Mansfield
Bill Hunter	1965	U.S. Military Academy (Army), Utah
Stan Skowron	1965	Mansfield
Steve Pallo	1965	Shippensburg
Mark Blair	1966	Delaware
Bob Portante	1967	U.S. Military Academy (Army)
Greg Skowron	1968	Mansfield
Mike Nagy	1970	Shippensburg
Dave Rizzo	1972	Juniata
Ralph DeMarco	1973	James Madison
Robert Mucciola	1973	Washington & Lee
Jeff Slatcoff	1973	Washington & Lee
Kevin Berkey	1973	West Virginia University
Bill Elko	1977	Arizona State University, Louisiana State
Rodger Shepko	1978	Lafayete
Brian Petrilla	1978	Indiana University of Pennsylvania, (IUP)
Paul Romanchock	1986	University of Maryland
Frank Blair	1987	St. Francis (Loretto)
John Drzewiecki	1987	St. Francis (Loretto)
Virgil Palumbo	1987	U.S. Naval Academy
Chris Palumbo	1989	St. Francis (Loretto)
Jason Ott	1992	Gannon
Aaron Korhut	1994	Carnegie Mellon
Chip Hanik	1994	Slippery Rock
Eric Korhut	1994	St. Francis (Loretto)
Neil Vatavuk	1994	St. Francis (Loretto)
Randy Ott	1994	St. Francis (Loretto)
Nathaniel Davis	1995	Lebanon Valley
Ron Mash	1995	Mansfield
Nick Rizzo	1999	University of Pitt., Washington & Jefferson
Frank Tallyen	2000	Waynesburg
Tom Wozniak	2001	Thiel
Keith Slezak	2001	Mansfield
Philip DeMarco	2002	Lycoming
Jarrod Mock	2002	Carnegie Mellon
Chris Perkosky	2003	Thiel
Brock Seese	2004	Seton Hill
Grant Seese	2005	St. Vincent
Joshua Horner	2005	Shippensburg University, St. Vincent

Windber High School Football Players Who Played Professional Football

Throughout this 94 year history of Windber High School Football only a few very talented players have reached the professional ranks. The following list gives the player's name, last year of high school football, position played at the professional level, college or colleges attended, number of games played, and the professional team or teams played for.

The position played and number of games played by an individual- with an asterisk in front of their name were obtained from the *2005 Pennsylvania Football News Resource guide*.

Name	Position	Games	College	Professional Team (Year)
*Gerald "Snitz" Snyder (1924)	OL	23	Maryland	New York Giants (1929-30)
*Bill Farkas (1935)	HB	?	University of Pittsburgh	Semi-Pro: Warren Red Jackets
*Joe Pierre (1938)	OE, DE	10	University of Pittsburgh	Pittsburgh Steelers (1945)
*Pete Gorgone (1938)	HB	9	Muhlenberg	New York Giants
*John Badaczewski (1939)	OG, DG	82	Case-Western Reserve	Boston Yanks, Chicago Cardinals Washington Redskins (1946-1953) All-National Pro League Team (1947)
*Gene Heeter (1958)	TE	25	West Virginia University	New York Jets (1963-65) Originally signed by San Diego Chargers
Robert Oyler (1960)	DL	10	Southern Methodist University	Semi-Pro: Dallas County Rockets Free Agent: Washington Redskins
*Bill Elko (1977)	OG, NT	29	Arizona State University Louisiana State	San Diego Chargers and Indianapolis Colts (1983-87)
Frank Blair (1987)	OL	16	St Francis (Loretto)	Johnstown Jackals Arena Football

Windber High School Football All-State Selections

The list of Windber High School football players who have been selected as All-State players was obtained from the *2005 Pennsylvania Football News Resource Guide*. The PFN Resource Guide has listed the all state teams dating back to the inception of each of the three organizations that named such teams. These three organizations include; Associated Press, Untied Press International, and Pennsylvania Football News.

According to the research done by PNF, the Associated Press first selected an All-State Team in 1939, and continues to do so today. However, the format of selecting teams changed in 1988, from an overall selection to a Big School/Small School format and in 2003, the Associated Press decided to select teams according to each of the four classifications: AAAA, AAA, AA and A.

The UPI named their first teams in 1952 and decided to discontinue naming all-state teams in 1984. Also, according to research done by PNF, United Press International named Pennsylvania All-State Teams, and found there were few duplicated names on both the AP and UPI rosters.

The Pennsylvania Football News began naming their all-state teams in 1998, the initial year of their newspaper. The PFN was the first to name all-state teams in all four classifications and remain the only group to name a first, second, and third team for both offense and defense for each of the classifications.

The following Windber High School Football Players have been selected as All-State Players:

Associated Press (Over All Format)

Team	Name	Position	Year
1st	Nunzio Marino	Back	1943
1st	Frank Kush	Tackle	1947
2nd	Earl Ripple	Back	1939
2nd	Ray Torquato	Center	1942
2nd	Anthony DiMuzio	Guard	1944
2nd	John Yocca	Guard	1946
2nd	Bernard Washko	Back	1950
2nd	Steve Kush	Guard	1961
3rd	Paul Kutch	QB	1945
3rd	Paul Kutch	Back	1946
3rd	Fred Green	End	1953

Appendix IV — A Reflection on Windber High School Football

Associated Press (Small School Format)

Team	Name	Position	Year
1st Defense	Philip DeMarco	DL	2001
1st Defense	Philip DeMarco	DL	2002
1st Defense	Josh Kotula	Linebacker	2006
2nd Defense	Frank Tallyen	LB	1999
2nd Defense	John Curlej	Punter	2001
2nd Defense	Josh Kotula	All-Purpose Back	2005
3rd Defense	Steve Slatcoff	DB	2002

United Press International

Team	Name	Position	Year
2nd Offense	Edward Hordubay	Tackle	1953

Pennsylvania Football News (Class A)

Team	Name	Position	Year
1st Offense	Luke Wozniak	Place Kicker	1998
1st Offense	Robby Kolson	WR	2000
1st Defense	Philip DeMarco	DL	2001
1st Defense	Steve Slatcoff	DB	2002
1st Defense	Philip DeMarco	DL	2002
2nd Defense	Frank Tallyen	LB	1999
2nd Defense	Frank Tallyen	LB	2000
2nd Defense	Steve Slatcoff	DB	2001
2nd Defense	John Curlej	Punter	2001
2nd Offense	Brock Seese	OL	2004
3rd Defense	John Curlej	Punter	2002
3rd Defense	Matt Wilson	DB	2004

Windber High School Football Pennsylvania Big "33" Football Classic Selections

The Pennsylvania Big "33" Football Classic originated in 1957, it is considered one of the finest scholastic All-Star games in the United States. No game was played in 1957, however, there has been one played each year since and in some cases two games were played. The game is usually played in July of the year following the scholastic football season, thus, the year indicated would be the player's graduation year as opposed to the football year played.

The following Windber High School Football Players were selected to this very prestigious All-Star Classic.

Chuck Webb	**1957**
Steve Kush	**1962**
Richard Zepka	**1971**
Paul Romanchock	**1987**

PSFCA All-Star Classic

In 2001 the PSFCA established an All-Star Classic, which is held each year at Mansion Park in Altoona. This all-star game originated in order to recognize players in the region from the class AAA, AA, and A schools.

The following Windber High School Football Player was selected to this regional All-Star game:

Jeff Slatcoff   2001

Tribune-Democrat
All Scholastic Team (1943-1967)
Player-Scholarship Award (1968-1991)
All-Area High School Football Team (1992-2007)

From 1943 through 1967, *The Johnstown Tribune* and later *The Johnstown Tribune-Democrat* newspaper annually honored the top high school players in the Johnstown area. The inaugural team in 1943 was selected by the high school football coaches of Cambria and Somerset Counties in collaboration with the Tribune. In later years the coverage area of the Tribune expanded and players from 36 schools in a five-county area were eligible and 22 were selected for the All-Scholastic Football Team. This selection process, based entirely on the player's football talents, was done by the coaches of the 36 schools nominating players worthy of this honor. Players selected for the First team and Alternate (2nd Team) were picked by the staff of the Tribune's sport department.

Windber High School Football
All Scholastic Team Members (1943-1967)

Inaugural Team 1943

First Team	Joe Campitell-Tackle, Joe DelSignore-Guard
	Arthur Toth-Center, Walter Cominsky-QB
	Nunzio Marino-Fullback
Second Team	Anthony DiMuzio-Guard

This first Tribune-Democrat All Scholastic Team with five starters from the same school is unprecedented in the 25 year history of this All-Star format. No other school has ever had this many players selected for the first team.

1944-First Team- Anthony DiMuzio-Guard
1945-First Team-Paul Kutch-QB, Steve Leonardis-Tackle
1946-First Team-Frank Kush-Guard, Paul Kutch-QB, John Yocca-Tackle
  Second Team-Nick Mehalko-Center

1947-First Team-Frank Kush-Tackle

The selection of Kush as a tackle on the 1947 Team and his selection of guard on the 1946 Team is unprecedented in the 25 year history of this All-Star format. No other player has ever been selected for two different positions.

1948-Second Team- Tom Sharpe-Halfback

1949-First Team- Ron "Link" Younker-Fullback
Second Team- Anthony Campitell-End

1950-First Team- Bernard Washko-Fullback
Second Team- Robert DeBiase-Center, John Sasko-Guard

1951-No Selections

1952-First Team- Bill Martell-Guard
Second Team- Terry Fagan-Fullback

1953-First Team- Edward Hordubay-Tackle
Second Team- Terry Fagan-Fullback

1954-First Team- Andy Hancharik-Halfback
Second Team- Joe Hordubay-Tackle, Bob Dutzman-Guard

1955-First Team- Roy "Pete" Seese-Fullback
Second Team- Charles Finnegan-End

1956-First Team- Chuck Webb-End
Second Team-Art Palumbo-Halfback

1957-First Team- Al Tavalsky-End
Second Team- Bob Zvolerin-Guard

1958-First Team- Tom Marron-Halfback, Bob Minitti-Quarterback
Second Team- Chuck Shuster-Center

1959-First Team- John Boruch-End
Second Team- Tom Bossi-Center

1960-Second Team- Pete Roscetti-End

1961-Second Team- Steve Kush-Guard

1962-First Team- James Bartholomew-Tackle

1963-No Selections

1964-First Team- Ronald Vitucci-End

1965-First Team- Bill Hunter-Halfback

1966-First Team- Phil DeMarco-Guard

1967-No Selections

In 1968 *The Tribune-Democrat* took a bold and progressive step in recognizing the outstanding achievements of the scholastic football player. This departure from the 25-year-old format resulted from recognizing the need to include scholarship and leadership along with football ability as requirements to be considered for this All-Star Team. The number of players selected went from 22 to 45 and were chosen from 45 schools participating in the program which field football teams of the 51 schools in a six county area of the *Tribune-Democrat's* circulation.

The award winners are chosen by the high school principals and football coaches with eligibility being limited to seniors with football ability, scholarship, and leadership being prime considerations with the emphasis on football ability. The new name of this All-Star team is The Tribune-Democrat Player-Scholarship Award.

Windber High School Football Player-Scholarship Award (1968-1991)

1968-Anthony Rizzo-Fullback
1969-Jim Lashinsky-Quarterback
1970-Anthony Slatcoff-Quarterback
1971-Dave Bencie-Fullback
1972-Bill Garland-End
1973-Kevin Berkey-Quarterback
1974-Dennis Mash-Fullback
1975-Stephen Bencie-Fullback
1976-Ray Palumbo-Quarterback
1977-Dale Tomlinson-Quarterback- Defensive End
1978-Mike Pascovich-Offensive-Defensive End-Place Kicker
1979-Steve Costantino-Fullback-Linebacker
1980-Todd Hoffman-Quarterback-Linebacker
1981-Paul Gentile-Running Back-Defensive Back
1982-John Niovich-Offensive Tackle-Linebacker
1983-Bill Gearhart-Offensive End-Safety
1984-Gene Mattis-Offensive Lineman-Defensive End
1985-Curt Manges-Running Back-Defensive Back
1986-Paul Romanchock-Quarterback
1987-Virgil Palumbo-Running Back
1988-Dave Ondesko-Placekicker, Brian Horner-Punter
1989-Eric Romanchock-Place Kicker
1990-Matthew Penrose-End-Linebacker
1991-Mike Moore-Quarterback-Safety

In 1992 The Tribune-Democrat decided to revert back to a format of selecting first and second teams for the selection of an All-Star Team with a few changes, these include; Offensive and defensive players of the year, coach of the year, first team offense and defense and a second team offense and defense. These all-stars were culled from a long list of worthy candidates, with significant input from coaches in the newspaper's 27-team coverage area. The basic rules used in the selection process were; Players could not be picked on both offense and defense, the all-area players would be selected by members of the sports department staff as well as free-lance writers who regularly covered area games, and consideration of statistical as well as subjective input included.

Windber High School Football
All-Area High School Football Team (1992-2007)

1992-First Team Defense- Jason Ott-Defensive End
1993-First Team Defense- Jake Grillo-Defensive Back
1994-First Team Defense- Chip Hanik-Lineman, Randy Ott-Defensive Back
1995-First Team Defense- Mike Pekala-Lineman
    Second Team Defense- Tony DiPaola-Defensive Back
1996-No Selections
1997-First Team Defense- Joe Pallo-Lineman
    Second Team Defense- Luke Wozniak-Punter
1998-First Team Offense- Joe Cannoni-Running Back, Jason Thomas-Lineman
   First Team Defense- Joe Pallo-Lineman, Like Wozniak-Kicker/Punter
    Second Team Offense- Nick Rizzo-Receiver
    Second Team Defense- Steve Sollenberger-Linebacker
1999-Offensive Player of the Year- Nick Rizzo-Quarterback
   First Team Defense- Frank Tallyen-Linebacker, Luke Wozniak-Kicker/Punter
    Second Team Offense- Robby Kolson-Receiver
    Second Team Defense- Jeremy Helman-Linebacker

2000-Offensive Player of the Year-Jeff Slatcoff-Quarterback
    First Team Offense-Robby Kolson-Receiver, Matt Hayes-Lineman
    First Team Defense-Frank Tallyen-Linebacker
        Coach of the Year-Phil DeMarco
2001-First Team Offense-Philip DeMarco-Lineman
    First Team Defense-Keith Slezak-Lineman, Steve Slatcoff-Defensive Back
        Second Team Offense-Josh Simon-Linebacker
2002-Defensive Player of the Year-Philip DeMarco-Lineman
    First Team Offense-Jarrod Mock-Wide Receiver
    First Team Defense-Steve Slatcoff-Defensive Back
        Second Team Defense-Jay Miller-Lineman
2003-Second Team Offense-Chris Perkosky-Lineman
        Second Team Defense-Jeff Thomas-Linebacker
2004-First Team Defense-Matt Wilson-Defensive Back
        Second Team Offense-Brock Seese-Offensive Line
2005-Defensive Player of the Year-Josh Kotula-Linebacker
    First Team Offense-C.W. Beckley-Lineman
    First Team Defense-Matt Wilson-Defensive Back
        Second Team Defense-Brenan Franchic-Lineman
2006-First Team Defense-Josh Kotula-Linebacker
    Second Team Offense-Matt Andrascik-Running Back
    Second Team Defense-Nick Berkey-Lineman
2007-First Team Defense-Jonathan Ferensic-Lineman

Bibliography

Alcamo, Frank P., **The Windber Story, A 20th Century Model Pennsylvania Coal Town**, Published by Frank P. Alcamo, 1983.

Armstrong, John, **The Way We Played the Game**, Sourcebooks, Inc., Naperville, Illinois, 2002.

Betcher, Larry, **My Home Town**, Essay for high school English class at Windber Area High School, 1985., used by permission of Larry Betcher.

Brabender, David J., Jr., **Ramblers, The History of Cathedral Prep Football**, Median Creative Group, A Division of Larson Texts, Inc., Erie, Pennsylvania, 2000.

Emmons, Mark, **The Last Chance Ranch**, Longstreet Press, Inc., Marietta, Georgia, 1996.

Freeman, Patrick J., **The Monster**, Essay for a creative writing course, 1986, used by permission of Patrick J. Freeman.

Gallagher, Jack, **A Boy's Life in Football, Pennsylvania**, Short Story, originally published in the 2003 Autumn issue of **Westsylvania Magazine**, used by permission of Jack Gallagher.

Hobba, Delores (DiGuilio), **Mighty Ramblers**, Cheer, 1964., used by permission of Delores (DiGuilio) Hobba.

Moose, February/March/April 2008, quarterly publication by Moose International. Article: **Ramblers Get Huge Media Coverage,** part of a front page story by the *Chicago Tribune* telling the story of Mooseheart football '07.

Pennsylvania Football News Resource Guide-2005, Publisher, Rich Vetock. P.O. Box 334, Revloc, PA 15948, E-Mail: rich@pafootballnews.com.

Windber High School "Stylus", Year Book, Annual Publication, 1923 to 2007.

Interviews

Charles William "Bill" Beckley, July 24, 2002.

Niles "Stud" Dalberg, August 7, 2002.

Irene (Geiser) Berkebile, October 3, 2006.

Phil DeMarco-January, 15, 2008

Newspapers

Bethlehem Republic

Bradford Journal

Chicago Tribune

Harrisburg Patriot

Hi-Times, Windber High School Newspaper

Johnstown Daily Tribune

Johnstown Tribune-Democrat

New York Daily News

The Evening Star, Washington, D.C., Newspaper

Windber Daily Era

Windber Weekly Journal

Internet

Chicago Tribune, **The Under Dogs**: Three part story of Mooseheart High School Football, Mooseheart, Illinois,. Retrieved February 6, 2008 from the internet:
   <http://www.chicagotribune.com/news/specials/chimooseheart>

Mooseheart Child City and School. Information about Mooseheart schools, Retrieved February 6, 2008 from the internet:
   <http://www.mooseheart.org/>

Siegfried History. 2000. University of Notre Dame, Retrieved December 1, 2002 from the internet:
   <http://www.nd.edu/~sieghall/history.htm>

Winthrop High School, Winthrop, Maine, Retrieved January 18, 2006 from the internet:
   <http://www.winthrop.k12.us/whs/index.htm>

Credits For Photographs

Listed below are the sources used for the photographs throughout the book. All photographs are identified in **bold** print. The photo is followed by the page number in the book, which is followed by the individual who contributed the photo or the source of the photo.

<u>Front Cover:</u> **Football:** Shaz Yuhas, **Colored photo of 1941 Game at Delaney Field:** Tom Congersky, **1925 photo of Jim Camille:** Geno Stevens, **2001 photo of Josh Simon:** Jerry Simon.
<u>Back Cover:</u> **1937 Championship Program and 1938 Program:** Gary DiGuilio, (Earl Ripple Scrap Book), **1948, 1958, and 1970 Programs:** Jim Boburchuk,(Steve Hritz-Scrapbook),**1961 Program:** Carl D. Mayer, **1988 Program:** Jake Oyler, **1990 Program:** John and Judi Pruchnic, **2000 Program:** Jerry Simon, **1933 Championship Program:** Bill Gorgon.

<u>Text</u>
1908 Team: page 13, 1937 *Hi-Times,* **1917 Team:** page 20, 1962 *Hi-Times*, **1923 Team:** page 23, 1923 *Stylus*, **1923 Banquet Booklet:** page 24, Carl D. Mayer, **Joe Congersky:** page 25, Tom Congersky, **Jim Cavacini:** page 30, 1934 *Stylus*, **1933 State Champions:** page 31, 1933 *Stylus*, **1934 Starting Offensive Line-up:** page 32, 1934 *Stylus*,
Ding and Duke: page 33, 1936 *Stylus*, **Touchdown Twins:** page 37, 1938 *Stylus,* **1937 State Champions:** page 39, 1938 *Stylus*, **1943 All Scholastic Team:** page 42, *Tribune Democrat*, **Nunzio Marino:** page 43, Geno Stevens, **1942 or 1943 Point Stadium:** page 44, Shaz Yuhas, **1961 Starting Offensive Team:** page 51, *Tribune Democrat*, Terry Heckler, **1973 Undefeated Team:** page 54, 1974 *Stylus*, **Bill Elko and Rodger Shepko:** page 55, 1978 and 1979 *Stylus*,
Paul Romanchock: page 56, 1987 *Stylus*, **Nick Rizzo:** page 58, 2000 *Stylus*, **Frank Tallyen:** page 58, 2001 *Stylus*, **Jeff Slatcoff:** page 58, 2001 *Stylus*, **Steve Slatcoff:** page 58, 2003 *Stylus*, **John Curlej:** page 59, 2003 *Stylus*, **Philip DeMarco:** page 59, Phil DeMarco, **Josh Kotula:** page 61, 2007 *Stylus*, **Recreation Park Diagram:** page 64, drawn by Frankie DiLoreto, **Recreation Park Grandstand:** page 64, Coal Heritage Museum, **Eugene Delaney:** page 65, Windber Era 1901 Illustrated Industrial Edition, **Delaney Field:** page 67, 1947-50th Anniversary Photo Book, **Game Action (3):**, page 68, Bill Gorgon, Shaz Yuhas, Jim Boburchuk (Steve Hritz Scrapbook), **Delaney Field:** page 69, Tom Congersky, **Windber Stadium:** page 70, Jim Cover, Jr., **Stadium Poster:** page 71, Carl D. Mayer, **1961 Game Action:** page 73, 1962 *Stylus*, **1971 Game Action:** page 74, Joe Yasko, **2006 Sidelines:** page 74, 2007 *Stylus*, **1914 Pitt Scrimmage:** page 77, *Johnstown Daily Tribune*, **Topographic Map:** page 78, Carl D. Mayer, **Cabins at Camp Hamilton:** page 81, Shaz Yuhas, **Camp Hamilton:** page 82, Jim Cover, Jr., **Camp Hamilton:** page 82, Carl D. Mayer, **Frank Kush and Monster:** page 85, *Tribune Democrat*, **Cabin Interiors:** page 87, A. J. Cannoni, **Larry Betcher:** page 105, 1986 *Stylus*, **Frank Kush:**, page 107, Geno Stevens, **Frank Kush:**, page 110, <u>Last Chance Ranch</u> by Mark Emmons, **Frank Kush:** page 111, Shaz Yuhas, **Baby Pictures:** page 114, Carl D. Mayer, **Dr. Rosenbaum:**, page 116, 1960 *Stylus*, **Manager Pictures:** pages 122 and 123, 1926, 1937, 1941, 1952, 1961,and 1975 *Stylus*, **Cheering Squads:** pages 126, 127, 128, 129, 130, 131,and 132, 1926, 1936, 1940, 1955, 1966, 1976, 1985, 1996, and 2001 *Stylus*, **Jim Hyde:** page 133, Shaz Yuhas, **Duke Weigle:** page 134, 1936 *Stylus*, **Joe Gates:** page 135, unknown newspaper article, **John Kawchak:** page 136, 1957 *Stylus*, **Joe Polansky:** page 138, Shaz Yuhas, **Phil DeMarco:** page 139, Phil DeMarco, **Kawchak's Letter:** page 142, Pat Freeman, **Shoe Shop:** page 143, Carl D. Mayer, **Souvenir Program:** page 147, Bill Gorgon, **Chrome Shovel:** page 149, 1958 *Stylus*, ***1938 Gang:*** page 150, Shaz Yuhas, **Carl Mayer:** page 151, 1961 and 1962 *Stylus*, **Heckler's Drawings and Caricatures:** pages 154-182, Terry Heckler, **1959 Starting Backfield:** page 182, *Tribune Democrat*, Terry Heckler, **1917 Team:** page 188, unknown newspaper article, **1920 Team:** page 191, 1961 Football Program, **1921 Team:** page 192, Bill Gorgon, **1922 Team:** page 193, Shaz Yuhas, **1923 thru 2004:** pages 194-277, 1924 thru 2005 *Stylus*, **2005 Team:** page 278, Cover Studio, **2006 and 2007 Teams:** pages 279 and 280, Life Touch, Hancock Studio.